Shire County Guide 5

WILTSHIRE

Mark Child

D0913847

Shire Publications Ltd

Published in 1995 by Shire Publications Ltd, Cromwell House, Church Street, Princes Risborough, Buckinghamshire HP27 9AA, UK.
Copyright © 1995 by Mark Child. First published 1984. Second edition 1987. Enlarged third edition 1995. Shire County Guide 5. ISBN 0 7478 0273 4.

Printed in Great Britain by CIT Printing Services, Press Buildings, Merlins Bridge, Haverfordwest, Dyfed SA61 1XF.

British Library Cataloguing in Publication Data:
Child, Mark.
Wiltshire. – 3 Rev.ed. – (Shire County Guides; No. 5).
I. Title. II. Series.
914.23104859.
ISBN 0-7478-0273-4.

Acknowledgements

The maps of Wiltshire on pages 4-7 and the plan of Salisbury on page 33 are by Robert Dizon. Photographs are acknowledged as follows: British Tourist Authority, page 69; Mark Child, pages 11, 30, 37, 61, 74, 111, 117, 119, 122, 124, 127, 131; *Salisbury Journal*, pages 64, 153; Science Museum, page 145; David Uttley, pages 55, 63; Geoffrey N. Wright, page 95. All other photographs, including the front cover, are by Cadbury Lamb.

Ordnance Survey grid references

Although information on how to reach many of the places described in this book by car is given in the text, National Grid References are also included in many instances, particularly for the harder-to-find places in chapters 3, 4, 5 and 9, for the benefit of those readers who have the Ordnance Survey 1:50,000 Landranger maps of the area. The references are stated as a Landranger sheet number followed by the 100 km National Grid square and the six-figure reference.

To locate a site by means of the grid reference, proceed as in the following example: Pewsey White Horse (OS 173: SU 171581). Take the OS Landranger map sheet 173 ('Swindon, Devizes and surrounding area'. The grid numbers are printed in blue around the edges of the map. In more recently produced maps these numbers are repeated at 10 km intervals throughout the map, so that it is not necessary to open it out completely.) Read off these numbers from the left along the top edge of the map until you come to 17, denoting a vertical grid line, then estimate one-tenth of the distance to vertical line 18 and envisage an imaginary vertical grid line 17.1 at this point. Next look at the grid numbers at one side of the map (either side will do) and read *upwards* until you find the horizontal grid line 58. Estimate one-tenth of the distance to the next horizontal line above (i.e. 59), and so envisage an imaginary horizontal line across the map at 58.1. Follow this imaginary line across the map until it crosses the imaginary vertical line 17.1. At the intersection of these two lines you will find Pewsey White Horse.

The Ordnance Survey Landranger maps which cover Wiltshire are sheets 173, 174, 183 and 184. Very small areas of the county are found on maps 163, 172 and 185.

Cover: *Old houses around the church at Westbury.*

Contents

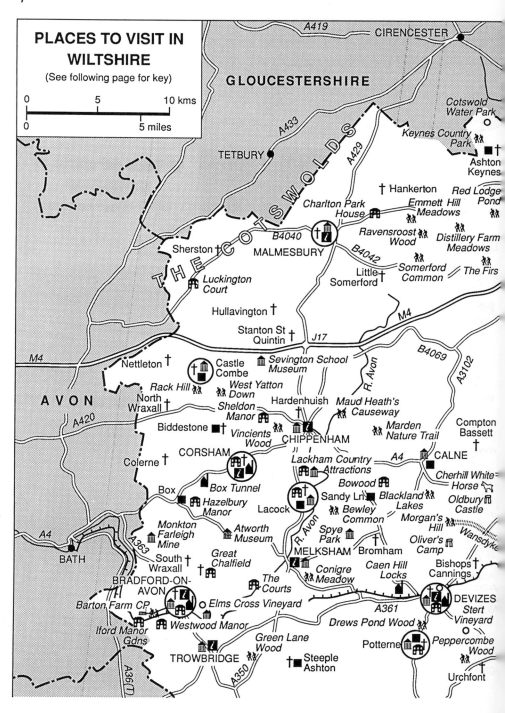

4

PLACES TO VISIT IN WILTSHIRE

(See following page for key)

0 ········ 5 ········ 10 kms
0 ········ 5 miles

GLOUCESTERSHIRE

CIRENCESTER

A419

Cotswold Water Park

Keynes Country Park

Ashton Keynes

TETBURY

A433

A429

THE COTSWOLDS

B4040

† Hankerton

Red Lodge Pond

Charlton Park House

Emmett Hill Meadows

Ravensroost Wood

Distillery Farm Meadows

Sherston †

MALMESBURY

B4042

Little Somerford

Somerford Common

The Firs

Luckington Court

Hullavington †

Stanton St Quintin †

J17

M4

B4069

A3102

M4

Nettleton †

AVON

A420

Castle Combe

Rack Hill

North Wraxall †

West Yatton Down

Sevington School Museum

Hardenhuish

Sheldon Manor

Maud Heath's Causeway

Marden Nature Trail

Compton Bassett †

Biddestone ■ †

Vincients Wood

CHIPPENHAM

R. Avon

CALNE

CORSHAM

Colerne †

Lackham Country Attractions

Bowood

A4

Cherhill White Horse

Box

Box Tunnel

Lacock

Sandy Ln

Blackland

Oldbury Castle

Hazelbury Manor

Bewley Common

Morgan's Hill

Wansdyke

BATH

A4

A363

Monkton Farleigh Mine

Atworth Museum

Spye Park

MELKSHAM

Bromham

Oliver's Camp

Bishops Cannings †

South Wraxall †

Great Chalfield

Conigre Meadow

Caen Hill Locks

BRADFORD-ON-AVON

The Courts

DEVIZES

Stert Vineyard

Barton Farm CP

Elms Cross Vineyard

A361

Drews Pond Wood

Peppercombe Wood

Iford Manor Gdns

Westwood Manor

Green Lane Wood

Potterne

TROWBRIDGE

A350

Steeple Ashton

Urchfont

A36(T)

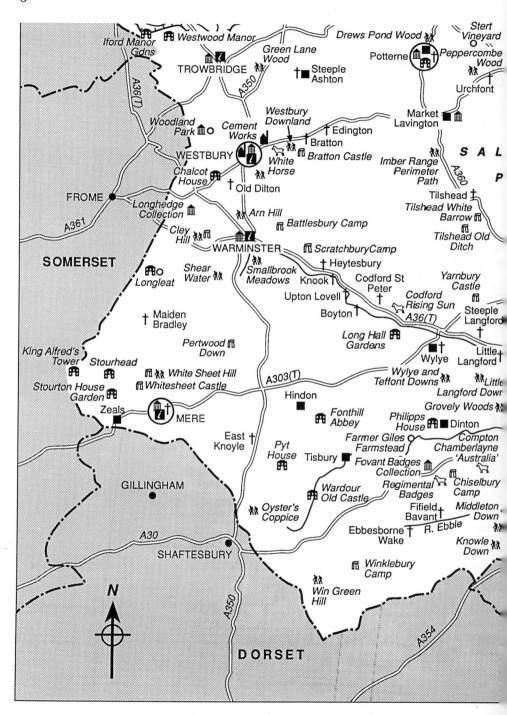

Iford Manor Gdns
Westwood Manor
Drews Pond Wood
Stert Vineyard
Potterne
Peppercombe Wood
Green Lane Wood
TROWBRIDGE
Steeple Ashton
Urchfont
Woodland Park
Westbury Downland
Market Lavington
Cement Works
WESTBURY
Edington
Bratton
Bratton Castle
White Horse
Imber Range Perimeter Path
S A L
P
Chalcot House
Old Dilton
Tilshead
Tilshead White Barrow
FROME
Longhedge Collection
Arn Hill
Battlesbury Camp
Tilshead Old Ditch
Cley Hill
WARMINSTER
Scratchbury Camp
SOMERSET
Heytesbury
Shear Water
Smallbrook Meadows
Yarnbury Castle
Longleat
Knook
Codford St Peter
Upton Lovell
Codford Rising Sun
Steeple Langford
Maiden Bradley
Boyton
A36(T)
Little Langford
Pertwood Down
Long Hall Gardens
King Alfred's Tower
Stourhead
White Sheet Hill
A303(T)
Wylye
Wylye and Teffont Downs
Little
Langford Dowr
Stourton House Garden
Whitesheet Castle
Hindon
Grovely Woods
Zeals
MERE
Fonthill Abbey
Philipps House
Dinton
East Knoyle
Pyt House
Tisbury
Farmer Giles Farmstead
Compton Chamberlayne
'Australia'
GILLINGHAM
Wardour Old Castle
Fovant Badges Collection
Regimental Badges
Chiselbury Camp
A30
Oyster's Coppice
Fifield Bavant
Middleton Down
SHAFTESBURY
Ebbesborne Wake
R. Ebble
Knowle Down
Winklebury Camp
Win Green Hill
A350
A354
N
D O R S E T

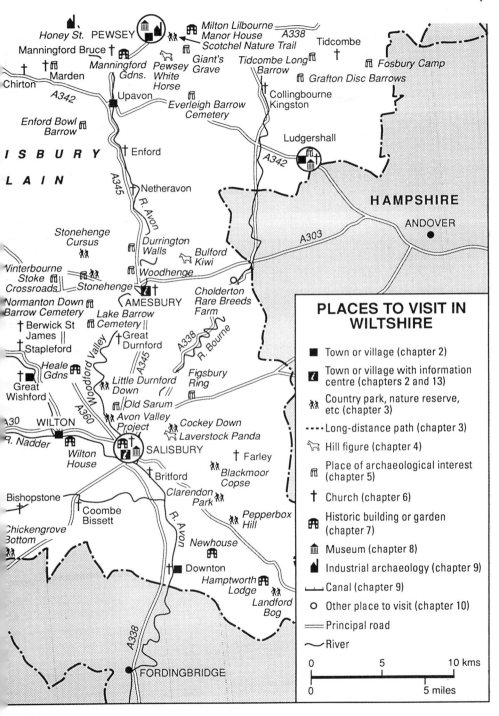

Honey St. PEWSEY
Milton Lilbourne
Manor House — A338
Scotchel Nature Trail
Tidcombe
Manningford Bruce
Giant's Grave
Tidcombe Long Barrow
Fosbury Camp
Chirton
Marden
Manningford Gdns.
Pewsey White Horse
Grafton Disc Barrows
A342
Upavon
Everleigh Barrow Cemetery
Collingbourne Kingston
Enford Bowl Barrow
Enford
Ludgershall
I S B U R Y
Netheravon
A342
L A I N
A345
R. Avon
HAMPSHIRE
ANDOVER
Stonehenge Cursus
Durrington Walls
Bulford Kiwi
A303
Vinterbourne Stoke Crossroads
Woodhenge
Stonehenge
Cholderton Rare Breeds Farm
Normanton Down Barrow Cemetery
AMESBURY
Lake Barrow Cemetery
Berwick St James
Great Durnford
R. Bourne
A338
Stapleford
Heale Gdns
Little Durnford Down
Figsbury Ring
Great Wishford
A345
Woodford Valley
Old Sarum
A360
Avon Valley Project
Cockey Down
Laverstock Panda
A30
WILTON
SALISBURY
Farley
R. Nadder
Wilton House
Britford
Blackmoor Copse
Bishopstone
Clarendon Park
Coombe Bissett
Pepperbox Hill
Chickengrove Bottom
R. Avon
Newhouse
Downton
Hamptworth Lodge
Landford Bog
A338
FORDINGBRIDGE

PLACES TO VISIT IN WILTSHIRE

■ Town or village (chapter 2)

🅸 Town or village with information centre (chapters 2 and 13)

Country park, nature reserve, etc (chapter 3)

---- Long-distance path (chapter 3)

Hill figure (chapter 4)

Place of archaeological interest (chapter 5)

† Church (chapter 6)

Historic building or garden (chapter 7)

🏛 Museum (chapter 8)

Industrial archaeology (chapter 9)

Canal (chapter 9)

O Other place to visit (chapter 10)

Principal road

River

0 _____ 5 _____ 10 kms

0 _____ 5 miles

Preface

Welcome to the Shire County Guide to Wiltshire, one of over thirty such books, written and designed to enable you to organise your time in the county well.

The Shire County Guides fill the need for a compact, accurate and thorough guide to each county so that visitors can plan a half-day excursion or a whole week's stay to best advantage. Residents, too, will find the guides a handy and reliable reference to the places of interest in their area.

Travelling British roads can be time consuming, and the County Guides will ensure that you need not inadvertently miss any interesting feature in a locality, that you do not accidentally bypass a new museum or an outstanding church, that you can find an attractive place to picnic, and that you will appreciate the history and the buildings of the towns or villages in which you stop.

This book has been arranged in special interest chapters, such as the countryside, historic houses or archaeological sites, and all these places of interest are located on the map on pages 4-7. Use the map either for an overview to decide which area has most to interest you, or to help you enjoy your immediate neighbourhood. Then refer to the nearest town or village in chapter 2 to see, at a glance, what special features or attractions each community contains or is near. The subsequent chapters enable readers with a particular interest to find immediately those places of importance to them, while the cross-referencing under 'Wiltshire towns and villages' assists readers with wider tastes to select how best to spend their time.

1
A portrait of Wiltshire

Wiltshire is famous for Avebury, Stonehenge, Moonrakers, the great bustard and lardy cake. The bustard, now recalled on the county's coat of arms, was a fast-running, turkey-sized bird which roamed in large flocks over Salisbury Plain but had died out in Wiltshire before the close of the nineteenth century. True natives have a slow drawl, an interesting way with the English language and a propensity for keeping themselves to themselves. Whether or not this explains why the county has been relatively slow to exploit its huge tourist potential is hard to say. But Wiltshire has a great deal to offer visitors and is especially suitable for short-break holidays.

Wiltshire is an inland county of 1344 square miles (348,070 hectares). It is fifteenth in size amongst the counties of England and at the 1991 census had a population of 573,000. At the beginning of the twentieth century the population was 273,869, about one-third more than in 1801. Wiltshire has always been a predominantly rural county and there are still large areas in the centre and east which are hardly less sparsely populated than they were a hundred years ago, and as a whole the overall density of people is only half the national average.

In general terms the area is going through a period of population expansion and business development. During the 1980s the population grew at a rate which was three times the national average. Business expansion is taking place at either end of the county – around Salisbury in the south and Swindon in the north – and along the line of small towns on the western side.

Six thousand years of man

People have left evidence of their existence in Wiltshire since the old stone age, although most of the prehistoric remains throughout the county come from the neolithic, bronze age and iron age communities. The first set the pattern of agriculture, the second established patterns of society and trade, and the third maintained territorial defences. By the immediate pre-Roman period named tribes had emerged with their own boundaries in the area: the Atrebates in the north-east, the Dobunni in the north-west, the Dorotriges in the south, and the Catuvellauni. Vespasian conquered the area for Rome and Roman settlements were established at *Cunetio* (Mildenhall), *Verlucio* (Sandy Lane) and *Sorbiodunum* (Old Sarum), from which five Roman roads radiated. Around fifty villa sites are known. The uplands and the river valleys continued to be the favoured areas of settlement, the latter for their obvious communication benefits, the former as great natural clearings in an otherwise wooded landscape.

With the Saxons came a long period of struggle for the area. The Gewissas, who approached from the south, are one group known to have established themselves. Rival Saxon forces fought each other as well as the Britons, but West Saxon supremacy over central Wiltshire was assured by Cynric's defeat of the old inhabitants at Old Sarum in 552. Just four years later, led by Ceawlin, the West Saxons ranged north and defeated the Britons at Barbury Castle near present-day Swindon. Ceawlin was himself to be beaten in 592 on the downs above Alton Barnes. The kingdom of Wessex was by now well established, although skirmishes with Mercia – such as an engagement with the West Saxons at Great Bedwyn in 675 – were part of the pattern of the next two centuries. In 652 Cenwealh's victory for the West Saxons at Bradford-on-Avon expanded their territory into Somerset.

This part of Wessex, together with the extreme south-west of England, remained untouched by the first half century of Viking raids around Britain but came under attack from other kingdoms. Mercia was an ever-present problem, and in 802 a group called the Wilsaetas, led by Weohstan, met raiders from Mercia. The nucleus of Wiltshire was formed of an area occupied by the Wilsaetas, West Saxon settlers in the Wylye valley. Their name, and so that of the county, is derived from Wilton, which was their chief town and where Egbert of Wessex had his palace. A decisive battle took place at Ellandune (Wroughton) in 823 when Egbert defeated the aggressor Beorwulf of Mercia.

Alfred was defeated by the Vikings at Wilton and at the opening of 878 was forced to flee from Chippenham in the face of Guthrum's surprise attack. Rallying at Athelney, Alfred engaged and defeated Guthrum in 878 at the battle of Ethandune, close by Edington. Returning to Chippenham, Guthrum was besieged for fourteen days before submitting to the humiliation of Alfred's terms. When the Danes returned early in the eleventh century, it was Swein who sacked both Old Sarum and Wilton. In 1016, led by Cnut, they engaged Edmund at Sherston but before the year was out Edmund was dead and Wessex transferred its allegiance to the Danish king.

In 1146 the Constitutions of Clarendon were drawn up by Henry I and his bishops near Salisbury. The forests and chases of Wiltshire were favourites of the hunting royalty from the time of John of Gaunt, and medieval monarchs held court variously throughout the county. For example, William I was at Salisbury in 1086, Henry I at Marlborough in 1110, and the Plantagenet kings from Henry III to Richard III all enjoyed hunting around the palace at Clarendon. Part of the conflict between Stephen and the Empress Maud in the twelfth century took place on Wiltshire soil with the county divided: the king fortified the abbey at Wilton whilst Bishop Roger of Salisbury garrisoned Devizes, Sarum and Malmesbury for the Empress; Marlborough was also held in her name. In a later period, James II had his headquarters at Salisbury in 1688.

Battle lines were also drawn across Wiltshire in the English Civil War. Marlborough sided with Parliament and was attacked in 1642. Other notable engagements included Roundway Down, Devizes, where in 1643 Sir William Waller was defeated by the Royalists under Lord Wilmot. In the same year Lady Blanche Arundell with about fifty fighting men and servants withstood Sir Edward Hungerford's force of 1300 at Wardour Castle for five days. Garrisoned by Parliament after Blanche's honourable surrender, the castle was ruined by her own son's bombardment in pursuit of the enemy! In 1655 Penruddocke's uprising at Salisbury, although unsuccessful, made Cromwell rethink his attitude to Royalist sympathisers.

There have been some ecclesiastical events of note. In 957 the Witan held at Bradford-on-Avon recalled Dunstan from exile to become Bishop of Worcester. In 978 a Witan met at Calne to settle the question of celibacy amongst the clergy, Dunstan then being in favour of the motion. In 1450 the unpopular Bishop Ayscough of Salisbury was dragged from William Edington's collegiate church and stoned to death on a nearby hill.

Landscape and countryside

The north-west tip of Wiltshire extends into a band of Jurassic oolitic limestone which runs diagonally from Chesil Bank on the Dorset coast to the mouth of the Humber. This is the stone which provided Gloucestershire with buildings from silvery white to honey brown. It furnished the grey stone which built Bath in Avon and in Wiltshire Bradford-on-Avon and Corsham, near both of which it was quarried. It was also used to build the artisans' railway village in Swindon. These deposits have been worked for a long time. The famous Box stone was reputed to have been discovered by St Aldhelm, whose name is linked with Malmesbury Abbey and the Saxon church at Bradford-on-Avon.

Swindon, the county's largest town, lies in the north Wiltshire plain. It is built on clay which overlies the limestone and runs from the mid-west of the county across the north into Oxfordshire. The further east and south one goes from the limestone belt the more important is brick in the fabric of the buildings and the greater the use of flint. The county's northern escarpment leads from the Marlborough Downs into the Vale of Pewsey; the southern escarpment adjoins Salisbury

The Vale of Pewsey, from Pewsey Down Nature Reserve close to Walker's Hill.

Plain, an area of flat open downland.

The southern two-thirds of the county is mostly chalk. This retains very little surface water and so was preferred for colonisation. Small villages occur frequently along the spring lines on the downlands where greensand intersects the chalk to allow wetter fertile valleys. There is a spur of upper greensand and gault which virtually divides the county across its centre but otherwise follows the southerly line of the clay. The whole of the chalk area appears as undulating downland with open vistas and wide horizons, covered in places by sandstone boulders known as sarsens or 'grey wethers'.

When ploughed, the crumbly earth has a white sheen and is mixed with pieces of dark brown flint. As one travels southwards, this intractable material is increasingly used in buildings which, particularly in the mid-Wiltshire villages, have a chalky feel. But chalk is not strong and is too porous to be used for construction to any great extent. Flint is mixed with limestone in the county's walls, with brick in the south-east and east, and it predominates in many small buildings in the south. It is sometimes used decoratively to very great effect and adds considerable visual character to the county.

Chalk has helped to preserve the lynchet-terraced slopes laid out by farmers on, for example, Fyfield Down. And for more than a thousand years men have kept sheep on the springy downland turf, where their runs have helped to shape the landscape. The resulting unimproved chalk downland – greater tracts than anywhere else in England – is a rich heritage of wildlife and vegetation. Parts of it, as well as other diverse and significant habitats throughout the county, are now being managed as nature trails and nature reserves, many of which are open to the public.

Agricultural activities are recalled in the place-names which once marked isolated homesteads. Even today small farmhouses and outbuildings occupy folds between the smooth, gently rounded downland slopes that descend into dry valleys such as the Vale of Pewsey. The Marlborough Downs and the slopes of Cranborne Chase are under arable cultivation as they have been for centuries. The rises have isolated bushes along their lengths and clusters of trees at the summits. These frequently surround the burial mounds – bell barrows, bowl barrows, disc barrows, pond barrows, saucer barrows and long barrows – which are as much a feature of the county as the sheep. Burial mounds would be even more numerous but for the ploughs of past generations which were less inclined to conservation than our own.

With the exception of Savernake Forest, one has to travel beyond Salisbury Plain to the boundaries with other counties to find large wooded areas. Certainly beeches surround the little villages in the south of the county where only the church towers and perhaps the gables of flint and limestone manor houses rise above them. But the main wooded areas are south-west of Warminster at the ancient Great Ridge Wood, the northern tip of Cranborne Chase where it enters the county south-west of Salisbury, and north-east through Grovely Wood towards the A350 between Warminster and Shaftesbury. The wooded areas indicate underlying deposits of clay, which are difficult to cultivate.

The tourist in Wiltshire can find a number of distinct areas to visit, as well as many specific attractions in the landscape. For the walker there are about 4000 miles (6000 km) of trackways and public footpaths, although they may, particularly on the Marlborough Downs, find themselves sharing part of the way with mountain bikes – for even these now have designated trails.

Agriculture and industry

Industry is now business. Throughout Wiltshire the old industries have mostly gone and their sites have been taken over by business parks and office developments, providing convenient units for housing medium to light engineering, commerce, consumer products, telecommunications, pharmaceuticals and the ever increasing service, legal and financial industries seemingly needed to maintain and sustain it all. Only in Swindon, Wiltshire's key conurbation on the M4 corridor, are there reawakened echoes of a true engineering heritage, very much part of the town's future. Elsewhere in the county business diversification is creeping around the peripheries of most small towns, quietly but relentlessly changing the business face of Wiltshire.

Anyone writing about industry in Wiltshire as recently as the 1960s would have found most of the county little changed from the beginning of the twentieth century. Four main canals – the Kennet & Avon which cuts the county in two, the Wilts & Berks, the Thames & Severn which just clips its northern boundary, and the Somerset Coal Canal – are a key to the traditional industries of the county and reminders of the need to move materials and provisions through a predominantly agricultural landscape before the age of railways.

The Thames & Severn, which opened in 1789, enters north Wiltshire east of Latton and continues past Inglesham to the Thames at Lechlade. Two of its characteristic round houses remain on this stretch at Marston Meysey and Inglesham. The Wilts & Berks Canal, opened by stages between 1801 and 1810, ran between Semington and Abingdon via Melksham, Lacock, Wootton Bassett and Swindon, with branches to Chippenham and Calne. Like the railways after, it employed so many navvies in its construction that for a while the population of Swindon doubled. There are several areas where the course of this canal can be followed, although in Swindon it is now a shopping precinct.

The Somerset Coal Canal, established in 1794, linked with the Kennet & Avon at Limpley Stoke, serving collieries south of Bath until the railways came. The Kennet & Avon Canal, which was authorised by an Act of Parliament in 1794 and opened in 1810, enters the county just north of Limpley Stoke and leaves it just west of Hungerford. Along its length are many of the county's industrial sites. A short canal, the North Wiltshire, was opened in 1819 and ran the 9 miles (14 km) between Swindon and Latton, linking the Wilts & Berks with the Thames & Severn.

The canals declined with the coming of the railways and in particular the Great Western Railway in the mid nineteenth century – an enduring industry on which Swindon was to be virtually dependent for more than a hundred years. The line reached the marshlands north of the town in 1840. Brunel's station, of which there are now barely any traces, was built over the next two years and the railway works followed almost at once. The locomotive, carriage and wagon works were part of a site of over 320 acres (130 hectares) and at their height employed some 14,000 men. Much of the area where they worked is now large-scale urban redevelopment, twentieth-century amenities, housing, services and shops built on decades of blood, sweat and ash.

Landlocked Wiltshire has always been known for sheep farming on an enormous scale, dairy cattle and pig raising. Many of the smaller towns owe their existence either to the livestock itself or to processing the products of agriculture. At Warminster there was a great corn market. Melksham is at the heart of an extensive dairy-farming area; Calne is renowned for bacon – which also played a large part in the economies of Chippenham and Devizes; Wootton Bassett is famed for milk production. Bradford-on-Avon was the county's centre for broadcloth weaving and there were cloth industries at Melksham, Calne, Westbury and Trowbridge. Rope and sack making was carried on at Melksham and Marlborough, and there was a tannery at Downton. Wilton has long been associated with carpets. Lace was made at Malmesbury, silk at Devizes and at Mere, where flax was also spun and cheesecloth made. Stables were established, particularly in the north of the county, and racehorses were bred and trained on the downs.

One of the most famous bell foundries in all England, that of the Cor family and later the Wells family, was at Aldbourne, a little downland village renowned also for the country crafts of willow plaiting and straw plaiting. From 1694 to 1826 Aldbourne bells were supplied to many counties in southern England. At Salisbury, too, there was a succession of bellfounders between the fourteenth century and the eighteenth, and also for brief periods in Devizes and Warminster.

Brewing was a staple industry throughout Wiltshire, unsurprising in an agricultural county and in an area such as Swindon, where it is said that men working in the railway hot shops in the nineteenth century would drink up to 10 pints (5.7 litres) of ale each morning before starting work at 6 a.m. Today there are breweries in Devizes, Trowbridge, Upper Stratton, Swindon and Mildenhall.

Brickmaking was a considerable industry at West Lavington for nearly three hundred years. There were iron-ore quarries at Seend and stone quarries at Box, Chilmark, Corsham and Monkton Farleigh. Stone from the great freestone quarries hereabouts was used extensively in church building throughout the county and in the 'stone towns' near the quarry sites.

Some 92,000 acres (37,000 hectares) of Wiltshire is Ministry of Defence land, the army having been connected with Salisbury Plain since 1897 and particularly active since the Second World War. Yet the area is archaeologically and ecologically of great importance and the visitor now more than ever can benefit from restricted access within this sensitive area.

The Caen Hill flight of locks on the Kennet & Avon Canal near Devizes.

2
Towns and villages

Aldbourne

Pronounced 'Auburn', this large village lies within the chalky folds of the Marlborough Downs, almost enveloped in ploughed fields speckled with flint. It is close by Aldbourne Chase, the green area where King John is said to have hunted. The small cottages with their plaster walls of pastel shades and the larger houses of flint and brick are pretty but show how difficult it was to find freestone hereabouts. Some of the walls are made from the sarsen stones of the downs. The village is arranged around the green, cross and duck pond, dominated by the church. Thomas Goddard's little sixteenth-century manor house at Upper Upham may well be on the site of an earlier structure and of the hunting lodge associated with John of Gaunt.

Aldbourne was famous for its bell foundry which, between 1642 and 1826, made a succession of bells. Many are still in use in Wiltshire and surrounding counties. The country crafts of willow and straw plaiting continued there until well into the twentieth century.

Church of St Michael, page 78.

In the locality: Chilton Foliat church, page 82; Liddington Castle, page 71; Ramsbury church, page 93.

All Cannings

Church of All Saints, page 78; Rybury Camp, page 73.

Alton Barnes

Adam's Grave, page 68; Alton Barnes White Horse, page 62; church of St Mary the Virgin, page 78; Honey Street, page 137; Kennet & Avon Canal, page 137; Knap Hill, page 70; Pewsey Downs National Nature Reserve, page 56.

Alton Priors

Church of All Saints, page 78.

Amesbury

Early closing Monday; market Wednesday, at the George Hotel car park.

A small town with a few Georgian buildings, once well-known for the manufacture of clay tobacco pipes, Amesbury has existed since the ninth century, situated on the Salisbury Avon and surrounded by Salisbury Plain. Legend has it as both the birth and burial place of Ambrosius Aurelianus, and it is said that Guinevere came to the former abbey at Arthur's death. The present building on the site dates from about 1830 but there are some eighteenth-century features in the grounds. The two gatehouses, Kent House and Diana's House, are probably all that remains of early seventeenth-century work. There is an exceptional cruciform church. Close by is Vespasian's Camp, an iron age hillfort, so named by Stukeley.

Church of St Mary and St Mellor, page 78.

In the locality: Bulford Kiwi, page 63; Cholderton Rare Breeds Farm, page 140; Durrington Walls, page 69; Enford church, page 86; Great Durnford church, page 87; Heale Gardens and Plant Centre, page 106; Netheravon church, page 92; Stonehenge, page 75, Stonehenge Down, page 59; Upper Avon Valley, page 59; Woodford Valley, page 61.

Ashton Keynes

Ashton Keynes is a pretty Cotswold-style village amidst flat meadows, built in a series of rectangles and largely part of a conservation area. The young river Thames wanders by as a gentle stream, forcing people to cross to their homes by numerous little footbridges which add great charm to a backdrop of eighteenth- and nineteenth-century stone houses. The remains of four ancient crosses attest to the village's former strategic importance.

Many of the houses have fine gardens which are well worth visiting when they hold an open day.

Church of the Holy Cross, page 79; **Cotswold Water Park**, page 140; **Keynes Country Park**, page 53; **Upper Waterhay Reserve**, page 59.

Atworth

Atworth Museum, page 123.

Avebury

Avebury is a compact village almost entirely within neolithic earthworks and in an area which abounds in antiquities. Although it is more impressive than Stonehenge, the area cannot be seen from one vantage point and it seems to have attracted little attention before being noted by John Aubrey. The village divides the stone circle into sections and most of the standing stones were broken up in the eighteenth century and used for boundary and cottage walls, in which they may still be seen. The method used was to heat the sarsens on huge bonfires and then pour cold water along marked lines. The extent and form of the standing stones which may once have radiated from the earthworks has never been satisfactorily determined. Speculation was started by William Stukeley, the eighteenth-century antiquary. His conjectural plan of the area was designed to advance his 'serpent' theory, in which stone avenues ended in circles at the beast's head and tail. The village includes the stone circle, museums, manor, church, craft shop and National Trust shop in a former grain store. The Red Lion pub has a well in one of the dining rooms and a cider press in the car park. There are walks along footpaths to local field antiquities and refreshment rooms in the village.

Alexander Keiller Museum, page 123; **Avebury Henge Monument**, page 68; **Avebury Manor**, page 100; **Avebury Manor Gardens**, page 100; **church of St James**, page 79; **Great Barn Museum of Wiltshire Life**, page 124; **Silbury Hill**, page 74.

In the locality: Alton Barnes White Horse, page 62; Berwick Bassett church, page 79; Broad Hinton White Horse, page 62; Cherhill White Horse, page 63; Oldbury Castle, page 72; The Sanctuary, page 73; Wansdyke, page 60; West Kennett Avenue, page 75; West Kennett Long Barrow, page 76, Windmill Hill, page 76; Winterbourne Bassett church, page 99.

Berwick Bassett
Church of St Nicholas, page 79.

Berwick St James
Church of St James, page 79.

Berwick St John
Winklebury Camp, page 77.

Biddestone

This is everyone's idea of an English village. Attractive stone-built tiled eighteenth-century cottages and larger houses with fine gateposts, walled front gardens, gables and mullioned windows group around the wide village green and duck pond. The seventeenth-century Manor House has older outbuildings and a large garden which sometimes opens under the National Gardens Scheme. Pool Farmhouse, of similar date, has a gazebo on the garden wall. The village school building, village inn, old stone barn and village pump beneath a tiled conical little roof on posts all add to the charm.

Church of St Nicholas, page 80.

Bishops Cannings
Church of St Mary the Virgin, page 80.

Bishopstone
Church of St John the Baptist, page 80.

Blunsdon St Andrew

Here Blunsdon Abbey, a magnificent riot of nineteenth-century gables, spires and high chimneys, was reduced to a ruin by fire in 1904. Around the remains there is now a large residential caravan park. On the other side of the Roman road to Cirencester is **Broad Blunsdon**, which almost begins with Blunsdon House Hotel, an award-winning family-owned hostelry of international standing which grew out of a chance encounter with bed and breakfast when it was just a farmhouse! Otherwise Broad Blunsdon is a picturesque village of cottage architecture with wonderful views across the north Wiltshire plain.

Swindon & Cricklade Railway, page 138.

Bowerchalke
Knowle Down, page 53.

Box
St Aldhelm is credited with discovering the famous Bath stone, extensively quarried for centuries around Box and used in the great Georgian building boom at Bath. This is a stone village on the south side of a steep valley carved out by the By Brook. Nearby, a large Roman villa was excavated.

Box Tunnel, page 136; **Hazelbury Manor**, page 106.

Boyton
Church of St Mary, page 80.

Bradford-on-Avon
Early closing Wednesday; market Thursday, at the library car park, and (for antiques) Thursday at Holy Trinity church hall.
The town which grew up around the 'broad ford' rises in steep tiers, gable upon gable, on the slopes above the river. The narrow roads are lined by grey buildings in mellowed Bath stone. The best buildings, like the wool merchant's house on Druce's Hill and the Chantry, were put up in the seventeenth and eighteenth centuries. Flemish weavers who settled here in the fifteenth century began a period of great prosperity. The wealth from the cloth trade combined with good limestone, quarried locally, to produce two centuries of varied domestic architecture. The Hall in Woolley Street, built by a rich clothier in about 1610, is a fine country mansion. In contrast are the weavers' cottages with their rounded gables at Dutch Barton, and the gabled houses with decorative bargeboards in the narrow pedestrian way known as the Shambles, close by the bridge. The bridge was put up in the fourteenth century and rebuilt in the seventeenth, retaining original work in the central arches. The lock-up on the bridge was formerly a chapel. The riverside mills were built to make cloth by machinery

in the nineteenth century, and some are now used by the rubber industry.

Barton Farm Country Park, page 49; **Bradford-on-Avon Museum**, page 124; **Bradford-on-Avon Wharf**, page 136; **church of St Lawrence**, page 81; **Elms Cross Vineyard**, page 140; **Kennet & Avon Canal**, page 137; **Tithe Barn**, page 100.

In the locality: The Courts, page 103; Great Chalfield church, page 87; Great Chalfield Manor, page 106; Iford Manor Gardens, page 107; Monkton Farleigh Mine, page 129; South Wraxall church, page 94; Westwood Manor, page 121.

Bratton
Bratton Castle, page 68; church of St James the Great, page 81.

Bremhill
Maud Heath's Causeway, page 54.

Brinkworth
The Firs Nature Trail, page 52; Somerford Common Nature Trail, page 58.

Britford
Church of St Peter, page 81.

Brixton Deverill
Pertwood Down, page 73.

Broad Chalke
Chickengrove Bottom, page 49; Middleton Down, page 55.

Broad Hinton
Broad Hinton White Horse, page 62.

Broad Town
Broad Town White Horse, page 62.

Bromham
Church of St Nicholas, page 82.

Bulford
Bulford Kiwi, page 63.

Calne
Early closing Wednesday; market Friday, at Pippin car park.

The bridge at Bradford-on-Avon supports a lock-up, which was previously a chapel.

Calne is first mentioned in the will of Edred, who died in 955. The Witan met here in 978 to debate celibacy of the clergy as advocated by Dunstan. When the floor collapsed, killing or injuring several, the Archbishop remained safe on a beam. This was seen as divine approval for his views. Before the meat business of C. & J. Harris came in 1770 to revive and later dominate the town's dwindling market and economy, it was an important centre in the making of broadcloth and other aspects of the woollen industry. Situated on the road between London and Bath, it became a profitable coaching town where inns proliferated to cater for the traveller. Today Calne is a stone-built town, centred on its market place, with several Georgian frontages. Harris's five-storey building dominates all, overshadowing the town hall and the Lansdowne Arms with its long Georgian frontage.

Atwell-Wilson Motor Museum, page 124; **Blackland Lakes Nature Reserve**, page 49.

In the locality: Alexander Keiller Museum, page 123; Avebury Henge Monument, page 68; Avebury Manor, page 100; Avebury Manor Gardens, page 100; Bowood, page 100; Bromham church, page 82; Cherhill White Horse, page 63; Compton Bassett church, page 84; Great Barn Museum of Wiltshire Life, page 124; Marden Nature Trail, page 54; Morgan's Hill Nature Reserve, page 55; Oldbury Castle, page 72; Spye Park Stables Museum, page 125; Wansdyke, page 60.

Castle Combe

Castle Combe is renowned as one of the most picturesque villages in Britain. Bye Brook winds its way through the village, passing beneath the little triple-arch bridge under the main street. The old houses and quaint cottages are of mellowed limestone and press on to the road. Some are gabled or have dormer windows, with stone-tiled roofs which are uneven and mossy. The seventeenth-century Dower House at the end of the main street is of particular interest, as are the old White Hart inn and the weavers' cottages in Water Lane. Also stone-tiled is the pyramidal roof of the market cross, its beamwork supported by stone posts. The village lies deep in a hanging valley, the wooded slopes providing the perfect backdrop for the stonework. Its origins lie on Castle Hill, where there was a Roman fort. The Danes, who came later, were finally routed at nearby Slaughterford. After the Norman Conquest the area belonged to the de Dunstanvilles, but of the Norman castle of about 1140, from which the village takes its name, only fragments remain. In the church are Walter de Dunstanville's tomb and effigy of 1270. The manor passed to the Scrope family in the fourteenth century and remained with them for five hundred years. Their seventeenth-century manor house is now, with later additions, an hotel. In the fifteenth century Castle Combe was an important weaving centre. There is a popular motor-racing track on the outskirts.

Castle Combe Museum, page 125; **church of St Andrew**, page 82; **Rack Hill Nature Trail**, page 56.

In the locality: Nettleton church, page 92; North Wraxall church, page 92; Sevington School Museum, page 125; West Yatton Down, page 60.

Castle Eaton
Church of St Mary, page 82.

Charlton
Charlton Park House, page 102.

Cherhill
Cherhill White Horse, page 63; Oldbury Castle, page 72.

Chilton Foliat
On a fast road to Hungerford, just over the border, this is a charming little village in wooded surroundings amidst the water meadows of the river Kennet. Thatched cottages, timbered buildings and Georgian brick houses all contribute to the charm, and the seventeenth-century Bridge House beside the river is an interesting oddity. Other attractive buildings include the eighteenth-century rectory next to the church and the red brick, late Georgian Chilton House nearby.

Church of St Mary, page 82; **Littlecote House**, page 111; **Littlecote Roman Villa**, page 71.

Chippenham
Early closing Wednesday; market Friday, in Bath Road; cattle market Friday, Cocklebury Road.

There was a Saxon market place here, between the Forest of Chippenham and Melksham and the Forest of Braden, favourite hunting grounds of the Wessex kings. Alfred lived here before the Danes established it as their headquarters, but they were defeated at the battle of Ethandune in 878. Chippenham was granted its charter in 1554. The area was disafforested in 1630 but the market continues, one of the greatest in Britain. Now a light industrial town, Chippenham was once a centre of the cloth trade. Broadcloth was made there between the seventeenth and early twentieth centuries. Cattle, sheep and pigs were sold in the old market place, where the restored fifteenth-century town hall still stands, bearing the borough arms dated 1776. The present town hall was built by Sir Joseph Neeld in the nineteenth century. There are a number of timber-framed houses of the sixteenth and seventeenth centuries, as well as stone-built Georgian examples, gabled and stately. The best are around the old market place and in St Mary Street. The present bridge over the Avon, built in 1966, replaced one constructed in the eighteenth century around one three centuries older. Here stagecoaches used to stop for refreshments and fresh horses at the Georgian Angel inn, on their journeys between London and Bath. Chippenham was the home of Ludovic Muggleton, a tailor who, with John Reeve, founded a religious sect called the Muggletonians in the seventeenth century.

Hardenhuish church, page 88; **Sheldon Manor**, page 118; **Vincients Wood Nature Trail**, page 59; **Yelde Hall Museum**, page 125.

In the locality: Bewley Common, page 49; Biddestone church, page 80; Bowood, page 100; Castle Combe church, page 82; Castle Combe Museum, page 125; Corsham church, page 84; Corsham Court, page 102; Fox Talbot Museum of Photography, page 127; Lackham Country Attractions – Agricultural Museum and Gardens, pages 110 and 128; Lacock Abbey, page 110; Lacock church, page

Cottages alongside the Bye Brook at Castle Combe, once voted the prettiest village in England.

Chirton

Chiseldon

Chittoe

Cholderton

Clyffe Pypard

Codford St Peter

Colerne

Collingbourne Kingston

Compton Bassett

Compton Chamberlayne

Coombe Bissett

Corsham
Early closing Wednesday; market Tuesday, at the Methuen Arms hotel car park.

In this small town there are an exceptional number of buildings of the seventeenth and eighteenth centuries, in cream-coloured Bath stone, now mellowed to perfection. The limestone was dug from underground quarries in the neighbourhood, the same as that which came out of Box Tunnel to the west, constructed by Brunel in 1836-41 for the Great Western Railway. High-quality large Georgian houses mix with low cottages, including a row of former weavers' dwellings in High Street. They date back to the fifteenth century and are gabled, some with bay windows. High Street has a number of impressive houses with sharp gables and mullioned windows, notably Tedburys of about 1632 on the east side. The L-shaped almshouse range, founded by Margaret Hungerford in 1668, is interesting and includes the master's house. In the churchyard is buried Sarah Jarvis, who died in 1753, aged 107. The market cross was destroyed in 1778 and five years later the town hall was built as a market hall. Typically, it had open arches and a central pediment bearing the Methuen arms. The arches were filled in, one forming a lock-up, and the building was raised one storey in 1882 when it became the town hall. Other buildings of note include Jaggards, which was built by Richard Kington between 1641 and 1680, and the seventeenth-century Pickwick Manor.

Church of St Bartholomew, page 84; **Corsham Court**, page 102; **Underground Quarry**, page 138.

In the locality: Atworth Museum, page 123; Biddestone church, page 80; Box Tunnel, page 136; Colerne church, page 83; Hazelbury Manor, page 106; South Wraxall church, page 94.

Corsley
Longhedge Collection, page 125.

Cricklade
Early closing Saturday.

Close to the source of the Thames, this is the northernmost town in the county, and the only one situated on the river. The ancient Forest of Braden once extended almost to the river and before disafforestation in the seventeenth century the Hospital of St John Baptist enjoyed the right of vert. Of this thirteenth-century foundation there are scant remains in the fabric of the Priory by the bridge. The town stands on the Roman road between Cirencester and Silchester but is now by-passed by the modern road between Cirencester and Swindon. Evidence of Roman occupation has been found in and around the town, with villas to the north and south-east. In later Saxon times it had its own mint. One of the legends associated with the town suggests that St Augustine met the Brit-

ish bishops there in about 603. It was an important outpost of Wessex, fortified in the ninth century. Some of these earthworks are visible and have been excavated. The Danes plundered in 905, and again a century later. In 1155 Henry II granted the townspeople a universal toll-free charter, in recognition of the time they sheltered his mother from Stephen's troops. Most of the domestic architecture of interest occurs in the altered seventeenth- and eighteenth-century buildings in the main street. Beside St Sampson's churchyard is Robert Jenner's gabled school, founded in 1651. Close by is the market cross, whilst St Mary's churchyard includes a fourteenth-century cross. The clock in the High Street was put up in 1897 to commemorate Queen Victoria's Diamond Jubilee. The town's main link with nearby Swindon occurred late in the nineteenth century when Daniel Gooch, the railway engineer, was the town's member of Parliament for twenty years. Within walking distance is the former junction of the Thames & Severn Canal (opened 1789) and the Wilts & Berks Canal. A closely guarded area is one of the few homes of the snakeshead fritillary, a rare plant. The Cricklade Music Festival is an annual event which takes place in September.

Church of St Mary, page 84; **church of St Sampson**, page 84; **Cricklade Museum**, page 126.

In the locality: Ashton Keynes church, page 79; Castle Eaton church, page 82; Cotswold Water Park, page 140; Emmett Hill Meadows, page 52; Keynes Country Park, page 53; New Farm Meadow, page 55; Purton church, page 93; Purton Museum, page 130; Red Lodge Pond, page 57; Swindon & Cricklade Railway, page 138; Upper Waterhay Reserve, page 59.

Devizes
Early closing Wednesday; markets Thursday and Saturday at The Shambles, and Thursday in the Market Place; (antiques) Tuesday, The Shambles.

Devizes is a town to be explored and details of a 'town trail' are available. Here, between Salisbury Plain and the Marlborough Downs, three boundaries met (*ad divisas* means 'at the boundaries') and Bishop Roger built a castle in 1120. The present 'castle' is a nineteenth-century mansion. The town grew around the original castle and when it fell into ruins in the sixteenth century the stones were used to build houses. The line of part of its outer defences may be seen in the shape of some roads. These include Monday Market Street, with its fifteenth-century timber-framed Porch House, and Sheep Street. In St John's Alley timber-framed houses closely overhang the cobbles and lead towards the Norman church, and St James's is Perpendicular. It is beside the Crammer, a supposedly bottomless pond which has occasionally dried up!

There was a popular corn market in the spacious market place, where an inscription on the cross of 1814 tells the cautionary tale of Ruth Pierce of Potterne. She agreed to buy her share of wheat but, withholding her money, claimed she had paid and wished to drop down dead if she had not. On repeating the oath she expired, with the money still in her hand.

Most of the best buildings are now of the eighteenth century, even if some, like the Bear Hotel, have earlier origins. There lodged the infamous Judge Jeffreys, and the painter Sir Thomas Lawrence was the son of a former innkeeper. Many famous people made this a fashionable place in which to stay. Other eighteenth-century buildings include Northgate House, the Queen's Head, the Elm Tree hotel, the Black Swan hotel, New Hall, Brownstone House and Greystone House. Nineteenth-century buildings reflect the role of Devizes in commerce and administration: the Town Hall, Assize Court, Market House and brewery. The fine architecture includes the warehouses by the Kennet & Avon Canal, which have been turned into a leisure complex and include a tourist information office at the Devizes Canal Centre. The canal runs through the town and just to the west is raised 230 feet (70 metres) by means of twenty-nine locks. The history of the area is best reviewed at the museum in Long Street.

Broadleas Gardens, page 102; **Caen Hill Locks**, page 136; **Canal Forge**, page 136; **church of St John**, page 85; **Devizes Mu-** seum, page 126; **Devizes Wharf**, page 137; **Drews Pond Wood Project**, page 51; **Kennet & Avon Canal**, page 137; **Kennet & Avon Canal Museum**, page 126; **Wadworth Shire Horses**, page 141.

In the locality: All Cannings church, page 78; Alton Barnes White Horse, page 62; Avebury Henge Monument, page 68; Avebury Manor, page 100; Avebury Manor Gardens, page 100; Bert Watts Museum, page 130; Bishops Cannings church, page 80; Bromham church, page 82; Chirton church, page 83; Honey Street, page 137; Marden church, page 91; Market Lavington Village Museum, page 129; Morgan's Hill Nature Reserve, page 55;

The market cross at Devizes records the cautionary tale of Ruth Pierce.

Oliver's Camp, page 72; Peppercombe Wood, page 56; Porch House, page 118; Potterne church, page 93; Rybury Camp, page 73; Stert Vineyard, page 141; Urchfont church, page 98; Wansdyke, page 60; Wiltshire Fire Defence and Brigade Museum, page 130.

Dilton Marsh
Chalcot House, page 102.

Dinton
Set in the Nadder valley, west of Salisbury, this village is known for four houses which belong to the National Trust, and for its proximity to the iron age hillfort called Wick Ball Camp. Philipps House is open to the public. Hyde's House, near the church, is thought to have been the birthplace of Edward Hyde, Earl of Clarendon, a seventeenth-century Lord Chancellor. It was built in the sixteenth century, but the front was remodelled in the eighteenth. Little Clarendon is a small fifteenth-century house, gabled and buttressed. Lawes Cottage, a seventeenth-century stone building, was once the home of William Lawes, the composer.

Philipps House, page 118.
In the locality: Farmer Giles Farmstead, page 140; Grovely Woods, page 52; Wylye and Teffont Downs, page 61.

Donhead St Mary
Oyster's Coppice, page 55.

Downton
Downton is an ancient borough and market town right on the Hampshire border, where its extension into The Borough straddles the lower Avon. Although it was once one of the larger settlements in the county, and modestly expanded from the 1960s, the central area with its wide and pretty green and thatched timber-framed cottages has not lost its village feel. The High Street curves down to the site of Henry de Blois's castle of 1138 for the Bishops of Winchester. To the south is the site of a Roman villa, and to the east is a series of concentric mounds known as The Moot. The private Moot House is a pedimented, late seventeenth-century building of stone quoins and mauve brick. Downton was famous for its Cuckoo Fair in the spring, a livestock fair in the late summer which attracted dealers from Wiltshire, Hampshire and Dorset, and its staple industry of tanning.
Church of St Lawrence, page 85.

Durrington
Durrington Walls, page 69; Stonehenge Cursus, page 75; Woodhenge, page 77.

East Kennett
Overton Hill, page 73; The Sanctuary, page 73.

East Knoyle
Church of St Mary, page 85.

East Tytherton
Maud Heath's Causeway, page 54.

Ebbesborne Wake
Church of St John the Baptist, page 85.

Edington
Church of St Mary, St Katherine and All Saints, page 86.

Enford
Church of All Saints, page 86; Enford Bowl Barrow, page 70.

Everleigh
Everleigh Barrow Cemetery, page 70.

Farley
Blackmoor Copse, page 49; church of All Saints, page 86.

Fifield Bavant
Church of St Martin, page 87.

Fonthill Gifford
Fonthill Abbey Ruins, page 103.

Fosbury
Fosbury Camp, page 70.

Fovant
Chiselbury Camp, page 69; Fovant Badges Society Collection, page 126; Fovant Regimental Badges, page 64.

Along a secluded road in Fonthill Gifford stand these attractive estate cottages.

Fyfield
Devil's Den, page 69; Fyfield and Overton Downs, page 70.

Great Bedwyn
This is a large village to the south-east of Savernake Forest; there was a Roman settlement here and it had city status in Saxon times. Now it retains the appearance of the small Wiltshire town it was when it sent two members to Parliament, had a market hall and traded by way of the Kennet & Avon Canal and then the railway.

Church of St Mary, page 87; **Crofton Beam Engines**, page 136; **Great Bedwyn Stone Museum**, page 126; **Kennet & Avon Canal**, page 137.

In the locality: Chisbury Camp, page 69; Ham church, page 87; Wilton Windmill, page 139.

Great Chalfield
Church of St All Saints, page 87; Great Chalfield Manor, page 106.

Great Durnford
Church of Andrew, page 87.

Great Wishford
Opposite the churchyard Sir Richard Howe's village school of 1722 stands next to Sir Richard Grobham's rebuilt former almshouses of 1628. These two buildings with tiled roofs and little dormer windows are a wonderful sight, the former of red brick with stone quoins and the other of banded stone with mullioned windows. There are still cob walls, and a walk along the three roads which converge on the churchyard will reveal many attractive houses, including the early eighteenth-century brick and stone parsonage, and the oak tree which sheltered the meetings of the Wishford Oak Apple Club.

Church of St Giles, **Wishford Magna**, page 99; **Grovely Woods**, page 52.

Ham
Church of All Saints, page 87; Ham Hill, page 52.

Hankerton
Church of the Holy Cross, page 87.

Hardenhuish
Church of St Nicholas, page 88.

Heytesbury
Church of St Peter and St Paul, page 88.

Highworth
Early closing Wednesday; market Saturday, in the Market Place.
Before the plague came in 1666 Highworth was a market town of greater importance than nearby Swindon. It was loyal to Charles I in the Civil War and was routed by Fairfax on his return from his victory at the battle of Naseby. The fortified church was besieged with cannon, and many townspeople were

Broad pavements flank the wide main street in Hindon, laid out as a market town in the thirteenth century.

killed or wounded. Both the market and the municipal government were transferred elsewhere, and the town was not greatly enlarged before the large suburban housing estates. The best buildings are around High Street and the square, where there are some from the seventeenth and eighteenth centuries. Of particular interest are the Jesmond House Hotel and Highworth House. The former is reputed to be haunted, as are the church and old passages under High Street. Local legend has it that one of the old houses in High Street, formerly a butcher's shop, supplied the first consignment of meat to reach London after the Great Fire. Highworth remains a quiet town of unpretentious stone buildings, with smaller cottages in the streets behind, built around its church on a hill 400 feet (120 metres) above sea level. There are good views over part of the Vale of White Horse, and the hill descends towards the nearby boating centre and Thames-side walks of Lechlade and Inglesham.

Church of St Michael, page 88; **Highworth Museum**, page 127.

In the locality: Castle Eaton church, page 82; Inglesham church, page 88; Lechlade Meadows and Riverside Park, page 54; Roves Farm, page 141; Stanton Fitzwarren church, page 96.

Hindon
Picturesque but never prosperous, despite its medieval potential, its former status as a market town and Parliamentary borough, and the prospects for development afforded by its position as a staging post on the London to Exeter road in the nineteenth century, Hindon was planned as a town in the thirteenth century by the Bishops of Winchester, who laid out the road system which it retains to this day: a wide street on a hill with large eighteenth-century houses on either side. There is little of note hereabouts earlier than Georgian, for in 1754 a disastrous fire destroyed most of the village. This gave the opportunity to rebuild using the fine limestone from the nearby Tisbury quarries where it could be afforded, and rubblestone mix for cottage architecture where it could not.

Hinton Parva
Church of St Swithin, page 88.

Holt
The Courts, page 103.

Huish
Gopher Wood, page 70.

Hullavington
Church of St Mary, page 88.

Imber
Imber Range Perimeter Path, page 52.

Inglesham
Church of St John the Baptist, page 88; Lechlade Meadows and Riverside Park, page 54.

Kilmington
White Sheet Hill, page 76.

Knook
Church of St Margaret, page 89.

Lacock
One of England's most beautiful villages, Lacock was given to the National Trust by Matilda Talbot in 1944. The few narrow winding streets run off or around the wide High Street in a square, connecting everyone with the church in a picturesque backwater. They are lined with old timber-framed, stone or brick buildings. Most were put up between the fourteenth and eighteenth centuries and they include one house with a cruck frame and the timber-framed Porch House in High Street. Others may have sharp gables, decorated overhangs, projecting eaves or dormer windows, presenting a combination of quaint frontages, as in Church Street. There is the fifteenth-century Angel inn, with sixteenth- and seventeenth-century additions, and, close by, a house with a fourteenth-century doorway. Lacock village is full of minor architectural detail from the early timber framework to the Georgian pediment and is a delight to explore. Some of the cottages in the village were former weavers' dwellings. Note the Red Lion hotel, an ambitious building for this village, put up early in the eighteenth century, opposite the fourteenth-century tithe barn and near the lock-up.

Bewley Common, page 49; **church of St Cyriac**, page 89; **Fox Talbot Museum of Photography**, page 127; **Lackham Country Attractions – Agricultural Museum and Gardens**, pages 110 and 128; **Lacock Abbey**, page 110.

In the locality: Spye Park Stables Museum, page 125.

Landford
Hamptworth Lodge, page 106; Landford Bog, page 53.

Langley Burrell
Maud Heath's Causeway, page 54.

Laverstock
Cockey Down, page 50; Laverstock Panda, page 65.

Liddington
Liddington Castle, page 71.

Little Bedwyn
Chisbury Camp, page 69.

Little Durnford
Little Durnford Down, page 54.

Little Langford
Church of St Nicholas, page 90; Little Langford Down, page 54.

Little Somerford
Church of St John the Baptist, page 90.

Luckington
Luckington Court, page 113.

Ludgershall
Much of the area was acquired by the army and Tidworth Camp is nearby. Anything of interest is in Castle Street. The Norman castle which housed the Empress Maud in 1141 has been in ruins for centuries. Ludgershall was a former market town and part of the carved market cross survives, rebuilt on a brick base and protected by iron railings. Two-storey

The remains of the market cross in the centre of Ludgershall.

brick almshouses, put up in the seventeenth century, are near the castle.

Church of St James, page 90; **Ludgershall Castle**, page 71; **Ludgershall Museum**, page 128.

Lydiard Millicent
Church of All Saints, page 90.

Lydiard Tregoze
Church of St Mary, page 90; Lydiard Park, page 114.

Maiden Bradley
Church of All Saints, page 90.

Malmesbury
Early closing Thursday.
It is from the historian William of Malmesbury that we learn that a monastery was established here in 640. William was not a native of the town but went there to be educated and stayed as librarian at the monastery. Today the abbey dominates the town. The early settlement was on a hill, on what was almost an island formed by the Bristol Avon and one of its tributaries. Around these natural defences the town was later fortified. Athelstan granted its first charter in 924. In the tenth century a monk called Oliver (or Elmer in some accounts) descended from one of the abbey towers with wings strapped to his arms and legs, determined to fly. He broke his legs but escaped with his life. In 1588 Thomas Hobbes, the philosopher, was born at Westport, now a suburb.

By the fifteenth century Malmesbury was a weaving centre and prospered as such into the eighteenth century. From early in that period comes the restored market cross, of about 1490, at the end of the High Street. It is over 40 feet (12 metres) high and comprises a lantern with figures beneath trefoil-headed canopies, above eight open arches with a groined roof. Above the arches are battlements; the lantern is supported by flying buttresses, and everywhere there are ogee arches, crockets and finials. It is a beautiful structure. By St John's Bridge are the seventeenth-century almshouses on the site of the thirteenth-century hospital of St John of Jerusalem. Of the original foundation, a blocked doorway remains. The town hall in Cross Hayes is gabled, and the narrow roads which run around it have buildings in Cotswold stone with stone-tiled roofs. Many are of the seventeenth and eighteenth centuries and, of the latter, there is a former four-storey cloth mill by the bridge.

Athelstan Museum, page 128; **Malmesbury Abbey**, page 91; **Malmesbury Abbey Parvise Museum**, page 129.

In the locality: Charlton Park House, page 102; Hankerton church, page 87; Hullavington church, page 88; Little Somerford church, page 90; Sherston church, page 94; Somerford Common Nature Trail, page 58; Stanton St Quintin church, page 96.

Manningford Abbots
Manningford Gardens and Nursery, page 115.

Manningford Bruce
Church of St Peter, page 91.

Marden
Church of All Saints, page 91; Marden Henge Monument, page 72.

Market Lavington

Although a long busy village with a thriving population, Market Lavington's fame is very largely in its past. This former market town beneath the northern escarpment of Salisbury Plain was a centre for sales of sheep and corn well into the nineteenth century. For three hundred years brickmaking was one of the staple industries hereabouts, then malting and brewing. It is also the home of a family of downland dewpond makers.

Market Lavington Village Museum, page 129.

In the locality: Imber Range Perimeter Path, page 52; Peppercombe Wood, page 56.

Marlborough

Early closing Wednesday; markets Wednesday and Saturday, High Street.

Marlborough has been an important place since the Roman occupation, when there was a station 1¹/₂ miles (2.4 km) east at Mildenhall (*Cunetio*). There was a mint at Marlborough in Norman times and kings hunted in the vast royal forest of Savernake. A borough since 1204, this market town has an exceptionally wide High Street. It was once on the stage-coach route between London and Bath. Interesting buildings, some with fine eighteenth-century façades, line both sides of the High Street and there is a church at either end. There was fighting here in the Civil War. The older, timber-framed buildings are to be found in the lanes beyond the High Street, because central Marlborough was devastated by fire in 1653, 1679 and 1690. After these fires thatched roofs were banned in the town by Act of Parliament. One survival of the fire

Malmesbury viewed across the river Avon from the cloth mill.

Left: *The house in Marlborough in which William Golding lived.* Right: *St Peter's church at the west end of the town is used as a community centre.*

was a group of houses on the north side above what is known as the Colonnade. These pillars are still there, fronting shops and beneath some fine gabled architecture. The Hermitage in the High Street dates from early in the seventeenth century, whilst the Castle and Ball inn is only slightly younger. Marlborough College was founded in 1843 and stands on the site of the old castle. 'Maerl's Barrow', in its grounds, is the legendary burial place of Merlin. The Mop Fair, a pleasure fair, takes place in the main street during two weekends in October. The redundant church of St Peter and St Paul, where Cardinal Wolsey was ordained in 1498, is in a municipal precinct and houses craft stalls and a coffee shop.

Church of St Mary, page 92; **Marlborough College Natural History Collection**, page 129; **Marlborough White Horse**, page 65; **Merchant's House**, page 115; **Postern Hill**, page 56.

In the locality: Alexander Keiller Museum, page 123; Alton Barnes White Horse, page 62; Avebury Henge Monument, page 68; Avebury Manor, page 100; Avebury Manor Gardens, page 100; Chiseldon church, page 83; Crofton Beam Engines, page 136; Great Barn Museum of Wiltshire Life, page 124; Great Bedwyn church, page 87; Great Bedwyn Stone Museum, page 126; Hat Gate, page 52; Martinsell Hill, page 72; Mildenhall church, page 92; Ogbourne St George church, page

93; *Preshute church, page 93; Savernake Forest, page 58; Wansdyke, page 60.*

Marston Meysey

This is the most northern village in the county, bounded on one side by the swelling river Thames, and mostly laid out beside one long street. Cotswold-style architecture here includes stone cottages and larger seventeenth-century farmhouses. Close by are the remains of a roundhouse of 1789, one of several on the Thames & Severn Canal, and there is a humpback bridge.

Melksham

Early closing Wednesday.
Melksham has much improved its shopping facilities and social amenities. Previously it appeared to be an uninteresting place whose greatest claim to fame was its failure to become a popular spa. Saline and chalybeate springs were discovered there and in 1815 attempts were made to market the town as a spa. The converted pump room remains and a crescent of houses on the Devizes road attests to this period. The town was once cut off by the Forest of Melksham and Chippenham, as it would have been when the heavily buttressed tithe barn was built in the fourteenth century. This was subsequently used as a school but has been converted to accommodate old people. Although in the twentieth century both light and heavy engineering have come to Melksham, it remains a market town with dairy farming as the traditional industry. It was once a centre of the cloth trade but there is little domestic architecture of interest to show for it. Some attractive limestone houses stand around High Street and the square, built in the seventeenth and eighteenth centuries, and King Street has some Georgian examples with mullioned windows. The town hall, which has a tall, pedimented entrance, was built in 1847. Also nineteenth-century is the King's Arms hotel in Market Place. Perhaps more pleasing aesthetically is the balustrade on the late eighteenth-century bridge over the river Avon. There is a fine fifteenth-century manor house at Beanacre.

Conigre Meadow, page 50; **Melksham Historical Collection**, page 129.

In the locality: Atworth Museum, page 123; Bewley Common, page 49; Bromham church, page 82; Fox Talbot Museum of Photography, page 127; Great Chalfield church, page 87; Great Chalfield Manor, page 106; Kennet & Avon Canal, page 137; Lacock Abbey, page 110; Lacock church, page 89; Spye Park Stables Museum, page 125.

Mere

Early closing Wednesday.
Downland and wooded hills engulf this little stone town, built on the borders with Dorset and Somerset and named after John Mere. The impressive tower of St Michael's church rises from the centre, overshadowed only by Castle Hill, although the castle built on it in 1253 has long gone. Close by is Whitesheet Hill with its iron age hillfort, in an area which is now a nature reserve. There are a number of small Georgian houses and a long one of the fifteenth-century called the Chantry. Here was once a school kept by William Barnes, the

The round house, used by clothmakers, at Melksham.

Dorset poet. Charles II stayed at the George hotel, as it then was, on his escape from the battle of Worcester in 1651. The Ship inn, made out of a seventeenth-century mansion, has fine wrought ironwork, including a sign by Kingston Avery, maker of the church clock. It includes John Mere's badge. The strange clock-tower was erected on the site of the old market house in 1866.

Church of St Michael, page 92; **Mere Museum**, page 129.

In the locality: East Knoyle church, page 85; King Alfred's Tower, page 107; Maiden Bradley church, page 90; Stourhead Gardens, page 119; Stourhead House, page 119; Stourton House Garden, page 120; Whitesheet Castle, page 76; White Sheet Hill, page 76; White Sheet Hill Nature Trail, page 60.

The statue of King Alfred in Pewsey High Street was erected to commemorate the coronation of George V.

Middle Woodford
Heale Gardens and Plant Centre, page 106; Woodford Valley, page 61.

Mildenhall
Church of St John the Baptist, page 92.

Milton Lilbourne
Giant's Grave, page 70; Manor House Garden, page 115.

Minety
Distillery Farm Meadows, page 51; Emmett Hill Meadows, page 52; Ravensroost Wood, page 57.

Monkton Farleigh
Monkton Farleigh Mine, page 129.

Netheravon
Church of All Saints, page 92.

Nettleton
Church of St Mary, page 92.

North Wraxall
Church of St James, page 92.

Norton Bavant
Scratchbury Camp, page 74.

Ogbourne St Andrew
Ogbourne Round Barrow, page 72.

Ogbourne St George
Church of St George, page 93.

Old Dilton
Church of St Mary, page 93.

Pewsey
Early closing Wednesday; market Tuesday, High Street car park.
This small town grew up around an island settlement, once encircled by the river. The name is derived from *Pevisigge*, 'little island'. It is situated on the Salisbury Avon, just below the Kennet & Avon Canal. King Alfred gave lands there and, as the result of one such bequest, Pewsey belonged to Hyde Abbey, Winchester, until the Dissolution.

Alfred's statue has stood at the junction of the three main streets since 1913. It was put there to commemorate the coronation of George V in 1911. The town is the metropolis of the lush Vale which divides the county across its width and to which it gives its name. It is surrounded by pretty little thatched villages and hamlets, and Pewsey itself still has small thatched shops in the main street. Note, too, the cast-iron sign of the Phoenix inn and the church on the hill. Pewsey is well-known for its annual carnival, which began in 1898 and takes place in September.

Church of St John the Baptist, page 93; **Jones's Mill Reserve,** page 53; **Kennet & Avon Canal,** page 137; **Pewsey Heritage Centre,** page 130; **Pewsey Wharf,** page 138; **Pewsey White Horse,** page 65; **Scotchel Nature Trail,** page 58.

In the locality: Alton Barnes church, page 78; Alton Barnes White Horse, page 62; Alton Priors church, page 78; Honey Street, page 137; Manningford Bruce church, page 91; Manningford Gardens and Nursery, page 115; Manor House Garden, Milton Lilbourne, page 115; Marden church, page 91; Martinsell Hill, page 72; Pewsey Downs National Nature Reserve, page 56; Upper Avon Valley, page 59; Wansdyke, page 60; Wilcot church, page 99; Wilton Windmill, page 139; Wootton Rivers church, page 99; Wootton Rivers Lock, page 139.

Potterne

Just south of Devizes, the busy A360 bends its way through the village, which is forever inscribed in folklore by one of its former inhabitants – Ruth Pierce, who lied, died and is remembered on Devizes market cross. Here are the offices of the Wiltshire Fire Service, a cluster of timber-framed houses, and cottages which press hard upon the twisting road. Next to the Porch House is another, very unusual timber-framed building.

Bert Watts Museum, page 130; **church of St Mary,** page 93; **Porch House,** page 118; **Wiltshire Fire Defence and Brigade Museum,** page 130.

Preshute
Church of St George, page 93.

Purton

Victorian attempts to create a spa here might have made more of Purton when nearby Swindon was still quite small, but only the little octagonal pump room of 1859 survived. Quite a long village, Purton is in several parts, beginning with the stone-built barn, the manor house and the picturesque area around the churchyard wall. In the High Street, around the centre, there are some interesting buildings including the Institute of 1875, now the library. Further along is an early eighteenth-century stone building which developed from commercial home-brewing origins into the Angel Inn of today. Then the village is taken over by housing, before the 'modern' end. Above all this is the imposing brick-built and pedimented former workhouse of 1838, latterly the North View Hospital for mentally handicapped ladies.

Church of St Mary, page 93; **New Farm Meadow,** page 55; **Purton Museum,** page 130; **Red Lodge Pond,** page 57.

In the locality: Swindon & Cricklade Railway, page 138.

Ramsbury

Close to the eastern border of the county, in the beautiful Kennet valley, is this large old village where a bishopric was created in 909 and where in 1846 a famous building society held its first meeting. In the 166 years before it was transferred to Old Sarum, the bishopric of Ramsbury provided three archbishops of Canterbury: Odo, Siric and Aelfric. The Ramsbury Building Society took as its logo the ancient elm tree which stood near to its head office in the village square, surrounded by streets which follow the medieval line. Many of the buildings are of brick and flint, used in bands, with stone, or randomly, although some of the cottages are timber-framed. Of interest is Parliament Piece, a late seventeenth-century house by the church, so called because of an association with one of Cromwell's parliaments. Ramsbury Manor, of about 1676, is an impressive brick building of nine bays, pedimented with hipped roof and stone dressings, in its own grounds.

Church of the Holy Cross, page 93; **Ramsbury Meadow,** page 57.

*In the locality: Aldbourne church, page 78;
Chilton Foliat church, page 82; Littlecote
House, page 111; Littlecote Roman Villa,
page 71.*

Redlynch

Newhouse, page 117.

Salisbury

*Markets: Tuesday and Saturday, Market
Square; (antiques) Tuesday, United
Reformed Church; (antiques) daily,
Catherine Street; (cattle) Tuesday, Ashley
Road.*

Salisbury is Wiltshire's only city. It is smaller
than the industrial sprawl of Swindon, and the
perfect antidote to it. The present city was
founded because bad weather, a shortage of
water and disputes with the military authorities compelled the clergy to leave the former,
exposed site at Old Sarum and establish a
new cathedral in a more suitable place. Work
went ahead from 1220, the townspeople followed the clergy, and in 1277 Henry III
granted the first charter. Salisbury became an
important centre in the cloth trade and many
of the secular buildings extant originated during this period of wealth. The city preserves
its architectural heritage, and the modern
shopping centre of Old George Mall is in no
way an intrusion. Timber-framed medieval
buildings with overhanging gables and bow
windows stand side by side with fine Georgian stonework. Salisbury has a wide and
busy market place surrounded by big old
buildings, and its modern shopping centre.
Traders still cluster around the hexagonal
Poultry Cross in Butchers Row as they have
since it first afforded shelter in the fifteenth
century. The cross has open ogee arches, canopied niches and flying buttresses supporting a
spirelet. It is said to have been erected as an
act of penance. Close by is a fourteenth-
century inn, the Haunch of Venison.

The city has traditionally been divided between The Close, which is still locked at
night, and the commercial area which presses
hard against the medieval walls. The old town
was built on a grid system of six streets running east to west, crossed by five running
north to south. Each square of streets in the
grid was named after a prominent building in
it and the names of several streets such as Salt
Lane, Butchers Row, Fish Row, Ox Row and
Chipper Lane attest to their commercial origins.

The city is situated just north of the point at
which the rivers Avon, Nadder, Bourne,
Wylye and Ebble converge. It was fortified in
the fourteenth century, partly with stone from
the then derelict cathedral at Old Sarum. Parts
of the wall remain as well as the North Gate in
High Street and St Ann's Gate in St Ann
Street.

Many of the important buildings may be
taken in on a tour beginning at the North Gate
in High Street. First are the three timber-
framed buildings which form Beach's bookshop; next is the Old George hotel. It was
built about 1320 and Cromwell slept there in
1645. New Street has the New Inn, built in the
fourteenth century. In New Canal, the entrance to the cinema is John Halle's fifteenth-
century banqueting hall, restored by Pugin in
1834. The library in Castle Street was originally the market house. A little to the north-
east, in Salt Lane, is the Shoemakers' Guildhall of 1638. The Church House in Crane
Street belonged to a wool merchant and became the house of correction and workhouse.
In St John Street, the King's Arms is reputed
to be as old as the cathedral and the White
Hart hotel, the largest in the city, was an
important coaching inn where Henry VII is
said to have stayed. The Joiners' Hall in St
Ann Street was built in the seventeenth century and the Rose and Crown three centuries
earlier. Trinity Hospital in Trinity Street was
founded in 1379. The House of John à Port
was built in 1425 in Queen Street and the
Guildhall of 1795 was designed by Sir Robert
Taylor.

There are many old and attractive buildings in The Close and Choristers' Green,
which comprise the largest cathedral close in
England. The College of Matrons was
founded in 1682 for the widows of clergymen; Mompesson House is a National Trust
property; The Wardrobe houses a military
museum; North Canonry gardens go down to
the river Avon; King's House is another museum; there are also Leadenhall, the South

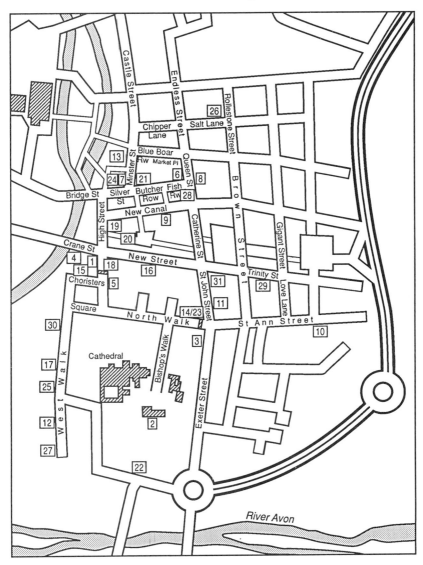

Salisbury street plan. Key: 1 Beach's Bookshop; 2 Bishop's Palace; 3 Bishop Wordsworth School Museum; 4 Church House; 5 College of Matrons; 6 Guildhall; 7 Haunch of Venison; 8 House of John à Port; 9 John Halle's Banqueting Hall (now Odeon cinema); 10 Joiners' Hall; 11 King's Arms; 12 Leadenhall; 13 Library (former Market House); 14 Malmesbury House; 15 Mompesson House; 16 New Inn; 17 North Canonry; 18 North Gate or High Street Gate; 19 Old George Hotel (Bay Tree Restaurant); 20 Old George Mall; 21 Poultry Cross; 22 Rose and Crown; 23 St Ann's Gate; 24 St Thomas's church; 25 Salisbury and South Wiltshire Museum (King's House); 26 Shoemakers' Guildhall (now the Pheasant); 27 South Canonry; 28 Tourist Information Centre; 29 Trinity Hospital; 30 The Wardrobe (regimental museum); 31 White Hart Hotel.

Canonry and the fourteenth-century Malmesbury House. At the thirteenth-century Bishop's Palace Charles II sat out the great plague of 1665, and from its gardens John Constable painted the cathedral.

Avon Valley Project, page 48; **Bishop Wordsworth School Museum**, page 130; **Church of St Thomas**, page 94; **Clarendon Park**, page 50; **House of John à Port**, page 106; **John Creasey Museum**, page 131; **Malmesbury House**, page 114; **Mompesson House**, page 115; **Old Sarum**, page 72; **Royal Gloucestershire, Berkshire and Wiltshire Regiment's Salisbury Museum**, page 131; **Salisbury and South Wiltshire Museum**, page 131; **Salisbury Cathedral**, page 94.

In the locality: Bishopstone church, page 80; Blackmoor Copse, page 49; Britford church, page 81; Chickengrove Bottom, page 49; Cockey Down, page 50; Coombe Bissett church, page 84; Downton church, page 85; Farley church, page 86; Figsbury Ring, page 70; Heale Gardens and Plant Centre, page 106; Knowle Down, page 53; Landford Bog, page 53; Laverstock Panda, page 65; Little Durnford Down, page 54; Middleton Down, page 55; Newhouse, page 117; Pepperbox Hill, page 56; Wilton House, page 121; Woodford Valley, page 61. See also Wilton, page 44.

Sandy Lane

On the busy A342 near to Bowood House and gardens is a tiny multi-layered thatch and tile sandstone village of small cottage gardens, thick hedges and tall trees. It came about when estate workers' dwellings were submerged in the making of Bowood's lake, and alternative homes had to be built for them. Here, too, are a unique little thatched church, the George Inn with eighteenth-century features and the village well beneath a pyramidal, tiled roof.

Sevenhampton

Roves Farm, page 141.

Sevington

Sevington School Museum, page 125.

Sherston

Church of the Holy Trinity, page 94.

South Wraxall

Church of St James, page 94.

Stanton Fitzwarren

This is one of Wiltshire's northern, Cotswold villages with Stanton House, although not built until 1935, continuing the theme. The Fitzwarrens were here by the mid eleventh century, where the Romans had settled before them. Good architecture and cottage-style gardens are still a feature.

Church of St Leonard, page 96.

Stanton St Quintin

Church of St Giles, page 96.

Stapleford

Church of St Mary, page 96.

Steeple Ashton

Much of the village was built in stone, on earlier foundations, with the profits from the wool trade before it declined during the second half of the sixteenth century. Untypical of the area it may be, but here is a perfect English village, notable for its juxtaposition of cottage and town architecture over several centuries. A good mixture forms an impressive backdrop to the triangular green. A weekly market began here in the middle of the thirteenth century, although the market cross is said to have originated in 1071. It is a column, put up in 1679 and since restored on several occasions, topped by a sundial which is thought to date from about 1714. It stands in the centre of the village next to the octagonal stone lock-up of 1773, with the usual-style domed roof. Notable buildings of character include the high ashlar-fronted Ashton House, whose façade of 1724 does not even hint at the fifteenth-century timber-roofed hall within. The timber-framed Old Merchant's Hall, with its herringbone arrangement of orange brickwork and leaded windows, is in stark contrast to the plain-fronted stone cottages. From here the vista is most impressive for it lifts the eye to the church, which lost its spire in 1670, as the focal point. Whether 'Steeple' is derived from the former impressive arrangement at the church or from

The Nadder valley and the village of Dinton.

The historic Castle and Ball Hotel, in Marlborough High Street.

the 'staple' of the wool trade is a matter of conjecture. The Old Vicarage, although externally of the early nineteenth century, is also of the fourteenth century in part. Steeple Ashton offers the visitor a number of short lanes and quiet corners flanked by a wide selection of historic buildings.

Church of St Mary, page 96.

In the locality: Green Lane Wood, page 52.

Steeple Langford

Church of All Saints, page 96; Yarnbury Castle, page 77.

Stert

Stert Vineyard, page 141.

Brunel's statue overlooks Brunel Plaza, the modern shopping development at Swindon.

Stockton

Long Hall Gardens, page 113.

Stourton

Stourhead Gardens, page 119; Stourhead House, page 119; Stourton House Garden, page 120; Whitesheet Castle, page 76.

Stratton St Margaret

What is left of the old village lies mostly between the Crown inn and the church, lining part of the Roman road which runs between Cirencester and Winchester. It was once a large parish of several hamlets, extending to the boundary of nineteenth-century Swindon. Now it is virtually a suburb, having given up much land to its sprawling neighbour. In living memory it has lost much interesting cottage architecture to the demands of modern housing and light industry. Its inhabitants were traditionally engaged in agriculture and later brickmaking, for there were several brickworks within the parish. The Crown and the Jacob's Ladder in Ermin Street are hostelries which may well have existed as such early in the eighteenth century, and the New Inn in Swindon Road is an example of an early nineteenth-century public house which came about to serve the needs of people who worked on the nearby Wilts & Berks Canal. There is a square stone dovecote of *c.*1600 in Pigeon House Lane.

To the north-west is **Upper Stratton**, where, at Kingsdown, the famous family brewery of Arkells celebrated its 150th anniversary in 1994. The Boundary House, built in 1894 in Beechcroft Road, is an architectural oddity.

Church of St Margaret, page 96.

Swindon

Early closing Wednesday. Markets: Tuesday, Friday and Saturday, Fleet Street car park; Wednesday, Saturday and Sunday, Dorcan market, Faraday Road, Dorcan; Thursday, Cavendish Square, Park South; Tuesday, Link Centre coach park, West Swindon; Sunday, Mannington Car Boot Market, off Mannington Roundabout, Great Western Way; Monday to Saturday, The Market Hall, Market Street; Saturday and Sunday, Marsh

Part of the planned village built at Swindon in the 1840s for the artisans and employees of the Great Western Railway Company. The church of St Mark was built by the railwaymen themselves.

Gate Market and Car Boot Sale, Marshgate; (antiques) quarterly, The Planks, Old Town. For details telephone: 01793 615915.

Swindon is the largest town in the county. Until the 1840s it was a small hilltop community which ran a market for cattle, sheep and horses and made cheese. Of that town little is left. The railway works which came to the plains below in 1842 established New Swindon; red brick buildings spread up the hill to meet the grey limestone buildings of the old town. Old and New Swindon were administratively joined in 1900. The town was dominated by the railway until after 1945, when industrial development attracted medium engineering. Sprawling monotonous council estates, built to house a sudden increase in population in the 1960s, still mark the town's periphery. The central area was redeveloped from the 1960s in piecemeal fashion, and this is still going on. Its big modern buildings, put up to house contemporary office businesses, are mainly out of harmony with each other, although smaller sensitive courtyard-type developments of more recent years are much of an improvement.

However, the stone railway village of about 1850, with its restored artisans' cottages, larger officials' houses and mechanics' institute – a planned Victorian village – should be visited. Close by is St Mark's, the railwaymen's church, built with their own hands. New Swindon town hall (1889-91), in Dutch seventeenth-century style, is an eccentric rarity and is now used as a reference library, contemporary dance studio and theatre and media arts complex.

In the old town, part of the Goddard estate, which once belonged to the lords of the manor, is open to the public. It includes the chancel and fragments of the town's original church of Holy Rood, open at specific times during the summer. The most attractive house is 42 Cricklade Street (1729), and other buildings of note here include Christ Church (1851), the adjoining hospital (1877) and some eighteenth-century buildings in High Street.

Features of Swindon are the murals and sculpture which have appeared all over the town in recent years, and which may be visited on Thamesdown Art Trails. There are currently more than forty murals on gable-end walls, beside car parks, on underpasses and in many other places. Some show long-gone Swindon life and personalities. They are the work of important local artists, groups

The picturesque village of Teffont Magna with its stream flowing in front of the cottages.

Tisbury has the largest medieval tithe barn in England.

and students. There are about fifteen groups of sculptures, which range from major work by internationally known artists to local craftsmen. They include many controversial pieces.

Teffont Magna

Tidcombe

Tilshead

Tisbury

This is a small town full of interesting old stone buildings and some quite exceptional ones. It grew up where the river Sem meets the river Nadder, now crossed by an early nineteenth-century bridge. Its economy benefited from the cloth trade and the high-

Left: *Number 64 Fore Street, Trowbridge, was the house of the clothier Thomas Cooper.* Below: *The tomb of Thomas Helliker, executed after the cloth riots of 1803.*

quality limestone quarries close by. The railway line helped Tisbury to gain supremacy over its immediate neighbours in the Nadder valley. Interesting buildings here include the seventeenth-century almshouses known as Vicar's Cottages, which have an upper storey of red brick added at Victoria's Golden Jubilee in 1887. Both Old House and Gaston House may be of late sixteenth-century or early seventeenth-century date, and the classical-style Tisbury House is about one hundred years later. At Place Farm, amidst a fine collection of fourteenth- and fifteenth-century buildings which once belonged to the Abbess of Shaftesbury, is the largest medieval tithe barn in England.

Pyt House, page 118.

In the locality: Chiselbury Camp, page 69; Compton Chamberlayne 'Australia' hill figure, page 64; Farmer Giles Farmstead, page 140; Fonthill Abbey Ruins, page 103; Fovant Badges Society Collection, page 126; Fovant Regimental Badges, page 64; Oyster's Coppice, page 55; Wardour Old Castle, page 120; Win Green Hill, page 60; Wylye and Teffont Downs, page 61.

Trowbridge
Early closing Wednesday; markets Tuesday, Thursday, Friday and Saturday, at the market precincts, and Thursday, at the football ground.

This is the administrative centre of the county. The wide Georgian-style façade of County Hall is the most impressive building, put up in Bythesea Road in 1940. Next in interest are probably the town hall and the market house, both mid-Victorian and both in continental styles. Of the castle which was besieged by Stephen in 1139 there are no remains, only the line of Fore Street following its rampart and ditch. There was a Saxon settlement here, but little expansion until Flemish weavers were imported in the reign of Edward III. By the fourteenth century it was the county's largest weaving centre, and later profits from the trade built the fine Georgian houses. These may be seen in The Parade, Fore Street and Roundstone Street where the frontages of stone-built, former merchants' houses are most impressive. With the coming of power looms, the redundant cloth workers rioted and burnt factories in the town and neighbourhood. The alleged leader, Thomas Helliker, was executed in 1803 on his nineteenth birthday and is buried in the churchyard. The cloth trade is still carried on in the town, as well as other light industry, and several nineteenth-century mill buildings can still be seen. There is an eighteenth-century lock-up. Matthew Hutton, who became Archbishop of Canterbury in 1757, was rector of Trowbridge from 1726 to 1730. A later rector was George Crabbe, the poet and naturalist, who held the office for the last eighteen years of his life to 1832. Sir Isaac Pitman, born here in 1813, was educated at the town's grammar school.

Green Lane Wood, page 52; **Trowbridge Museum**, page 133.

In the locality: Bradford-on-Avon church (St Lawrence), page 81; Bradford-on-Avon Museum, page 124; Bradford-on-Avon Tithe Barn, page 100; Bradford-on-Avon Wharf, page 136; The Courts, page 103; Great Chalfield church, page 87; Great Chalfield Manor, page 106; Kennet & Avon Canal, page 137; Steeple Ashton church, page 96; Westwood Manor, page 121; Woodland Heritage Museum, page 134; Woodland Park, page 141.

Upavon

The river is quite substantial here, and the village on its west bank grew up thatched and timber-framed where the Upper Avon begins its flow in earnest through the county. The traveller can still pursue an attractive course, following the river along the minor roads through East Chisenbury, Fittleton, Figheldean, Milston, Bulford and on to Amesbury. There are fine views from Upavon Airfield on the downs to the south-east and it was here that the Central Flying School of the Royal Flying Corps was opened in 1912. Perhaps the village's most famous son was the colourful Henry 'Orator' Hunt MP (1773-1835), revolutionary son of a local farmer.

Upton Lovell
Church of St Peter, page 98.

Urchfont
Church of St Michael, page 98; Peppercombe Wood, page 56.

Wanborough
Church of St Andrew, page 98.

Wardour
Wardour Old Castle, page 120.

Warminster
Early closing Wednesday; market Friday, at the central car park.

Built of local stone 400 feet (120 metres) above sea level at the edge of the Wylye valley, Warminster and its immediate neighbourhood have become well-known for alleged sightings of unidentified flying objects. To the east lie Battlesbury and Scratchbury Camps on the edge of Salisbury Plain, and Cley Hill is to the west. Between lies the small town. The long main street runs most of its length, interrupted only by the wide market place. An agricultural centre and market town, it was described by Daniel Defoe as 'without exception the greatest market for wheat in England'. It played a part in the cloth

The obelisk at Warminster.

The village pond at Urchfont.

industry and became well-known for glovemaking, retaining its agricultural connections and adding light industry. The Army School of Infantry is on the outskirts, as are the workshops of the Royal Electrical and Mechanical Engineers. It was at Warminster that Alfred assembled his army for the final onslaught against the Danes in 878. There are a number of eighteenth- and nineteenth-century cottages and houses. The stone-built grammar school was founded in 1707 by Thomas Thynne, Viscount Weymouth of Longleat, and has mullioned windows and a dormer roof. The doorway to the school house was originally designed by Wren for Longleat. The school's most famous pupil was Dr Thomas Arnold, the educational reformer, later headmaster of Rugby. Of the old coaching inns, the Bath Arms hotel and the Old Bell, which overhangs a colonnade, are noteworthy. The town hall was built in the reign of William IV and the nearby chapel of St Lawrence is a restored thirteenth-century foundation. A street monument, topped by an urn and formerly used as a water trough, was erected in 1781. Roman remains have been found around Pitmead, 2 miles (3 km) away, where two villas were discovered in 1786.

Arn Hill Nature Trail, page 48; **Battlesbury Camp**, page 68; **Cley Hill**, page 50; **Cley Hill Camp**, page 69; **Dents Glove Museum**, page 134; **Dewey Museum**, page 134; **Infantry and Small Arms School Corps Weapons Museum**, page 134; **Smallbrook Meadows**, page 58.

In the locality: Boyton church, page 80; Codford St Peter church, page 83; Heytesbury church, page 88; Imber Range Perimeter Path, page 52; Knook church, page 89; Long Hall Gardens, page 113; Longhedge Collection, page 125; Longleat House, page 113; Longleat Safari Park, page 140; Maiden Bradley church, page 90; Scratchbury Camp, page 74; Shear Water, page 58; Upton Lovell church, page 98.

Westbury

Early closing Wednesday; market Friday, at the football ground.

A moated site called Palace Green is sup-

Wilton's extraordinary church was built in Italian Romanesque style in 1844.

posed to have been where the kings of Wessex had a palace, and certainly the area has Saxon connections. This pleasant little town is close to the Somerset border, on the western edge of Salisbury Plain. There are a number of Georgian buildings around the market place and others grouped around the church beyond. All Saints is a Perpendicular cruciform church known for its unusual faceless clock, made by a local blacksmith in 1604, and a chained copy of the New Testament paraphrase by Erasmus. It has a ring of eight bells and a sanctus bell, one of the heaviest anywhere in the world. The old town hall was built in 1815 by Sir Massey Lopes, whose family name is recalled in the Georgian Lopes Arms hotel. Otherwise there is mostly cottage architecture of the nineteenth century in some quaint and picturesque corners away from the main street. Hereabouts is good sheep-grazing land and Westbury had a part in the medieval wool and cloth industry. It is known for leatherwork and glovemaking, to which has been added light engineering in recent times. The White Horse is 1½ miles (2.4 km) to the south-east on Bratton Down.

Donne Collection, page 134; **Westbury Cement Works**, page 138; **Westbury Downland**, page 60; **Westbury Swimming Pool**, page 138; **Westbury White Horse**, page 65.

In the locality: Bratton Castle, page 68; Bratton church, page 81; Chalcot House, page 102; Edington church, page 86; Imber Range Perimeter Path, page 52; Old Dilton church, page 93; Steeple Ashton church, page 96; Woodland Heritage Museum, page 134; Woodland Park, page 141.

West Kennett

West Kennett Avenue, page 75; West Kennett Long Barrow, page 76.

Westwood

Iford Manor Gardens, page 107; Westwood Manor, page 121.

Wilcot

Church of the Holy Cross, page 99; Kennet & Avon Canal, page 137.

Wilsford

Lake Barrow Cemetery, page 71; Normanton Down Barrow Cemetery, page 72.

Wilton

Early closing Wednesday; market Thursday, in the Market Place.
Nothing remains of the great capital of Saxon Wessex, royal residence and bishopric which gave its name to the county. Alfred founded the priory, dissolved in 1544, where Wilton House now stands. Wilton's most ancient association is with agriculture; it has three sheep fairs annually and is still the centre of the sheep trade in the area. The town hall of 1738 is in the Market Place. In 1844 T. H. Wyatt built an amazing church for Sydney Herbert, an Italian basilica in flamboyant Lombardic style. Internally it is a riot of decoration with twisted columns, marbles and mosaics, and there is some medieval glass from the continent. The Royal Wilton carpet factory was granted its royal charter by William III in 1699.

Wilton House, page 121.

In the locality: Berwick St James church, page 79; Bishopstone church, page 80; Chiselbury Camp, page 69; Compton Chamberlayne 'Australia' hill figure, page 64; Coombe Bissett church, page 84; Fifield Bavant church, page 87; Fovant Badges Society Collection, page 126; Fovant Regimental Badges, page 64; Grovely Woods, page 52; Little Langford church, page 90; Little Langford Down, page 54; Philipps House, page 118; Stapleford church, page 96; Steeple Langford church, page 96; Wishford Magna church, page 99; Wylye and Teffont Downs, page 61.

Wilton (near Marlborough)

Wilton Windmill, page 139.

Winterbourne Bassett

Church of St Katherine, page 99.

Winterbourne Dauntsey

Figsbury Ring, page 70.

The old town hall in the market place at Westbury was built by Sir Massey Lopes in 1815 and given to the town.

Winterbourne Monkton
Windmill Hill, page 76.

Winterbourne Stoke
Winterbourne Stoke Crossroads Barrow Group, page 77.

Wootton Bassett
Early closing Thursday; market Wednesday, at the town hall.
This was a market town of some importance in the days when nearby Swindon was just a village on a hill. Today there is little more than a half-mile long High Street on the road between Swindon and Chippenham. It has peripheral housing estates, built between the town and the railway line to the south. Most of the buildings of interest are in or around the High Street, in which the centre of attraction is the timber-framed town hall of 1700. Between 1446 and the Reform Bill of 1832 Wootton Bassett sent two members to Parliament, and it had a corporation until 1886. One MP was Edward Hyde, first Earl of Clarendon. Some of the houses are Georgian; the Cross Keys inn is dated 1742 and the Crown hotel is also of the eighteenth century.

Wootton Bassett Museum, page 135.

In the locality: Broad Town White Horse, page 62; Clyffe Pypard church, page 83; Dis-

The lock on the Kennet & Avon Canal at Wootton Rivers.

Wootton Rivers

Wroughton

The old village lies alongside and in between two hills where picturesque thatched cottages and quiet leafy corners are still to be found in parts like The Pitchens. But since the 1960s the area has been extended and developed as commuter land for Swindon. In comparison with much of this, the red brick cottage and town-house architecture put up between the wars looks positively attractive. This is a village with a long history, for it was here in 873 that the river Ray 'ran red with blood' when Egbert defeated Beornwulf in a decisive battle which planted the seed of monarchical succession in England. Agriculture traditionally paid the wages of Wroughton people, although from Victorian times to the 1930s there were also a number of racing stables. Wroughton-trained horses regularly won the Grand National and the village's most famous resident was perhaps Brown Jack, winner six times in succession of the Queen Alexandra Stakes at Ascot.

Wylye

Wylye is deep in flint and stone chequerwork country, with cottage walling of a type encountered all along the Wylye valley. This village of narrow roads, which were never built for motor traffic, lies to the south of the river, where it is now protected by a bypass. Grey stone buildings and walls with weathered orange tiles press hard against the roads.

Stone-built cottages in the village of Wylye.

It was traditionally a village concerned with agriculture and John Aubrey, the gossiping antiquarian, credits it with pioneering the water-meadow approach to farming early in the seventeenth century. Close to the bridge over the Wylye river is the old mill house.

Church of St Mary, page 99; **Wylye and Teffont Downs**, page 61.

Yatton Keynell
West Yatton Down, page 60.

Zeals
A network of little lanes which seem to go around in circles converges on the A303 at Zeals in the south-west of the county. The countryside is hilly, and wooded to the north-east. The village has many attractive small cottages and two buildings of real note: the almshouses and, to the east, Zeals House, which was built up in the nineteenth century around a medieval core. It was owned by the Chafyns and Chafyn Groves, one of whom built the Tudor-style gabled almshouses of brick in 1865, The house is big and attractive in its diversity of architectural features: tall chimneys rising above battlemented tower, oriel window and gables with large, square-headed windows below – a quite breathtaking group of buildings.

3

The countryside

The majority of nature reserves and nature trails mentioned in this chapter are either owned or managed under lease, licence or agreement by the **Wiltshire Wildlife Trust**, 18-19 High Street, Devizes SN10 1AT (telephone: 01380 725670), formerly the Wiltshire Trust for Nature Conservation. The Trust is a charity which was set up in 1962, and for the most part it allows unrestricted public access to its sites, where it rightly expects all visitors to follow the Country Code. The Trust produces a series of extremely good descriptive leaflets covering many of the sites. It is well worth intending visitors sending a stamped self-addressed envelope for details of the Trust and buying the modestly priced leaflets for the sites which interest them. This is also important because advance permission for access to some sites must be sought of private individuals, and the Trust's general leaflet indicates when this is necessary and of whom. Readers should also note that all the sites are rich in fauna and flora native to the particular environment, and that at each the Trust is engaged on a complex and ongoing programme of maintenance and development.

Throughout the county, local conservation groups are managing and maintaining small areas of the natural environment. The field office of the **British Trust for Conservation Volunteers** at Wyndhams, St Joseph's Place, Devizes SN10 1DD (telephone: 01380 729517), is the best point of contact for anyone who wants to locate the community conservation sites and groups in Wiltshire.

Arn Hill Nature Trail, Warminster (OS 183: ST 877465).

A 2 mile (3 km) long circular nature trail runs through the beech woodland, past an old limekiln and around the golf course off the A350 about 1 mile (1.6 km) north of Warminster town centre. Here is unploughed open downland where sheep have grazed for centuries and where the chalk was prepared for commercial use. The trail follows public footpaths through an area rich in chalkland flora and wildlife, and there are a number of fine viewpoints.

Avon Valley Project, Salisbury (OS 184: SU 135316).

South of Stratford sub Castle and near to Old Sarum, both sides of the Salisbury Avon to the north-east of Salisbury city centre provide a number of different habitats adjacent to each other. The nature reserve includes the river corridor itself, an area of reed beds and a water-meadow, both fast disappearing habitats and scarce in Wiltshire, grasslands and a small flood-plain willow wood. The area is owned by the Salisbury District Council and managed with advice from the Wiltshire Wildlife Trust consultancy. Visitors can walk between Salisbury City Centre and Old Sarum, passing through the Avon Valley Project nature reserve.

Barbury Castle Country Park, Burderop, Swindon (OS 173: SU 155761). Telephone: 01225 753641.

On the northern ridge of the Marlborough Downs are about 150 acres (60.6 hectares) of open land with breathtaking views of the Vale of the White Horse. Part of the ancient Ridgeway forms the northern boundary of the country park and the Ridgeway national trail marks the southern boundary and then passes through the Barbury Castle hillfort, from which the park takes its name (see page 68). Close by are the Celtic field system at Burderop Down, the medieval settlement on Barbury Down and a number of burial mounds associated with the hillfort. Within the park too are the possible sites of flint quarries. It is here that the battle of Beran Byrig is said to have taken place in AD 556, when the West Saxons under Cynric and Ceawlin trounced the British. The area was beloved of the writers Richard Jefferies and Alfred Williams, who are recalled by the memorial on a sarsen stone which was brought from Overton Hill near Avebury in 1939. The hillfort is grazed by sheep and the park is being managed as an important area for wildlife, walkers, naturalists and visitors, under a plan produced by the Wiltshire Wildlife Trust consultancy.

Barton Farm Country Park, Bradford-on-Avon (OS 173: ST 814604). Telephone: 01225 753641.

To the south of the town, off the B3109, this area mostly lies within a narrow strip of meadowland bounded by the Bristol Avon to the north and the Kennet & Avon Canal to the south. Running from the great tithe barn to the Avoncliff weir and aqueduct, it is about 1$\frac{1}{2}$ miles (2.4 km) long and comprises about 36 acres (14.5 hectares) of unspoiled countryside. Easily reached on foot from the town, this is a peaceful setting in which to picnic whilst visiting the area. The park includes land to the north of the river over Barton Bridge, the old packhorse bridge which was crossed by people bringing in tithes. Otherwise it may be approached by Pound Lane or by a path from the station car park. The area takes its name from the medieval farm which belonged to the Shaftesbury Abbey estate for over five hundred years and extended to both sides of the river Avon. The old granary and cow byre have been restored for visitors and the park is managed to produce hay. Habitats have been established to encourage wildlife, with advice from the Wiltshire Wildlife Trust consultancy.

Bewley Common, Lacock, Chippenham (OS 173: ST 935682). National Trust.

Situated on the steep rise of Bowden Hill on the approach to Lacock from the A342 at Sandy Lane, Bewley Common has been National Trust property since 1946. To the east are the wooded areas within the triangle of Chippenham to the north-west, Calne to the north-east and Bromham to the south. The common is an open space of several acres suitable for picnics, with fine views over west Wiltshire and the valley of the Avon. In favourable weather the panorama stretches from the Cotswolds to the Mendips.

Blackland Lakes Nature Reserve, Stockley Lane, Calne (OS 173: SU 007689). Telephone: 01249 813672.

Part of this commercial holiday and leisure centre off the A4 just east of Calne includes three small lakes, a nature walk and a wildfowl and bird sanctuary within a conservation area. Visitors who are not resident on the caravan and camping site are welcome to enjoy the lakes, with their collection of wildfowl, which now includes about thirty species of ducks and geese. Trees have been planted in spinneys, and within the conservation area many different habitats have been created to encourage indigenous flora and fauna.

Blackmoor Copse, Farley (OS 184: SU 234288).

Here is one of the Wiltshire Wildlife Trust's loveliest sites; part ancient oak woodland since medieval times, part former common ground, it is associated with an ancient field system. It has been managed by the Trust since 1963, comprises mainly oak and ash trees and includes a fifteen-year hazel-coppice rotation in its northern part. The copse is famed for its butterfly population, which includes a number of rare and beautiful woodland species, its birds and a wide range of mammals. It is located about 6 miles (10 km) east of Salisbury off a minor road between East Grimstead and Winterslow.

Chickengrove Bottom, Broad Chalke (OS 184: SU 040216).

This nature reserve, which is owned by a

local farming family who have managed it in the interests of nature conservation since 1967, is in the south of the county off the A354. Situated between Ox Drove and a Roman road to the north of the wooded Vernditch Chase, the reserve is some 20 acres (8 hectares) of chalk grassland surrounded by a coppice and scrub border. There is a breeding population of adders and lizards on this area of downland, which is managed under a Countryside Stewardship agreement and with advice from the Wiltshire Wildlife Trust.

Clarendon Park, Salisbury (OS 184: SU 181302).

About 2 miles (3 km) east of Salisbury there are several areas of unconnected woodland, all that is left of the royal forest of Clarendon. Of the great twelfth-century palace which was enjoyed by the Plantagenet kings there are mounds and ditches but little else. It was partly excavated in the 1930s. Access to the main area is by footpaths from Pitton in the north-east and Petersfinger to the south-west. Here a pagan Saxon cemetery was excavated in the early 1950s, revealing sixty-three burials and a quantity of military and personal items.

Cley Hill, Warminster (OS 183: ST 838448). National Trust.

The National Trust beauty spot here is centred on an iron age hillfort some 3 miles (5 km) west of Warminster off the A362 to Frome. The property comprises more than 80 acres (32.3 hectares) of chalk upland and includes tumuli. From 800 feet (244 metres) above sea level there are fine views and it is not surprising that a beacon was lit here to warn of the approaching Spanish Armada.

Since 1965, when the first siting was claimed, Cley Hill has been a meeting place for spotters of 'unidentified flying objects' (UFOs).

Clouts Wood, Wroughton (OS 173: SU 136800).

Lining the steep chalk hillside to the south-west of the valley, Clouts Wood is reached from Red Barn Hill on the A4361 out of Wroughton. A 1½ mile (2.4 km) track runs around and through a woodland of mainly oak and ash, now protected as a Site of Special Scientific Interest. The southern part is owned by the Science Museum, which has its Wroughton outpost close by, and the northern part is privately owned. The Wiltshire Wildlife Trust has managed the area as a nature reserve since 1983.

Coate Water Country Park, Marlborough Road, Coate, Swindon SN3 6AA (OS 173: SU 177829). Telephone: 01793 490150.

This large country park and nature reserve is centred on the 72 acre (29 hectare) lake which from 1822 was a reservoir supplying water to the Wilts & Berks Canal. On hot summer days it may be crowded with people enjoying a whole range of facilities; there is boating on the lake, a children's playground and giant sandpit, pitch and putt and angling. There are barbecue areas and fine views of the downs. Waterfowl and other birds abound and there are country walks. The naturalist and writer Richard Jefferies was born at Coate Farmhouse and the reservoir features in his work. What remains of the stone circle he discovered is to the east of the lake at Day House. The entrance to the park is off the A345 just south-east of Swindon.

Cockey Down, Laverstock (OS 184: SU 173320).

On the north-west facing slope of fine chalk downland, just over a mile north-east of Laverstock, from which it is reached along a public footpath, Cockey Down is associated with an ancient field system. There are good views over the Bourne valley and the area is rich in chalkland flowers and butterflies. This is a Wiltshire Wildlife Trust nature reserve.

Conigre Meadow, Melksham (OS 173: ST 901637).

Just where the river Avon enters Melksham, the Wiltshire Wildlife Trust is engaged in restoring a riverside meadow. This work includes the creation of a new pond, laying a new footpath and marking out a nature trail.

Clouts Wood near Wroughton is a Site of Special Scientific Interest.

Cotswold Country

The north-west corner of the county is Wiltshire's Cotswold area, ranging from Castle Combe in the south through Corsham to Chippenham, north to Malmesbury and then across the north of the county. The clay vale which supports Trowbridge and Swindon as well as the infant Thames gives way to a chalk plateau and then deeply wooded hanging valleys to the west. Drystone walls wend their way across the landscape. The towns and villages here share the same band of good building stone as Gloucestershire and Oxfordshire. Many were also engaged in the medieval wool trade. The result of the profits of this trade and the good building material can be seen in the fine stone villages of the area, set in rolling downland and wooded countryside. Some, like Biddestone, are clustered around the village green and pond. Particularly picturesque are those along the border with Avon and Gloucestershire: Easton Grey, where John Aubrey was born, Alderton,

Grittleton, Luckington, Littleton Drew, Ashton Keynes, where a number of little bridges cross the Thames, and Cricklade with its magnificent church tower.

Distillery Farm Meadows, Minety (OS 173: SU 032896).

Just south of Minety village off the minor road to Brinkworth, the Wiltshire Wildlife Trust's gate sign announces an area of traditional flower-rich hay meadows with public access to a total of five fields. Visitors are asked to keep to the edge of the fields when hay is growing.

Drews Pond Wood Project, Devizes (OS 173: SU 007597).

The site was bought by the county asylum in 1884 and the wood is now owned by the Regional Health Authority. Since 1990 volunteers have carried out conservation work, coppicing and traditional woodland management.

Emmett Hill Meadows, Minety (OS 173: SU 011903).

To the east of Upper Minety there are two adjacent meadows of varied soils which have never been treated with herbicides or artificial fertilisers. A stream separates them and a pond has been dug in order to encourage aquatic wildlife. The site was bought by the Wiltshire Wildlife Trust in 1987 and is designated a Site of Special Scientific Interest. It can be reached off the B4040 road between Cricklade and Minety. The site is hard to find. Please keep to the rights of way which lead to the reserve.

The Firs Nature Trail, Brinkworth (OS 173: SU 047865).

This area was once part of the royal forest of Braydon. At one time cleared of trees, it was planted with conifers, which went to the sawmills at Purton during the First World War, and was replanted with oak and ash in the 1920s. The wood was opened to the public in 1992. It is owned by Hills of Swindon Ltd and managed by the Braydon Forest Project. Here is a circular walk in a damp area on Oxford clay, which is immediately north of Webb's Wood off the B4696 road.

Green Lane Wood, Trowbridge (OS 173: ST 886576).

East of Trowbridge and reached off the A350 between Semington and West Ashton, this is an ancient woodland of oak, field maple and hazel, abounding in wild flowers, birds and butterflies. It is a Wiltshire Wildlife Trust reserve.

Grovely Woods, Great Wishford, Salisbury (OS 184: SU 062348).

This ancient forest between the Wylye valley to the north and east and the Nadder valley to the south may be approached off the A36 between Salisbury and Stapleford or the B3089 between Wilton and Dinton. There are many footpaths and bridleways into and through the wood, and part of the Roman road from Old Sarum (*Sorbiodunum*) runs through the centre of its western section. The large iron age settlement close to Ebsbury Hill, Grovely Castle and field system, the Barford

Down and Grovely Hill field systems, as well as other, lesser earthworks, lie within the woods and their downland perimeter.

Ham Hill, Ham, Hungerford (OS 174: SU 333616).

In the 1920s the author's father and his schoolboy friends used to chase the rabbits down Ham Hill until the animals lost their footing, bowled over, broke their necks and were taken home for the pot. The huge field mushrooms to be found here have long been served on the villagers' breakfast tables. This is a very steep area of chalk downland, with orchid flora and a notable butterfly population. Access to Ham Hill is by permission only, except for members of the Wiltshire Wildlife Trust.

Hat Gate, Savernake Forest (OS 174: SU 212642).

The old Cheltenham to Andover railway line crossed the Kennet & Avon Canal and passed to the south of Savernake Forest. No longer in use, this site presents a wide variety of chalk downland fauna and flora.

Imber Range Perimeter Path (OS 184: SU 009510).

Deep into Salisbury Plain is the deserted village of Imber, closed to the public in 1943 and since used by the army for live firing. 'Imber on the down, four miles from any town' ran the old rhyme, and it is said that in bad weather the village was often isolated. Yet Imber is in an area of archaeological significance and one which in spite of – perhaps resulting from – military ownership has preserved an important abundance of fauna and flora. The Imber Range Perimeter Path is a 30 mile (48 km) circular walk around the edge of the Imber Range military firing and training area. It has distinctive waymarkers which take the walker adjacent to the Westbury White Horse and Bratton Camp, the Westbury chalk quarries, the UFO spotters' Cradle Hill, and the hillforts at Battlebury and Scratchbury. There are breathtaking views of the countryside at every one of them. The path also passes close to the Arn Hill Nature Trail.

The Imber Range military area on Salisbury Plain contains the village of Imber, which was closed to the public in 1943.

Jones's Mill Reserve, Pewsey (OS 173: SU 170611).

This reserve is reached off the B3087 northeast of Pewsey. It has been owned by the Wiltshire Wildlife Trust since 1980. Fed by the river Avon, the site comprises fen grassland and wet willow woodland with marshland plants, on former water-meadows.

Keynes Country Park, Ashton Keynes, Swindon (OS 163: SU 027958). Telephone: 01285 861459.

There are three public nature reserves centred around the Cotswold Water Park (see page 140). Keynes Country Park has a nature walk, bird hide and information displays. The park also has numerous lakeside walks, picnic sites, a children's playground and beach (open June to September, weather permitting). Neigh Bridge Country Park has a riverside walk beside the young Thames, angling and a picnic area. At Friday Island there is a 'tropical' location for hire for private functions or businesses (telephone: 01285 770226). There is plenty of space for spectators and participants and easy access to some charming villages and walks around this part of north Wiltshire

Knowle Down, Bowerchalke (OS 184: SU 032226).

The village of Bowerchalke is almost completely surrounded by hills, except to the south where the valley joins the Vale of Chalke towards Cranborne Chase. The downs are highest to the south-west, where Knowle Down offers a nature reserve rich in wild flowers. The site is managed under a Countryside Stewardship agreement, with advice from the Wiltshire Wildlife Trust.

Landford Bog, Landford (OS 184: SU 259186).

Hereabouts is the most wooded part of the county, for Landford lies in the south-east corner close to the boundary with Hampshire and at the northern edge of the New Forest. Landford Bog is to the south of Landford village off the B3079 in an area of burial mounds. The reserve comprises a valley bog and wet heath with birch woodland. Noted for reptiles and dragonflies, the area is also frequented by many butterflies.

Lechlade Meadows and Riverside Park (OS 163: SU 213993).

In the north-east corner of the county, approached by the A361 Swindon to Burford road, a summer tourist resort has developed around the Thames-side town of Lechlade (Gloucestershire) and its seasonal boating fraternity. The course of the river Thames, which here forms the county boundary, may be followed by the towpath or through meadows in either direction. Apart from the Riverside Park itself, where there is plenty of space for family games and picnics, a most popular stretch is between Lechlade and Inglesham, where there are pleasant meadowland walks beside the river. Quieter stretches can be reached by a pathway opposite Inglesham church, and close by is one of the quaint round houses built along the Thames & Severn Canal.

Little Durnford Down, Little Durnford (OS 184: SU 129350).

Roads on either side of the river Avon closely follow its course between Amesbury and Salisbury. Chalk downland rises steeply from the river valley along the whole length of this section, affording splendid views. Little Durnford is opposite the village of Lower Woodford and is a Wiltshire Wildlife Trust reserve.

Little Langford Down, Little Langford (OS 184: SU 046348).

Close by Grovely Wood, the iron age hillfort of Grovely Castle and the associated field system, Little Langford Down is a north-facing downland surrounded by deciduous woodland. It is noted for flowers and butterflies. Contact Wiltshire Wildlife Trust for parking details (telephone: 01380 725670).

Marden Nature Trail, Chippenham (OS 173: ST 962723).

The trail runs roughly parallel with the river Marden, a tributary of the Bristol Avon. It utilises a 4 mile (6 km) stretch of the disused railway line between Calne and Chippenham from a point near the remains of the Cistercian Stanley Abbey. It is particularly interesting for the varied fauna and flora along its length.

Marlborough Downs

The gentle undulating downland (sometimes called the Wessex Downs) between Swindon in the north and the Vale of Pewsey to the south, and between Calne and the eastern boundary of the county, offers the best opportunities for walkers and ramblers. The huge chalk escarpments are free-draining. Although the chalk is too porous to be used structurally, the land, probably by reason of its elevation, has supported communities from the earliest times. The old tracks across the ridges are numerous and easy to follow and take the walker past many sites of archaeological interest. Marlborough, itself a town worth exploring, is a good base for such activity. There are particularly good views from the northern ridge of the downs. A feature of this area is the sarsen stones, variously called 'grey wethers' or 'druid stones', to be found on Overton Down and Fyfield Down, to the north-west of Marlborough, and to the west on National Trust land at Piggle Dene.

Maud Heath's Causeway, near Chippenham (OS 173: ST 952756).

In 1474 Maud Heath, a trader at Chippenham market, provided sufficient funds to build and maintain a causeway between Wick Hill, near Bremhill, and Chippenham. The 4^1/2 mile (7 km) long causeway passes through the Avon valley, which was frequently flooded, her home parish of Langley Burrell and those of Kellaways and Tytherton. Mostly it is at road level, but at Kellaways the stone path is raised some 6 feet (1.8 metres) or so on sixty raised arches. There an inscribed sundial with a ball finial marks the way. Where a railway line was built at right-angles to the path, a narrow pass was constructed beneath to preserve the right of way. At the top of Wick Hill is Maud Heath's monument, where her statue stands with staff and basket above a pillar. The inscription on the stone was translated from the original Latin in 1827 by William Lisle Bowles, the parson poet of Bremhill. Bowles,

Maud Heath's Causeway at Kellaways is raised above the road, which was subject to flooding. The causeway was funded by Maud, a market trader, in the fifteenth century.

together with the Marquis of Lansdowne, paid for the monument to be erected in 1838. There is another inscribed stone where the causeway ends at Chippenham.

Middleton Down, Broad Chalke (OS 184: SU 049233).

In the south-west of the county there is an area of rolling chalk downland, coombs and little villages in the folds, strung out along the watercourses. Less than a mile south of Broad Chalke is the Wiltshire Wildlife Trust's 65 acre (26.3 hectare) reserve on Middleton Hill, which it acquired in 1988. Here are two steep-sided coombs running east—west, linked by the side of a much larger valley. The downland reserve includes areas of gorse, trees and shrubland.

Morgan's Hill Nature Reserve, Devizes (OS 173: SU 028672).

Morgan's Hill, south of Calne, is in an area rich with burial mounds, just south of a Roman road and adjacent to Wansdyke. It includes the site of a former chalk quarry now colonised by those plants which have adapted to the thin chalky soil, as well as woodland, scrubland and a variety of grasses. The Wiltshire Wildlife Trust acquired the site in 1989. Footpaths link the area with Cherhill Down (Oldbury Castle and Cherhill White Horse) and Avebury to the north-east. Access to this nature reserve is from the Smallgrain Plantation private site.

New Farm Meadow, Purton (OS 173: SU 082887).

This is a large hay field by Purton Common, managed in consultation with the Braydon Forest Project, on behalf of Hills Aggregates Ltd. Contact the Wiltshire Wildlife Trust for other details (telephone: 01380 725670).

Oyster's Coppice, Donhead St Mary (OS 184: ST 894259).

This wet alder woodland has a varied ground flora rich in ferns and plenty of birds.

At Barbury Castle, on the downs north of Marlborough, is the Ridgeway long-distance footpath.

Pepperbox Hill, Salisbury (OS 184: SU 218252). National Trust.

This is National Trust land reached off a minor road to the east of the A36, about 5 miles (8 km) south-east of Salisbury. There is a wooded area below and about 70 acres (28.2 hectares) of downland afford a dramatic panorama over parts of Wiltshire, Hampshire and Dorset and even, it is said, to the Isle of Wight when conditions are favourable. A plaque gives a plan of the area. The hill is named after the shape of a small, slate-roofed octagonal brick tower called Eyre's Folly which was built on the down in 1606. The building has bands of bricks between each stage for decoration, and the windows are blocked up.

Peppercombe Wood, Urchfont (OS 173: SU 038574).

This small strip of woodland north of Urchfont is famed for its colourful display of flowers in spring.

Pewsey Downs National Nature Reserve (OS 173: SU 115635).

This is a walker's paradise at the west end of the Marlborough Downs. There are exceptional views over the Vale of Pewsey, the rich and fertile valley on a bedrock of upper greensand which separates the Marlborough Downs from Salisbury Plain. The reserve rises 800 feet (244 metres), stretches either side of the road between Marlborough and Alton Barnes, covers some 400 acres (161.6 hectares) and is especially noted for its rare plant and insect life. This is herb-rich downland which has for centuries been grazed by sheep, thus supporting an amazing diversity of flora and wildlife. The reserve runs between Tan Hill in the west and Knapp Hill in the east, where there is a car park, taking in Milk Hill, the Alton Barnes White Horse, Walker's Hill and Adam's Grave long barrow. The Ridgeway crosses it, running northwards east of Walker's Hill, and Wansdyke clips the north-west edge of the reserve.

Postern Hill, Marlborough (OS 173: SU 196680).

At the north-west corner of Savernake Forest, approached off the A346, is the main caravan and picnic site in the area. (There is a smaller official picnic area at Hat Gate in the extreme south-west of the forest; see page 52.) A forest trail of up to 3 miles (5 km) begins at Postern Hill.

Rack Hill Nature Trail, Castle Combe (OS 173: ST 843763).

The picturesque village of Castle Combe

lies astride the Bye Brook, in a beautiful valley that is steeply wooded to the east of the village. Rack Hill lies about half a mile (800 metres) to the south-west and the nature trail is on the south-west facing slope of limestone downland which overlooks the village. Here are oak, ash, beech, hazel and field maple. The land is privately owned and has been a reserve since 1976. Keep to the public footpath.

Ramsbury Meadow, Ramsbury (OS 174: SU 273714).

The river Kennet runs to the south of the village of Ramsbury, and in 1980 a piece of adjacent water-meadow was given to the Wiltshire Wildlife Trust.

Ravensroost Wood, Minety (OS 173: SU 023882).

All around this area are remnants of the royal forest of Braydon. At 96 acres (38.7 hectares), the Wiltshire Wildlife Trust's wood 1¹/₂ miles (2.4 km) south of Minety is one of the larger areas of woodland, and its history has been particularly well recorded. It is mostly an area of mature oak trees with a hazel shrub layer, growing on wet clay. There are several ponds. This is an ancient woodland where roe deer are amongst the amazing diversity of wildlife, and more than 160 species of ground flora have been recorded. The Trust is managing the area as compartments of high forest and coppice with standards.

Red Lodge Pond, Braydon (OS 173: SU 055888).

This is an area of woodland through which runs the river Key and its tributary. A pond and meadow within the Forestry Commission plantation comprise the nature reserve, rich in amphibians and dragonflies.

The Ridgeway

This prehistoric highway can be seen in several broken sections throughout the county, notably the last part from Alton Barnes to Overton Hill near Avebury. Beyond that it becomes a designated National Trail, leaving the county north-east of Liddington Hill on its 85 mile (137 km) journey across the Oxfordshire and Berkshire Downs and on to Ivinghoe Beacon, Buckinghamshire. Its way through Wiltshire is marked by points of archaeological interest and by a wide range of different habitats for wildlife, and there are fine views throughout its length. In places it is up to 40 feet (12 metres) wide and lined by ancient hedgerows. From Overton Hill it runs north along the summit of Hackpen Hill and then north-east past Barbury Castle. At this point the footpath deviates southwards along Smeath's Ridge to Ogbourne St George, where it again runs north towards Liddington Hill and the minor road out of the county, which for a while follows the original course of the Ridgeway.

River Ray Parkway, Swindon. Telephone: 01793 493553.

This is an 8 mile (13 km) recreational and conservation route. It skirts the south and south-west edge of Swindon between Coate Water Country Park and Moulden Hill, with its distant view of Cricklade. The route is equally a reminder of the town's history and industrial heritage and of the efforts being made to re-establish wildlife habitats and in nature conservation. The route was planned roughly to follow the course of the river Ray, utilising the bed of the former Midland & South Western Junction Railway line. Officially opened in 1991, it takes the visitor through or past new conservation areas like Casso's Wood, Rivermead and Rotary Wood, by established woodland, geological sites, meadows and marshlands, open spaces, modern housing estates and office developments, and nature reserves. Distinctive green and gold heritage signs point the way and indicate the features along its length. The Parkway incorporates the Old Town Rail Path, a footpath and cycleway established early in the 1980s, and is itself intended to become part of a longer route which will link Cricklade to the north with the Wiltshire Downs. The project is part of the Borough of Thamesdown's Great Western Community Forest project.

Salisbury Plain

The Plain is the largest chalk plateau in Britain and is about 20 miles (32 km) square.

It was once open sheep country, the haunt of highwaymen, and the territory of the great bustard, a large bird, preserved examples of which may be seen in the Salisbury Museum. In season large fields of wheat stretch into the distance, and elsewhere it is made up of bleak scrubland or rough grassland with occasional groups of trees. Much of it belongs to the army. There are training areas and firing ranges, and some newer footpaths have been provided to compensate for the old ones which were incorporated into military property. One is liable to encounter 'tank crossings', and groups of military vehicles may sometimes be seen waiting in isolated clumps of trees just off the road. The flora is particularly rich in areas to which the public are denied access and, far from being driven out, birds and animals have learnt to live and flourish beside all the military activity. The Plain is more or less bounded by the roads which run from Salisbury north-east towards Andover, north-west through Ludgershall to Upavon, virtually west to Westbury and thence south-east to Salisbury. The A303 crosses from east to west, whilst three main roads run southwards, converging on Salisbury. In part at least, these closely follow the courses of rivers, on which are to be found a close succession of small villages and hamlets largely unchanged throughout the twentieth century. The southern section has a number of clear chalk streams where there is plenty of fishing for the enthusiast.

Savernake Forest, near Marlborough.

The surviving 2300 acres (929 hectares) are only a fraction of the pre-Conquest forest which became an area of sport for kings. It is situated on an undulating chalk plateau which forms the extreme north-east edge of Salisbury Plain. The main area for the visitor is bounded by the A4 Marlborough to Hungerford road and the A346 to the south-west. There are oaks and avenues of beech trees planted by 'Capability' Brown, including the 3 mile (5 km) long Grand Avenue, and the Eight Walks which radiate geometrically from the centre. The only statutory footpath runs north from Cadley church, but there is a network of others – as well as minor roads and rides – which give access to glades, verges and parts of the forest where visitors with due consideration for fauna and flora may go on foot. In the dense parts there are many unusual species of plants and wild birds, and roe and fallow deer may be seen. The classical monument in the south-east corner was put up by Thomas Bruce, Earl of Ailesbury, reputedly to commemorate George III's recovery from madness.

Scotchel Nature Trail, Pewsey (OS 173: SU 164600).

At the north-east of the town, where the river Avon meets the railway embankment, are a reserve and nature trail owned and maintained by the Pewsey Parish Council, which bought the land in 1982. The trail is adjacent to a water-meadow, reed beds and watercress beds. The trail twice crosses the river.

Shear Water, Warminster (OS 183: ST 850422).

This is a well-known 38 acre (15.3 hectare) lake in dense woodland to the south-east of the Longleat estate, approached from minor roads off the A350 south of Warminster. It was made in 1791 to the design of Francis, Duke of Bridgewater. The lake is used for sailing and other water activities including fishing. There are a number of walks around the woodland.

Smallbrook Meadows, Warminster (OS 183: ST 878443).

Since 1989 the Wiltshire Wildlife Trust has leased and is managing a number of wet meadows, in partnership with West Wiltshire District Council, close to the centre of the town and the course of the river Wylye. Much of the 35 acre (14 hectare) reserve is marshy grassland, tall sedges and reeds, and there is a large pond, created in 1989, to attract aquatic animals and water birds. Several small areas of woodland within the reserve and the hedgerows which border it provide particularly varied habitats for a wide variety of wildlife.

Somerford Common Nature Trail, Brinkworth (OS 173: SU 026863).

This is one of the largest remaining fragments of the Forest of Braydon and is now owned by the Forestry Commission. Since 1970 the Wiltshire Wildlife Trust has managed part of it as a nature reserve with a 1¼ mile (2 km) nature trail around each of its three sections. These include conifer plantations and deciduous woodland with coppiced areas throughout.

Stonehenge Down (OS 184: SU 070430 to 160430). National Trust.

The main feature in the landscape of Salisbury Plain, typical of the whole 'spine' of the county, is the early and middle bronze age bell, bowl and disc barrows. These burial mounds have yielded important artefacts, which are now in the county's museums. The area enclosed by the approximate rectangle of roads linking Amesbury, Durrington, Shrewton and Winterbourne Stoke is particularly rich in all kinds of burial mounds. Fine collections may be seen in the barrow cemeteries on Normanton Down, Wilsford Down and Winterbourne Stoke.

Upper Avon Valley

Nowhere else is it more obvious how important the river was to establishing communities. From Pewsey, where the Salisbury Avon is but a stream, south to Amesbury its course is closely followed by the A345 to the west. After Upavon a web of minor roads to the east links a series of peaceful and attractive villages which have grown up at almost every turn in the river. This is the most attractive region for the visitor to explore. Picturesque and gently wooded backdrops set off rural architecture, interesting churches and ancient sites, with small farms and thatched cottages dotted around the countryside. Worth visiting are Manningford Bruce, Manningford Bohune, North Newnton, Charlton, Rushall, Upavon, Enford, Fittleton, Netheravon and Durrington.

Upper Waterhay Reserve, Ashton Keynes (OS 173: SU 068937).

The most northerly of the Wiltshire Wildlife Trust's reserves is on the flood plain of the young river Thames, which enters the county just west of Ashton Keynes. It is well-known as the site of the creamy-coloured snakeshead fritillary, which until the mid twentieth century grew on acre after acre in this area, despite being a favourite flower for picking. Almost lost since, it is now growing on the fine well-managed reserve together with a wide variety of other flowering plants.

Vincients Wood Nature Trail, Chippenham (OS 173: ST 898733).

A medieval woodbank runs through this piece of old woodland on the western edge of Chippenham. The nature trail is about one mile (1.6 km) long within an area composed mostly of oak, ash and field maple, with willows bordering the stream to the north. It runs through dense woodland, a small grove of aspen and a hazel coppice. Here the Wiltshire Wildlife Trust has embarked upon a programme of removing sycamores, thinning the weakest of the oak and ash, coppicing and creating glades to allow the widest range of flowers to grow.

The Ailesbury column in the Savernake Forest.

Wansdyke

The origin and purpose of this two-part bank and ditch, created in the Dark Ages, are obscure. A defensive earthwork, dated between the fifth and seventh centuries, it may well mark the one-time limit of Wessex where the 10 mile (16 km) eastern stretch runs through Wiltshire. It might have been a Romano-British defence against the Saxons or, more likely, a later Saxon point of division. The Wiltshire Wansdyke is impressive and may be walked for the whole of its length – a rewarding experience across the Marlborough Downs. It begins at Morgan's Hill north-west of Bishops Cannings, at the point of intersection with the Roman road between Bath and Mildenhall. It crosses the A361 almost at once and continues south-east, ending just east of Savernake Forest. Wansdyke may be seen at its best where it crosses the minor road between Alton Priors and Fyfield, just south of Boreham Wood.

Westbury Downland (OS 184: ST 900516).

To the east and south-east of Westbury, surrounding the white horse, are about 60 acres (24.2 hectares) of open downland above the northern escarpment of Salisbury Plain. There are fine views to the west and north, and places of archaeological interest abound. The iron age camp here is 750 feet (229 metres) above sea level, enclosing 25 acres (10 hectares) and a long barrow.

West Yatton Down, Yatton Keynell (OS 173: ST 852760).

This area of limestone downland is just south of the motor-racing circuit at Castle Combe, reached off the road between Castle Combe and Biddestone, at Long Dean. Please keep to the bridleway.

White Sheet Hill Nature Trail, Mere (OS 183: ST 799350).

Close to Stourhead, just off the B3092 out of Mere, is a nature trail on chalk downland which has been used by man since neolithic times. This trail runs through Whitesheet Castle and the neolithic causewayed camp to the north, around a disused eighteenth-century chalk quarry and through the Wiltshire

Wildlife Trust's nature reserve. The whole area is part of the Stourhead Estate, which has belonged to the National Trust since 1946. There are fine views.

Wiltshire Cycleways

There are six circular routes throughout the county, officially and collectively termed Wiltshire Cycleways and distinguished by blue route signs with white arrows. The largest, of 160 miles (257 km), roughly follows the shape of the county and links Salisbury, Great Bedwyn, Swindon, Malmesbury, Corsham, Bradford-on-Avon, Horningsham and Mere. The 145 mile (233 km) route runs around the top two-thirds of Wiltshire, between Swindon, Malmesbury, Corsham, Bradford-on-Avon, Horningsham, Wilton, Salisbury and Great Bedwyn. At 140 miles (225 km) in length, the third longest route encompasses the lower two-thirds of the county, linking Bradford-on-Avon, Devizes, Great Bedwyn, Amesbury, Salisbury, Mere and Horningsham. The route around Salisbury Plain is 125 miles (201 km) long, linking Salisbury, Great Bedwyn, Devizes, Bradford-on-Avon, Horningsham and Wilton. The 90 mile (145 km) trip skirts around and then passes through the north-east downland countryside between Swindon, Ramsbury, Great Bedwyn and Bishops Cannings before heading up through Lacock, Corsham and Malmesbury. At only 70 miles (113 km) long, the designated Cycleway around the south-east of the county below Salisbury Plain links Salisbury, Wilton, Horningsham and Mere. In addition, the lower third of the county is bisected by the Wylye Valley Cycleway, which runs between Horningsham in the west and Wilton to the east. The top third of the county has the Vale of Pewsey route which crosses the county from Corsham to Great Bedwyn. All of the Cycleways use minor roads, running through the county's most attractive and unspoilt areas.

Win Green Hill, near Shaftesbury (OS 184: ST 926206). National Trust.

At the extreme south-west of the county, Cranborne Chase, an area of ancient forest and upland, nudges into Wiltshire. It was

Wansdyke, where it crosses the minor road between Alton Barnes and Fyfield.

once a well-populated area, as evidenced by the field systems, burial mounds and other earthworks, but declined in the Dark Ages. In medieval times it was a royal chase. The National Trust's 38 acres (15.3 hectares) of land on tree-crowned Win Green Hill is, at 911 feet (277.8 metres) above sea level, the highest point on the Chase. There are breathtaking views to the Quantocks and across the width of the Isle of Wight.

Woodford Valley

The valley of the Avon between Amesbury and Salisbury is an area of picturesque and attractive villages. The region should be explored along the minor roads to the west of the A345, which follow the course of the river and join close to Old Sarum. The villages of note here include Wilsford, Great Durnford, Upper, Middle and Lower Woodford and Stratford sub Castle.

Wylye and Teffont Downs, Salisbury (OS 184: SU 007353).

The unclassified roads which cross the downland between Wylye and Dinton, with the Wylye valley to the north and that of the Nadder to the south, reach 650 feet (198 metres) above sea level and offer breathtaking views. Public footpaths and tracks cross the downs and link the two large wooded areas, Great Ridge Woods to the west and Grovely Woods to the east. Here there have long been sheep runs, and a wealth of wild flowers grows from the springy turf in summer, providing nectar for the insects. Close by is the iron age or Romano-British settlement of Hanging Langford Camp, with earthworks leading to the enclosure at Church End Ring. Across the road are the remains of the 'Celtic' field system on Wylye Down. The buildings hereabouts frequently include flint and stone chequerwork or may otherwise be of stone, thatched and gabled. Little stone bridges cross the stream in the Nadder valley. The pretty villages of Teffont Evias, Teffont Magna, Dinton and Chilmark are worth touring. The Chilmark quarries provided stone for Salisbury Cathedral, Wilton House and less grand dwellings in the villages.

4
Hill figures

Restoration of the Westbury White Horse in 1778 seems to have brought public attention to this kind of monument. The rolling downland of Wiltshire provided the most suitable landscape for display, especially where it overlooked vales below. Within the following century at least nine more were added, usually for no apparent reasons, by eccentric amateurs. Four of the known horses – Pewsey old horse, Rockley Down, Roundway Hill and Ham Hill – are now at best vague marks on the ground. But seven are still there, including the replacement cut at Pewsey in 1937. Visitors should note that none are as they originally were; successive scouring or even periods of neglect have had effects on them all. When they were built, the design was supposed to take into account the contours of the land and the foreshortening effect of distance from below. At close quarters they will always appear to be misshapen and they are best viewed from a distance. Most are in positions that naturally command fine views, and they are often associated with ancient settlements and close to trackways.

Alton Barnes White Horse, Marlborough (OS 173: SU 106638).

A high-stepping beast with an arched neck and docked, jaunty tail, this horse is 180 feet (55 metres) high and 165 feet (50 metres) long and has an eye circumference of 12 feet (3.7 metres). Reputed to be a copy of the horse at Cherhill, it was paid for in 1812 by Robert Pile of Manor Farm, Alton Barnes, so that his village might be on an equal footing with Cherhill and Marlborough. John Thorne, a journeyman painter, made a drawing of how the finished animal should look on the hill, set men to work and then made off with the twenty sovereigns he had been paid to get the job done.The horse, which in the event was cut by Mr Pile, stands on the southern slopes of the ridge between Walker's Hill and Milk Hill and is visible from Old Sarum. This area is rich in archaeological remains, and the horse is close to the Knapp Hill settlement, Adam's Grave long barrow and a number of round barrows.

Broad Hinton White Horse, Swindon (OS 173: SU 128749).

The Ridgeway, turning northwards along Avebury Down, follows the crest of Hackpen Hill, from where there are fine views, and thence runs past Barbury Castle. At the point where the minor road between Marlborough and Wootton Bassett intersects the Ridgeway on Hackpen Hill there is an odd-looking white horse. It is 90 feet (27 metres) long and 90 feet high, with ears like short horns, a raised tail and a gently trotting gait. It was carved out in 1838 by Henry Eatwell, the parish clerk, assisted by Robert Witt, the local publican. Alone amongst Wiltshire's nineteenth-century white horses, it is supposed to commemorate an event, the coronation of Queen Victoria. This figure is also known as the Hackpen White Horse.

Broad Town White Horse, Swindon (OS 173: SU 098783).

This animal is high-stepping into obscurity on a rise above Littleton Farm, on part of the upland ridge which connects Compton Bassett with Wroughton. It may soon be completely lost. The county's most northerly white horse, it is ascribed to William Simmonds, a farmer, who laid it out in 1863. What there is of it

Alton Barnes White Horse, near Marlborough.

measures 86 feet (26 metres) long by 61 feet (19 metres) high, with a badly misplaced eye and an erect, docked tail.

Bulford Kiwi, Salisbury (OS 184: SU 201440).

This famous bird was cut out on Beacon Hill, just north-east of Bulford barracks and amidst the army's firing ranges, in 1918. The vogue for cutting badges on the downland hereabouts, as a reminder of the regiments stationed locally during the First World War, was at its height. This one commemorates the occupation of Sling Camp by troops from New Zealand. The designer was Captain H. M. Clark, whose bird, 420 feet (128 metres) long with the letters NZ each 65 feet (20 metres) high beneath its beak, showed remarkable draughtsmanship in getting the correct perspective. In the vicinity of Beacon Hill are numerous barrows on land belonging to the army. The hill itself, being 625 feet (190 metres) above sea level, gives fine views across Salisbury Plain and may be approached via the A3028.

Cherhill White Horse, Calne (OS 173: SU 049695).

The eccentric Dr Christopher Alsop of Calne had this horse carved out in 1780. He is said to have shouted instructions through a megaphone whilst his helpers pegged out the shape on Cherhill Down with little white flags. The best view is from the A4, east of the village, where there is a fine climb on foot towards the horse and Oldbury Castle hillfort beyond. Said to be visible over 30 miles (48 km) away, the horse is 131 feet (40 metres) long and once had an eye filled with glass bottles to catch the sun. It appears to be trotting or pawing the turf.

Slightly to the south-east of the white horse on Cherhill Down is the **Lansdowne Monument**, an obelisk erected about 1845 by the third Marquis of Lansdowne to commemorate his ancestor Sir William Petty, It towers some 125 feet (38 metres) above the hill and may be seen 30 miles (48 km) away. The hill belongs to the National Trust.

Codford Rising Sun, Warminster (OS 184: about ST 984394).

Part of the same series as the Fovant Regimental Badges, this is a small version of the 'rising sun' badge used by the Anzac troops and was cut out by members of the Australian Commonwealth Military Forces stationed around Fovant in 1916. At one time maintenance was carried out on this badge at the expense of the Australian government.

Compton Chamberlayne 'Australia', Salisbury (OS 184:SU 005273).

This huge outline of Australia and Tasmania is also part of the Fovant group of hill figures, which were made about 1916 and restored in 1950. The work was done by members of the Australian Commonwealth Military Forces.

Fovant Regimental Badges, Salisbury (OS 184: SU 005273).

The long north-western slopes of Fovant Down, which at the intersection with Compton Down encompass the Chiselbury Camp iron age hillfort, provide the perfect setting for a remarkable series of regimental badges. They are designed to be seen from the Shaftesbury to Salisbury road (A30) and were made about 1916 by men who were billeted at the huge training and transit camps in the locality before going into action on the Western Front. The first to be cut out was the cap badge of the London Rifle Brigade, which apparently originated the idea. The last of this series was the device of the Young Men's Christian Association, which was put there by members of the forces in recognition of the spiritual guidance the YMCA had given to soldiers stationed at camps in the area

during the hostilities.

The volunteers worked between 4 a.m. and 7 a.m., and each badge took several months to complete. The *modus operandi* was either to dig deep outline trenches on the downland and then fill them with chalk, or to place chalk on the surface, adding bricks, tiles and broken crockery to make outlines. All of the former type have survived, but the rest have not. By 1919 there were twenty badges on the hillside between Sutton Mandeville and Compton Chamberlayne.

The badges were allowed to become overgrown during the Second World War, and in 1949 the Fovant Home Guard Old Comrades were asked by some of the London regiments to determine the condition of their badges and restore them. This was achieved by volunteers working in their own time, with payment at the then agricultural rate, out of the income from subscriptions. Over the next few years, eleven badges were worked on and two more were added.

There are now twelve emblems on the downs, reading from east to west: Map of Australia; the Royal Wiltshire Yeomanry; the Young Men's Christian Association; the 6th City of London Regiment; the Australian Commonwealth Military Forces Badge; the

The Royal Warwickshire Regimental badge cut into the chalk at Fovant during the First World War.

Royal Signals Corps; the Wiltshire Regiment; the London Rifle Brigade; the Post Office Rifles; the Devonshire Regiment; the 7th City of London Regiment; the Royal Warwickshire Regiment. The badges of the Wiltshire Regiment and the Royal Wiltshire Yeomanry were added in 1950 and that of the Royal Signals Corps in 1971. In 1963 the name of the Fovant Home Guard Old Comrades Association was changed to the Fovant Badges Society. Restoration has continued under the auspices of the society (telephone: 01722 714689).

Laverstock Panda, Salisbury (OS 184: SU 177312).

This piece of graffiti is now barely discernible. It was cut into the hillside to the east of Salisbury, on the land of Manor Farm northeast of Laverstock, where it could be seen from the London road. The panda's head, approximately 55 feet (17 metres) square, appeared overnight on 24th January 1969, with the initials UCNW carved to its left. A man telephoned the *Salisbury Journal* to say that it had been made by people representing the 'Union for Conservation of Nature and Wildlife'. Later the theory was put forward that the work had been done by students from the University College of North Wales, Bangor, whose symbol is a panda. This is the generally accepted explanation

Marlborough White Horse, Marlborough (OS 173: SU 185682).

This small horse, cantering across Granham Hill to the south-west of the town, almost where the A4 now meets the A345, was cut in 1804. It fell into neglect, was revived and altered in 1873 but still has a strangely shaped head and a very short tail. Although the horse is mentioned in the Marlborough College end-of-term song, the work was done by the boys at another school in the town. The original design and pegging out are attributed to William Canning, of the Manor House, Ogbourne St George, a pupil at Mr Greasley's school, who prevailed upon his contemporaries to cut out the shape and fill it in with chalk. The present dimensions are 61 feet (19 metres) long and 47 feet (14 metres) high.

Pewsey White Horse, Pewsey (OS 173: SU 171581).

The first horse here, reputedly with a rider, was cut on a western slope of Pewsey Hill, overlooking the Vale, about 1785. The architect of the scheme was Robert Pile, who was also responsible for the horse at Alton Barnes. Almost entirely lost from view, it was superseded in 1937 by the most beautifully proportioned and detailed horse in the county, designed by George Marples and made by the members of the Pewsey Fire Brigade. The horse was commissioned by the village organising committee for celebrating the coronation of King George VI. It stands close by the site of the original, about a mile (1.6 km) south of the town at a steep incline in the minor road to Everleigh. It is 66 feet (20 metres) long and 45 feet (14 metres) high and is shown trotting. Just east of Pewsey Hill is the Giant's Grave long barrow.

Westbury White Horse, Westbury (OS 184: ST 898516).

The Westbury or Bratton White Horse is the oldest in the county. It is in the most commanding position on Bratton Down, 60 acres (24 hectares) of open downland overlooking the Vale of Pewsey. The approach is via a minor road off the B3098, close by Bratton Castle, tumulus and long barrow. Legend associates the first horse here with a likeness of Swallow, Alfred's charger in his victory over the Danes at the nearby battle of Ethandune in 878. This horse was said to have been cut in outline, facing the opposite direction to its successor. According to the likeness of a stallion drawn by an antiquarian clergyman named Wise in 1742, this strange beast had a beak-like head and a long curving tail, crescent-shaped at the end. It had one very large eye and a saddle with two circles. If this is true, it might have been lost in the body of the present steed, which is known to be the work of George Gee, steward to Lord Abingdon, in 1778. The horse was further remodelled in 1853 and restored twenty years later. This placid beast, 180 feet (55 metres) long and 107 feet (33 metres) high, with an eye circumference of 25 feet (7.6 metres), has a deep body, short legs and a long limp tail.

5
Sites of archaeological interest

Wiltshire has been inhabited from the earliest times and has more field antiquities extant than any other county. Certainly lower palaeolithic man hunted here, and there is scant evidence of post-glacial mesolithic settlements, but with neolithic man came the first farming communities. These were the people who built the long barrows and the causewayed enclosures some five thousand years ago, leaving such enigmas as Avebury and Stonehenge – two of the most important monuments in Britain – and Silbury Hill, the largest prehistoric earthwork of its kind in Europe. The remains of their enclosures have been conjecturally identified as animal paddocks, ritual or community centres. They had largely given up the hunting life of their predecessors and farmed cereals, cattle, sheep and pigs. During the latter part of the neolithic period small groups of possibly elite people began using a new type of fine pottery vessel called a beaker and developed monuments called henges, which were of ceremonial use.

By the bronze age the dense forests were being cleared and settlements were established on the chalk uplands. The large number of various types of round barrow extant, with the knowledge that many have been lost, indicates how widely populated the area was. Commerce and trade provided wealth and lessened the dependence on farming for survival. Evidence for this exists in the rich jewellery and other ornaments recovered from bronze age burials. The iron age followed, with the construction of hillforts, numerous in Wiltshire, and the 'Celtic' field systems so often associated with them. The communities which had developed from the earliest hunters' territories in the river valleys had by now become hamlets and farmsteads adjacent to the rivers, where they have grown into the villages of today. Natural hilltops were fortified with ramparts, and settlement areas were grouped into tribal regions.

Thus the region which Vespasian conquered for Rome by AD 47 included scattered conmunities centred on hillforts as well as outlying settlement enclosures, farming adjacent land. The new military built a network of roads centred on their own bases at Mildenhall (*Cunetio*), Sandy Lane (*Verlucio*), and Old Sarum (*Sorbiodunum*), from which five roads radiated – to Badbury Rings, Somerset, London, Winchester and Exeter. Elsewhere in the county parts of the national road network were developed for military use but were invaluable in the exchange of trade between the communities. The Roman road between Gloucester and Silchester ran to the east of Swindon through Wanborough (*Durocornovium*). There are the sites of two Roman buildings at Cricklade, almost where this road enters the county, and excavations at Nythe Farm on the outskirts of Swindon have revealed buildings and burials. Here the road branches, the second route going through Mildenhall to Winchester. The road between London and Bath also passed through Mildenhall and Sandy Lane, close to Spye Park near Calne, where there are the remains of a villa.

As all these roads were built, some Roman landowners established farming or industrial estates known as villas. There are about fifty known villa sites in the county, of which the most interesting have been excavated at Atworth, Castle Combe and Truckle Hill, North Wraxall. Variously, they revealed rooms, baths, hypocausts and burials. The most interesting site for the visitor is at Littlecote, where a substantial Roman building with mosaic floors was discovered in 1730 and again in 1978. Since then excavations have continued, and the site is open to the public. There is other evidence of Romano-British settlement throughout the county, notably at Easton Grey and at Nettleton, which has been extensively excavated. There an early military base developed into a large community with a temple to Apollo. Other settlements are known to have existed at Berwick St John, Tollard Royal, Heytesbury, Teffont, Imber, Knook Castle at Upton Lovell, Bratton, Chisenbury Warren near Enford, and West Overton. Overton Hill revealed a first- and second-century settlement, as well as burials.

The first Saxons were in Wiltshire by the early sixth century and in 552 a force of them led by Cynric defeated the Britons at Old Sarum. They won another victory at Barbury Castle in 556. In 591 there was a battle close by Alton Barnes, and in 652 Cenwealh's victory at Bradford-on-Avon gave the West Saxons territory into Somerset. At this time Wiltshire became the centre of the kingdom of Wessex, and Wansdyke was probably built as part of its defence. The groups of farming communities were now organised into large estates and, at the close of the seventh century, the shire system began, with Wilton as the county town. It was here that Alfred encountered the Danes. Although he fortified a number of key towns against invasion, he was to be driven from Chippenham before inflicting a humiliating defeat on Guthrum at the battle of Ethandune near Edington in 878. The Danes returned to Wiltshire in 1003 under Sweyn to sack Wilton and Old Sarum, and again in 1016 for a battle near Sherston.

There is little extant from the Dark Ages. A pagan Saxon cemetery at St Edmund's church, Salisbury, produced up to thirty burials. The hillfort at Oldbury Camp on Cherhill Down was reoccupied after the Romans had gone, and at Yatesbury Field nearby were found skeletons and jewellery of the period. Similarly, a burial at Rodmead Hill, Maiden Bradley, included a sword, knives and a brass-bound bucket. A yew bucket, some jewellery and fragments of a wooden coffin comprised a Saxon burial in a bowl barrow at Roundway, Devizes. Old Sarum was a Saxon burgh; so too was Cricklade, where the shape of the defences may still be seen.

In the following gazetteer of sites, the number of the Ordnance Survey 1:50,000 Landranger map on which each site occurs is given, followed by the National Grid reference.

Adam's Grave, Alton Barnes (OS 173: SU 112633).

In a Nature Conservancy area on Walker's Hill, off a minor road between Alton Barnes and Lockeridge, is the neolithic long barrow called *Wodnes beorge* (Woden's barrow) in Saxon times. A footpath leads to the wedge-shaped mound, which is 200 feet (61 metres) long, 100 feet (30.5 metres) wide and 20 feet (6 metres) high, with flanking ditches and two sarsens of a former burial chamber. In the nineteenth century it was known as Old Adam, Little Eve being a stone nearby.

Avebury Henge Monument (OS 173: SU 103700). English Heritage and National Trust.

Most of the old village lies within the 28.5 acres (11.5 hectares) enclosed by the bank and ditch, now divided into four segments by the modern roadways which run through the original entrances. The ditch, once 55 feet (17 metres) deep, has gradually silted up but is very impressive. Immediately within this, ninety-eight sarsens formed the outer circle and inside them were two smaller rings. The northern one included a three-stone enclosure, known as The Cove. Many stones were damaged or buried during medieval times and others were broken up for building use in the eighteenth century. Only the western half of the site has been excavated. The positions of many key stones no longer in existence are marked by posts. The monument, which was altered at least twice, spans the period 2600–1800 BC. It was little regarded until John Aubrey became interested in the site during the seventeenth century. Avebury is a World Heritage site.

Barbury Castle, Wroughton (OS 173: SU 149763).

The iron age hillfort is the focal point of a country park (see page 48), reached via a minor road off the B4005 or on foot across open downland. Commanding fine views, it is adjacent to the Ridgeway and allied with a 'Celtic' field system. The oval site of 11½ acres (4.7 hectares) is enclosed by two banks and ditches, as well as other defences which may have been later additions. The site has yielded weapons, tools and chariot equipment. It may later have been the site of the victory by Cynric and Ceawlin over the Britons at Beran Byrig in 556. It now has a distinguishing clump of beech trees.

Battlesbury Camp, Warminster (OS 184: ST 898456).

This long-occupied iron age oval enclosure of 25 acres (10 hectares) has double and triple defensive ramparts following the line of the hill, above a series of lynchets. There are two entrances to the east and north-west with outworks, beyond which a pit containing the remains of an apparent massacre was found. The site is about one mile (1.6 km) east of Warminster and may be reached by footpath.

Bratton Castle, Bratton (OS 184: ST 899516).

This iron age hillfort is 750 feet (229 metres) above sea level on the chalk escarpment of Westbury Hill, less than a mile south-west of Bratton, where a minor road off the B3098 leads directly on to the site. Army ranges are close by. The fort is an irregular rectangle enclosing about 25 acres (10 hectares), protected by two banks (up to 35 feet [10.6 metres] high) and ditches with two entrances and outworks. Evidence of Romano-British occupation has been found here as well as elsewhere around Bratton. Within the hillfort there is a 250 foot (76.2 metre) long barrow which is about 12 feet (3.6 metres) high. It was believed that Guthrum may have withdrawn to Bratton Castle following his defeat by Alfred at the battle of Ethandune near Edington in 878.

Burderop Down, Chiseldon (OS 173: SU 164762).

Close by Barbury Castle hillfort, and reached in the same way, is a 'Celtic' field system on gentle downland. It covers about 140 acres (56.5 hectares) with banks defining the individual rectangular fields. The area is thought to have been in use from the iron age to medieval times.

The bank, ditch and part of the stone circle at Avebury.

Chisbury Camp, Little Bedwyn (OS 174: SU 279660).

This is an iron age earthwork, approached from the road between Great Bedwyn and Little Bedwyn. The hillfort, at the top of a steep escarpment some 650 feet (198 metres) above sea level, is a multivallate enclosure of about 15 acres (6 hectares) with entrances at the north-west and south-east. On the east side of the camp the remains of the flint-built St Martin's chapel, with thirteenth- and fourteenth-century work, were latterly used as a farm building.

Chiselbury Camp, Fovant (OS 184: SU 018281).

A univallate iron age hillfort at the junction of Fovant Down and Compton Down, with a semicircular outwork at the entrance to the south-east, encloses about 8.5 acres (3.4 hectares). A single rampart and ditch enclose the area and bivallate ditches extend from the outwork and the north side.

Cley Hill Camp, Warminster (OS 183: ST 838450).

This univallate hillfort, which encloses 17 acres (6.8 hectares), stands at 800 feet (244 metres) above sea level on an isolated chalk knoll amidst areas of woodland. It is reached via the A362 to Frome, some 2½ miles (4 km) to the west of Warminster. Two bowl barrows stand on the hill. A beacon was lit on the summit at the time of the Spanish Armada. The National Trust now owns 66 acres (26.6 hectares) of land hereabouts.

Devil's Den, Clatford Bottom (OS 173: SU 152696).

To the east and north-east of Avebury, around Fyfield Down and Overton Down, are the areas of sarsen stones known as 'grey wethers', natural deposits which scattered over the ground. The best way of seeing these is to walk from Avebury towards Clatford Bottom by Fyfield and then continue to the Devil's Den. This was a neolithic chambered long barrow, flattened by ploughing. What remains is a cromlech of four sarsen stones and a thick capstone, rebuilt in 1921, at the east end.

Durrington Walls, Durrington (OS 184: SU 150438).

Just south of its intersection with the A3028 at Durrington, the A345 bisects a wide circular henge monument known as Durrington Walls. It has been heavily ploughed and little can be seen today. During excavation it produced large quantities of grooved ware pottery, often used for ceremonial purposes. It dates from the neolithic period.

Enford Bowl Barrow, Enford (OS 184: SU 129516).

With a diameter of about 150 feet (45.7 metres) and a height of 17 feet (5.1 metres), this bronze age barrow on private land is a magnificent specimen, and one of the largest of its type in Britain. Legend has it that a golden chair is buried there.

Everleigh Barrow Cemetery, Everleigh (OS 173: SU 184561).

This is a mixed group of bronze age barrows on army ranges and reached via footpaths from the A342 road between Upavon and Andover. There are two bowl barrows, two bell barrows and a disc barrow.

Figsbury Ring, Winterbourne Dauntsey (OS 184: SU 188388). National Trust.

This univallate iron age hillfort of 5¹/₂ acres (2.2 hectares) is almost circular. Within the outer bank and ditch there is a concentric ditch which may have provided additional material for the ramparts. Entrances are to the east and west. The earthwork is located just off the A30 Salisbury to Winchester road. The site belongs to the National Trust, which owns 27 acres (10.9 hectares) of surrounding land.

Fosbury Camp, Fosbury (OS 174: SU 320565).

This iron age oval bivallate hillfort enclosed 26 acres (10.5 hectares) on Haydown Hill. It is 830 feet (253 metres) above sea level, partly in Oakhill Wood, and has an inturned entrance to the east.

Fyfield and Overton Downs (OS 173: SU 135715).

This area, almost halfway between Marlborough and Avebury, is a rich prehistoric landscape close to the Ridgeway. In 1908 the National Trust bought land at Piggle Dene, an area thick with sarsen stones, and these were further preserved from 1956 when Fyfield Down was made a National Nature Reserve. There are a few burial mounds, and at the centre is a large field system of banks forming rectangular fields. A walk of about 2 miles (3 km) from the A4361 at Avebury, or from various points along the A4 between West Kennet and Fyfield, sometimes passing standing stones, leads directly to the region of sarsen stones and field systems.

Giant's Grave, Milton Lilbourne (OS 173: SU 189581).

About 2 miles (3 km) to the south of the village, from where it is reached via a footpath, there is an unchambered neolithic long barrow with side ditches. It is oriented northeast—southwest on Milton Hill. Excavations in the nineteenth century disclosed remains of several skeletons and a leaf-shaped arrowhead.

Gopher Wood, Huish (OS 173: SU 139639).

Reached via footpaths off the minor road running north out of Huish, there is a bronze age cemetery comprising seven bowl barrows and a disc barrow. Excavations here revealed cremations, funerary deposits and jewellery.

Grafton Disc Barrows, Collingbourne Kingston (OS 174: SU 271563).

To the east of the village are three isolated bronze age disc barrows, of similar sizes. They are interesting because two of them overlap and are partly overlaid by a section of a later 'Celtic' field system.

Knap Hill, Alton Barnes (OS 173: SU 121636).

From the point at which Wansdyke crosses the road between Lockeridge and Alton Barnes and the latter village there is a particular concentration of notable archaeological sites. On the summit of Knap Hill, overlooking the Vale of Pewsey, is a neolithic causewayed enclosure. It consists of a length of ditch broken by at least five causeways, and radiocarbon-dated to 3450 BC. On its northern edge there is a small, roughly rectangular earthwork of late iron age date. There are two burial mounds beside the path at the foot of the hill near the road.

Lake Barrow Cemetery, Wilsford (OS 184: SU 109402).

This bronze age cemetery is one of the Stonehenge series and lies within and outside a beech wood to the south of Wilsford Down. Access is off the A303 south of Stonehenge, through an area full of burial mounds isolated and in groups. Lake Cemetery includes a neolithic long barrow about 140 feet (42.7 metres) long, four bell barrows, fifteen bowl barrows and two disc barrows. Most of them revealed cremations when they were excavated and one had traces of a wooden coffin.

Liddington Castle, Liddington (OS 174: SU 209797).

Liddington Hill, just south of the old Ridgeway and overlooking the Wanborough Plain, is traditionally the scene of Arthur's victory over the Saxons at *Mons Badonicus*. Three counties – Wiltshire, Oxfordshire and Gloucestershire – can be seen from this point on the northern edge of the Marlborough Downs. The univallate iron age hillfort comprises bank, ditch and counterscarp bank. It is oval in shape, enclosing about 7³/₄ acres (3.1 hectares) with an entrance to the south-east. Excavations have revealed that the rampart

was built in three phases from around 600 BC to the Roman period.

Littlecote Roman Villa, Littlecote House, Hungerford (OS 174: SU 297708). Telephone: 01488 684000.

The Littlecote Roman Research Trust is excavating an extensive and important Roman villa site in Littlecote Park, south of the B4192 near Chilton Foliat. The Trust provides guided tours and gives visitors the chance to see archaeological conservation in progress. The showpiece of the site is the amazing 'Orpheus' mosaic on the floor of a building which was probably a pagan chapel. It was found about 1730 and well recorded but it was thought to have been subsequently destroyed until it was rediscovered in 1978. It was restored in 1980 and is the largest mosaic on permanent diplay in Britain. Excavations around it are revealing the villa on which the Roman settlement was centred between the mid first and fifth centuries AD.

Ludgershall Castle, Ludgershall (OS 184: SU 264513).

The extensive and complex earthworks and the fragment of Norman keep at the northern

The remains of the Norman keep at Ludgershall Castle.

edge of the village date from the eleventh century. They are all that is left of a royal castle which continued to be altered and enlarged throughout the middle ages. The castle was associated with Henry I, and both the Empress Maud and her supporter the Earl of Gloucester were there during the period of civil strife in the reign of King Stephen.

Marden Henge Monument, Marden (OS 173: SU 091584).

At the northern edge of the village the Salisbury Avon on two sides and a bank and inner ditch on the other sides enclose about 35 acres (14.1 hectares) of neolithic oval earthworks in the Vale of Pewsey. There are entrances to the east and north-west; within the latter were found the post holes of a small timber circle 34 feet (10.5 metres) in diameter. This is the largest neolithic henge monument known in Britain.

Martinsell Hill, Pewsey (OS 173: SU 177639).

Reached via a minor road between Clench Common and Wootton Rivers off the A345 north of Pewsey, Martinsell Hill is steep-sided and, at 964 feet (294 metres), commands a good position overlooking the Vale of Pewsey from the southern ridge of the Marlborough Downs. The rectangular iron age hillfort on its summit encloses about 33 acres (13.3 hectares). It follows the shape of the hill to the east and the entrance is through a wooded area to the north-east.

Normanton Down Barrow Cemetery, Wilsford (OS 184: SU 118413).

The largest group of barrows in the region of Stonehenge is less than a mile to the south, around Normanton Down. They are close to the Lake Group, separated only by Wilsford Down, and within a triangle which has the richest concentration in the county. They may be reached from the A303 or A360 and comprise some twenty-five bowl, bell and disc barrows, with a long barrow to the south.

Ogbourne Round Barrow, Ogbourne St Andrew (OS 173: SU 188723).

A bowl barrow in the churchyard was re-used for pagan Saxon and medieval burials. It was excavated in 1885 and revealed about twenty skeletons as well as one in a wooden coffin with iron fitments.

Oldbury Castle, Cherhill (OS 173: SU 049693). National Trust.

With the white horse on its northern face, a group of barrows to the south, the Cherhill monument at the top and Oldbury Castle, Cherhill Down to the south of the A4 between Avebury and Calne is a most interesting place in an Area of Outstanding Natural Beauty. The 'castle' is an irregularly shaped, well-defended bivallate iron age hillfort enclosing about 25 acres (14.9 hectares) with an inturned entrance to the south-east. It is defended by sections of single and double rampart and ditch. In the nineteenth century excavation yielded iron age pottery, and the site was subjected to flint digging.

Old Sarum, Salisbury (OS 184: SU 138327). English Heritage.

Four Roman roads met at this important site, which the Romans named *Sorbiodunum*. The massive but recut outer ramparts and ditches of the iron age hillfort enclose 29$\frac{1}{2}$ acres (11.9 hectares) and the Normans added inner earthworks. It was a Saxon burgh which was given military and ecclesiastical importance by the Normans to the extent that, at the start of the medieval period, the hillfort had become the basis of a town with castle, cathedral and houses. There are fine views, and the remains of these buildings can be seen. The ecclesiastical buildings were abandoned during the first half of the thirteenth century, because of friction between the church and the military; a cathedral was begun at New Sarum (Salisbury) and the townspeople moved out. Even so, it was not until the Reform Act of 1832 that Old Sarum stopped returning two members to Parliament.

Oliver's Camp, Devizes (OS 173: SU 001646).

A small univallate promontory hillfort was built in the iron age on a spur between Beacon Hill and Roundway Hill north of Devizes. It is roughly triangular in shape, a single bank

Old Sarum Castle stands in the middle of a prehistoric hillfort.

and ditch enclosing an area of about 3½ acres (1.4 hectares) with an entrance at the east. Excavations uncovered two holes for gate-posts on each side. There are two bronze age round barrows at the south-west. The camp is named after Oliver Cromwell although there is no good reason other than a tenuous link in the Civil War battle of 1643 on nearby Roundway Down.

Overton Hill, East Kennett (OS 173: SU 119682).

The great stone avenue leads from Avebury to West Kennett, to the east of which lies Overton Hill, the Saxon *Seofan Beorgas* (Seven Barrows). At the point where the Ridgeway crosses the A4 there is a cemetery of two bowl barrows, three bell barrows and a triple barrow, with an exceptionally fine bell barrow close by. Excavations revealed that bronze age cremations made up most of the burials in this group.

Pertwood Down, Brixton Deverill (OS 183: ST 872374).

Just east of Monkton Deverill, and reached either from below the village or from a minor

road off the A350, this is a fine neolithic long barrow close to a field system and isolated burial mounds. The long barrow is 260 feet (79.3 metres) in length and there is a berm between the ditch and the mound. It is all very well preserved. Nearby there is a section of Roman road.

Rybury Camp, All Cannings (OS 173: SU 083638).

On a detached knoll called Clifford's Hill is a neolithic causewayed enclosure of two concentric oval ditches, overlain by an iron age hillfort with a single rampart and internal ditch, enclosing about 3½ acres (1.4 hectares). The camp is just south of Wansdyke, from which it may be approached by foot-path, 1½ miles (2.4 km) north-east of Allington.

The Sanctuary, Overton Hill, East Kennett (OS 173: SU 118679).

According to Stukeley, some stone circles at the end of the Avenue on Overton Hill were destroyed in 1724 and the raw material was sold, presumably for building. This was the Sanctuary, a ceremonial site to the south of

Silbury Hill is the largest man-made prehistoric mound in Europe.

the A4 at West Kennett. It was excavated in 1930, when seven concentric circles were traced. The outer circle was of stone, then came a timber fence-ring, then a stone and post ring and four more rings of timber. Together they probably formed a circular thatched building, dated to about 2500 BC. Concrete pillars now mark their positions, and the whole structure is thought to have been a wooden temple. This is a World Heritage site.

Scratchbury Camp, Norton Bavant (OS 184: ST 912443).

The companion to nearby Battlesbury Camp, overlooking the Wylye valley close to Heytesbury, this four-sided univallate hillfort encloses about 40 acres (16 hectares). There are three entrances, one in the north-west and two in the south-east. Within the iron age enclosure are a number of bronze age round barrows and there is the outline of a smaller, earlier hillfort on the site. There are strip

lynchets and another burial mound on Middle Hill between the two hillforts.

Silbury Hill, Avebury (OS 173: SU 100685).

On the A4, about a mile (1.6 km) from Avebury village, from which it may be reached by footpath, is the largest man-made prehistoric mound in Europe. Silbury Hill covers 5¼ acres (2 hectares) and is built on a spur of natural chalk. It is a truncated cone 139 feet (42.3 metres) high, 100 feet (30.5 metres) across its flat top, and with a base diameter of 550 feet (167.7 metres). Excavations between 1968 and 1970 determined that it was built in four phases, together with its ditch, during the neolithic period. Several archaeological investigations have failed to clarify its purpose. Samuel Pepys wrote that it was called 'Selbury' after a King Seall who was said to have been buried nearby. John Aubrey, whose interest in Avebury kindled it in others, brought Charles II to Silbury Hill in 1663.

Stonehenge, Amesbury (OS 184: SU 123422). Telephone: 01722 336855. English Heritage.

A circular sacred site within an area of important religious activity from neolithic times, Stonehenge was probably built in three phases. Around 2300 BC the slight outer bank, ditch and main inner bank were built with an entrance to the north-east. The naturally shaped sarsen Heel Stone was set up opposite, and within the bank cremations were interred, their positions marked by the so-called Aubrey Holes. The second phase, about 2200 BC, belonged to people using beakers, who built the Avenue and set up a double circle of blue stones within the earthworks. From this time the monument's axis pointed towards midsummer sunrise and midwinter sunset, thus establishing the wide-ranging speculation on its true purpose. During the third phase, about 2000 BC, the blue stones were removed, replaced by a circle of sarsens with lintels in pairs enclosing a U-shaped setting similarly arranged, then brought back again. An original plan for them seems to have been abandoned, and they eventually formed a circle between the sarsens and the horseshoe. The upright Altar Stone was added to the centre. Stonehenge is a World Heritage Site administered by English Heritage.

The Stonehenge Cursus, Durrington (OS 184: SU 110430).

A little to the north of Stonehenge is this unexplained rectangular enclosure, consisting of two parallel banks and ditches about 100 yards (91.5 metres) apart and 1 1/2 miles (2.4 km) long. Cursuses seem to have been ritual monuments associated with long barrows and the dead.

Tidcombe Long Barrow, Tidcombe (OS 174: SU 292576).

Close by the site of a Roman road below Tidcombe Down, there is a neolithic long barrow 185 feet (56.4 metres) long. Four sarsen stone uprights and roofing slabs at the south-east end are all that is left of the burial chamber, where excavations revealed a single skeleton.

Tilshead Old Ditch, Tilshead (OS 184: SU 011465).

All around Tilshead village there are military danger zones on army land. These are bisected by the A360 to Salisbury and at one point, about three-quarters of a mile (1200 metres) south of the village, the road is crossed by the bank and ditch known as 'Old Ditch'. The ditch, which forms the parish boundary in some places, may be traced in several sections as it runs east to west across the south of the village. There are a number of long barrows close by, including the longest example visible in Britain (OS 184: SU 023468). It is on Ministry of Defence land but can be clearly seen in a belt of trees, to the south of the Tilshead to Chitterne road at 021475.

Tilshead White Barrow, Tilshead (OS 184: SU 033468).

About three-quarters of a mile (1200 metres) south of the village, west of the A360 to Salisbury, there is a fine neolithic barrow, some 250 feet (76.2 metres) long and 155 feet (47.2 metres) at its widest point. It is about 8 feet (2.4 metres) high and lies within a ditch. The surrounding 3 acres (1.2 hectares) of land belong to the National Trust, which bought it in 1909.

West Kennett Avenue, Avebury (OS 173: SU 108690).

Originally there were more than two hundred standing stones set up in pairs, each of one tall and one wide sarsen, snaking a processional way of 1 1/2 miles (2.4 km) between the henge monument at Avebury and the Sanctuary on Overton Hill to the south-east. The work of neolithic people, *c.*2300 BC, it suffered a similar fate to the Avebury stone circles and the other great avenue which Stukeley described as going south-west towards Beckhampton. Part of the West Kennett Avenue was restored in 1934-5, when excavations found beaker burials at the foot of some of the stones. The twenty-seven sarsens now in place represent only the northern section of the avenue. It runs parallel to the B4003 from Avebury on land belonging to the National Trust.

Six concentric rings of wooden posts (now marked with concrete pillars) formed Woodhenge, a neolithic monument. In the centre was found the grave of a three-year-old child.

West Kennett Long Barrow, Avebury (OS 173: SU 104677).

Just south of the A4 near West Kennett is a fine, wedge-shaped burial mound 340 feet (104 metres) long and about 8 feet (2.4 metres) high with four lateral chambers and a burial chamber at the eastern end. The chambers are constructed of large sarsens and drystone walling, and huge capstones form the roof. It is easily accessible for inspection. The entrance is obscured by large sarsens and smaller flanking stones with which the mound was sealed after about one thousand years of use.

Whitesheet Castle, Stourton (OS 183: ST 804346).

About 1½ miles (2.4 km) north-northeast of the town, at the southern edge of Whitesheet Down, and reached by a footpath running between the B3092 and the B3095, this is a triangular iron age hillfort enclosing 14 acres (5.6 hectares). The defences are univallate, except to the north-east, where there are three sets of widely spaced ramparts.

White Sheet Hill, Kilmington (OS 183: ST 802352). National Trust.

A single bank and causewayed ditch of the neolithic period enclose an oval area of about 4 acres (1.6 hectares). A bronze age bowl barrow overlies the bank on the south-east side, with several more close by. Windmill Hill pottery was found here.

Windmill Hill, Winterbourne Monkton (OS 173: SU 087714). English Heritage.

About a mile (1.4 km) north-west of Avebury, and reached by a minor road off the A4361 through Avebury Trusloe, is one of the largest neolithic causeway enclosures in Britain. Enclosing about 21 acres (8.4 hectares), it consists of three concentric ditches, cut to different depths and different distances apart, and overlying an earlier settlement. Windmill Hill was a seasonal gathering place for the settlers in the region of the Marlborough Downs about 3300 BC. A bowl barrow and a bell barrow between the inner ditches are part of a small bronze age cemetery extending from the east of the camp. This is a World Heritage Site.

Winklebury Camp, Berwick St John (OS 184: ST 952217). Winklebury Hill lies just south-east of the village. The camp is a univallate iron age hillfort, unfinished but built in three phases and covering an area of 12 acres (4.8 hectares). It is surrounded by a ditch and a 40 foot (12.2 metre) rampart. The remains of a wattle and daub hut were excavated. A pagan Saxon cemetery containing thirty-one burials was excavated at the end of the nineteenth century. There are particularly fine views from this hilltop.

Winterbourne Stoke Crossroads Barrow Group (OS 184: SU 101417).

The most accessible of the Stonehenge barrow groups is just north of Longbarrow Crossroads, where the A360 and A303 meet about 1½ miles (2.4 km) east of Winterbourne Stoke. The neolithic long barrow of 240 feet (73.2 metres) gives its name to the place; otherwise there are about three dozen bell, bowl, disc, pond and saucer barrows, mainly in two roughly parallel lines, partly on National Trust property.

Woodhenge, Durrington (OS 184: SU 150434).

The site of this probable wooden building, south-west of Durrington just off the A345, was discovered by aerial photography in 1926. It was possibly roofed around the outside while being open to the sky at its centre. Today the holes in which the timber uprights once stood are marked by concrete pillars. The construction was of six concentric rings of post holes within an external bank and ditch, with an entrance to the north-east. This henge monument was built in the neolithic period and is about 250 feet (76.2 metres) in diameter. A central grave was revealed to be that of a child, and Windmill Hill pottery was found at the site.

Yarnbury Castle, Steeple Langford (OS 184: SU 035403).

This iron age hillfort was built on Salisbury Plain and is just north of the A303 about halfway between Wylye and Winterbourne Stoke. The hillfort is circular and has three ditches, the inner one being 50 feet (15.2 metres) deep, and double ramparts with a particularly elaborate entrance at the east. The area covered by the enclosure is 28.5 acres (11.5 hectares). Inside,there are traces of an earlier prehistoric earthwork. A sheep fair used to be held in the fort during the eighteenth century.

6
Churches

Aldbourne: St Michael. (On B4192 between Swindon and Hungerford.)

The building stands tall and long on its rise above the green, overshadowing the little row of cottages which incline downwards towards it, and in so doing give it an even more dominating aspect. There is a twelfth-century doorway, larger than on any other village church in the county, with zigzag moulding; otherwise it is externally almost all of the fifteenth century, with Richard Goddard's impressive tower and big, Somerset-type bell openings a joy to behold. Inside, the south arcade with its original billet decoration is Norman work, although the arches were remade and set up on thirteenth-century capitals and columns following a fire. Fine panelling on the soffit and sides of the arch into the south chapel is the only example of such work in this part of the county.

All Cannings: All Saints. (East of Devizes, south of the Kennet & Avon Canal.)

This is a large cruciform church, as was its Norman predecessor. Most of the outside is plain Perpendicular, except for the battlemented parapet of the south chapel and the south transept which were treated as one piece by the early Tudor builders and are richly done. The chapel was probably built around 1508 by Sir Richard Beauchamp, Lord St Amand. The interest in each aisle centres on the strangely decorated and inscribed monuments to members of the Ernle family, and a sumptuous wall monument of 1581 recalls Walter Ernle and his wife Jean. But the exceptional feature is the chancel, an elaborate reconstruction of mid thirteenth-century style by T. H. Wyatt in 1867.

Alton Barnes: St Mary the Virgin. (East of Devizes, north of the Kennet & Avon Canal.)

This is a pretty little church when seen from the south-west, against a backdrop of downland and meadows, framed in foliage and at the end of a cobbled path. Originally an Anglo-Saxon building and retaining its internal proportions, it now has a nave exterior of uniform pebbledash and a brick chancel of 1748. Pilasters and megalith quoins attest to its age, and internally there is much to enjoy: a rough fifteenth-century collar and tiebeam roof, a small three-decker pulpit, a west gallery crammed with tiered pews and reached by a winding wooden staircase, a reading desk and a baluster birdbath Georgian font.

Alton Priors: All Saints. (East of Devizes, north of the Kennet & Avon Canal.)

Its Perpendicular west tower rises invitingly across the fields, and there is a rewarding meadow pathway with two rustic stiles across the stream. On the south face of the tower a huge sundial keeps the time, which can be read some distance away. Most of the fabric is fourteenth-century, with only the twelfth-century chancel arch remaining from an earlier church. Inside there is the brass of a nun, dated 1528, and in the chancel are rustic Jacobean stalls put together in a very haphazard manner. The altar rails were made in the eighteenth century and, behind them, William Button rises naked from his marble tomb towards the gates of Heaven.

Amesbury: St Mary and St Mellor. (On A345 north of Salisbury.)

Here is a fine and imposing cruciform church without aisles, built mostly of flint with some chequerwork and stone blocks. The Norman nave was extended in the thirteenth century when the transepts were added. It is a textbook church for lancet windows and has a fine example of an early fourteenth-century window in the chancel. Worth visiting is the Jesus Chapel, an extension through the east wall of the north transept, built almost entirely in the thirteenth century.

All Saints' church at All Cannings contains fine monuments to the Ernle family.

Ashton Keynes: Holy Cross. (Off B4696 west of Cricklade.)

The treasure here is a richly decorated fourteenth-century stone reredos – a triptych with a vesica as the centrepiece. The chancel arch is big and wide, put up at the end of the twelfth century and widened at the restoration of 1876-7, when the chancel retained its thirteenth-century walls. Set against these, on the outside, are three shallow buttresses which may be Norman. The roof of the south porch is unusual in having a barrel vault, and another feature is the Transitional tub font with zigzag and big fleshy leaves.

Avebury: St James. (On A4361 between Swindon and Devizes.)

The church stands outside the great stone circle, a little to the north-west and on the way to the manor house and museums. High in what were once the outside walls of the Saxon church – made into aisles in the twelfth century – are the original, and unique, round windows. In restoring the circular lights in what proved to be their original positions, C. E. Ponting provided Avebury with features

found in no other church. None of the nineteenth-century restoration altered the dimensions of the Saxon nave, so here we have a textbook example. The walls were left intact even to the original string course which runs the length of the north wall. The splendid rood loft is a fifteenth-century survival, and the barrel-shaped tub font is Saxon in shape but Norman in decoration.

Berwick Bassett: St Nicholas. (Off A4361 south of Swindon.)

At the end of an overgrown pathway, past sarsens used as tombstones, is a little church declared redundant in 1972. The low two-stage tower, with its unusual blunt pyramidal cap, rises above the wilderness. Inside there is a thirteenth-century font, a restored fifteenth-century screen, a wooden pulpit, a clerk's desk and a lectern with little candle holders swinging mournfully in their sockets.

Berwick St James: St James. (On B3083 north-west of Wilton.)

This is a small low flint and stone church with a western tower, embattled and dated

1670. It is basically of the thirteenth century, although the north doorway is Norman, where one enters beneath a tympanum of green and white stone bands, which pales beside that of nearby Little Langford but must be older. The chancel is Early English, but most of what we see was rebuilt in the fifteenth century.

Biddestone: St Nicholas. (Off A420 west of Chippenham.)

More picturesque and quaint than of any real architectural interest, this little church lies at the end of a pathway lined with flowers. The most interesting external feature is the bell turret, a thirteenth-century arched base with a fifteenth-century octagonal stone spirelet. The font is a deep Norman tub with a band of chevron. The woodwork in the church is late Georgian and of light oak, and there are pine box pews and a west gallery supported by very slender pillars, which are more decorative than functional. The wall at the west end of the nave is lined with old and faded photographs of the church and its past incumbents.

Bishops Cannings: St Mary the Virgin. (Off A361 north-west of Devizes.)

This is a fine structure made all the more imposing by its situation in a wide expanse of flat ground. It is a large church, yet apparently covering the same ground plan as it did in the thirteenth century. A walk across the southern face takes in the work of several centuries from Early English to Perpendicular, probably begun by Bishop Joscelyn late in the twelfth century. Inside, the arcades show the development of Norman to Early English styles and decoration. But at no time did development stand still; there is evidence, for example, that windows were altered from lancets quite early on and substantial reconstruction took place over the next two centuries. This was an impressive church when it was first built and remains so today.

Bishopstone: St John the Baptist. (Southwest of Salisbury in the Ebble valley.)

This is a large cruciform church, almost entirely of the fourteenth century, in flint and stone with nave and chancel of equal lengths and a square embattled central tower. The exterior is dominated by fine reticulated and flowing window tracery of the period. It is a happy hunting ground for students of the ogee arch, to be found here in arches, niches, canopies and minor decoration. The chancel has a stone-vaulted ceiling made up of lierne ribs in two bays, and of interest also are the flamboyant fourteenth-century sedilia in the south wall of the sanctuary.

Boyton: St Mary. (Off A36 south-east of Warminster.)

Built of stone and flint in rough courses, this is a thirteenth- and fourteenth-century church of unusual ground plan with a north tower. Here in the Gilford Chapel is the great wheel window, an early geometric window of c.1280 which comprises circles within circles. 12 feet (3.6 metres) across, it is overpowering and quite out of harmony with the little chapel.

Bradford-on-Avon: St Lawrence.

In 1856 Canon Jones looked down the hill

The Saxon church of St Lawrence in Bradford-on-Avon was lost and not rediscovered until 1856.

Roman tiles form this Saxon arch at St Peter's church, Britford.

at Bradford-on-Avon and saw the shape of a little church amidst the cottages. He painstakingly collected the evidence of antiquaries, who agreed upon its great age if not its exact foundation. The paraphernalia of secular use within was removed and so were the buildings which obscured it. Then, in 1871, Canon Jones found evidence to suppose that this was the church which St Aldhelm built at the end of the seventh century. Other authorities have dated it between 950 and 1000, and some maintain it to be the original church restored in the tenth century. The building is nevertheless a blueprint for the dimensions by which we assess the possible Saxon origins of others: the extreme height in relation to the length, the tall narrow doorways and round arches, the double-splayed windows, the type of external arcading and the pilasters.

The church was built on the Celtic plan and completed at one time. It consists of square-ended chancel, nave and north porticus; of the one to the south only the former position is discernible. It has been used as a schoolroom and a three-storey dwelling. Restoration work has included two modern buttresses to keep the fabric intact. High above the chancel arch are two sculptured angels, reset in what is thought to be their original position, where they may once have attended the figure of Christ on the cross. Other fragments of Anglo-Saxon carving have been found hereabouts and in 1970 some of them – including pieces which may have come from the original altar – were made into a new one. Others which once formed part of a cross were placed above the east wall of the chancel.

Bratton: St James the Great. (On B3098 east of Westbury.)

This is an almost completely Perpendicular church, standing away from the village by the side of a valley. The walker has a long climb up many steps from the main street, the motorist by a narrow lane under the scrutiny of wildly delightful gargoyles – grinning beasts conceived at the hands of fifteenth-century masons. Battlemented like a fortress without, surprisingly compact within, it is Perpendicular in essence and feeling but not a one-period church. The 'Early English' chancel is a mid nineteenth-century rebuilding, the font – thought to have been a Saxon tub – was delicately cut by a mid-Victorian mason to look Norman, and the present crossing tower is on the bases of an earlier one.

Britford: St Peter. (Off A338 south of Salisbury.)

This church is in the midst of flat water-meadows and actually on an island formed by various waterways. The spire of Salisbury

Cathedral is in the distance, and the church is reached by a narrow lane with the sound of running water all along it and the smell of churchyard yews at the end. Its large crossing tower looms over a mostly fourteenth-century building, rebuilt in 1767 and restored by G. E. Street in 1873. It was then that three remarkable Anglo-Saxon doorways came to light, one turned with flat Roman tiles. The decorative work associated with these is some of the most important of its age in the county. Also of particular interest is a fine altar tomb with figures in niches. It is reputedly that of Henry Stafford, who was beheaded in Salisbury market place in 1483, and the figures are for the most part said to represent those people involved in his fate. There are the seventeenth-century pulpit, bench ends and pews, an Early English effigy in the chancel, the fifteenth-century parish chest and, outside, an attractive cluster of eightenth-century headstones in the churchyard.

Bromham: St Nicholas. (Off A342 between Devizes and Chippenham.)

One's first sight is of a short stone parapet spire, rising from within a low tower, put up about 1500 when the vogue for spires was on the wane. Richard Beauchamp, Lord St Amand, built a chantry chapel at Bromham although he is not buried here. It is very similar in style to the Beauchamp Chapel at St John, Devizes, and decorated without, very much like the chapel which bears his arms at All Saints, All Cannings. The licence for it was granted in 1492, and it is both a work of great beauty and a gem of high Gothic. Embattled and pinnacled with decoration and decorative mouldings, treated externally with the south transept and awash with grotesques and gargoyles, it is in stark contrast to the plain lancets of the Early English chancel. Inside, beneath the panelled wooden ceiling of the chapel, there is an impressive altar tomb which carries an alabaster effigy of Sir Richard Tocotes, who died in 1457. The tomb appears to have been defaced with names and dates ever since; one vandal had a most exquisite copperplate hand! The stained glass east window was designed by Burne-Jones and created by William Morris.

Castle Combe: St Andrew. (Off B4039 northwest of Chippenham.)

The church is a bonus in a beautiful place; the postcard view is from the bridge over the river, from where it stands high in the trees hard by the market cross and framed by the warm brown stone of the clustering houses. It is a wool church, begun in 1434 and built by someone who knew how to draw the eye up a tower. But it is now interesting only in particulars: the east Jesse window, the tall piers of the fourteenth-century nave arcade beneath a fine tiebeam roof with braces, the dark woodwork and the carved Perpendicular pulpit, and the font with its bookrest projection.

Castle Eaton: St Mary. (Off A419 north of Swindon.)

At a turn in the road is the lychgate, built between drystone walls and at the end of a lane which curves out of sight towards the meadows. It leads to the church with its massive and unique sanctus bell turret – an octagonal stone spirelet supported by four rectangular blocks of stone, put up in the thirteenth century. The tower is fifteenth-century, but otherwise the church has a thirteenth-century 'feel' externally – the date of the chancel. The north arcade is a curiosity, made of timber set on stone bases and inviting speculation that the original intention, to complete the work in stone, was not fulfilled. There is a carved oak post, dated 1704, which may once have supported a gallery, a fine Jacobean pulpit and some panelled woodwork. There is some reticulated tracery in the north chapel.

Chilton Foliat: St Mary. (On B4192 northwest of Hungerford.)

This is a little church of stone and flint which is easily missed because it lies back behind two walls. Its low tower is one of few in Wiltshire to have been put up in the thirteenth century, and although the church is Early English it was substantially rebuilt in the seventeenth century. This is the date of the wagon roof over the nave; the gallery – possibly a reconstruction – is dated 1694 and the same may be true of the Jacobean screen, a fine piece oddly arranged with baluster muntins yet Gothic tracery. The Victorian font is crammed with scenes from both the Old and New Testaments. Two contrasting memorials are an unidentified weathered knight in armour, and the startling nineteenth-century likeness in white marble of Francis Popham, who died at six months.

Chirton: St John the Baptist. (Off A342 south-east of Devizes.)

Here is a small village church, originally of the twelfth century, whose brown roof tiles shine almost gold in the sun. It has a number of good Norman and Transitional features, for example the richly decorated south doorway (with a fourtenth-century arch inserted and protected by a fifteenth-century porch), the late twelfth-century arcades and the early font. This is one of the best in the county and has the twelve apostles variously holding books beneath a decorated arcade, and St Peter has a key. This was a high standard of carving for the time, so delicately done that even now one can distinguish their features, the folds in their clothes and even their toes.

Chiseldon: Holy Cross. (Off A345 south-east of Swindon.)

There was a church here in Saxon times, but all that remains of it is what appears to be the head of a Saxon window, built on its side into the south-west pillar of the thirteenth-century nave arcade. But here we have an unusual fourtenth-century three-stage south tower porch, which is almost a detached tower because the clerestory runs right along behind it. Inside the church the walls are covered with tablets and minor memorials to local families.

Clyffe Pypard: St Peter. (South of Wootton Bassett.)

Beautifully situated beneath a wooded rise, this little fifteenth-century church has a great treasure: a canopied Jacobean pulpit of 1629, richly carved with its original bookrest. At the west end of the south aisle is an overpowering monument in white and orange marble to a children's benefactor, Thomas Spackman, a local carpenter who taught them how to read and write. The nave has a fine barrel roof with a cambered tiebeam.

Codford St Peter: St Peter. (Off A36 south-east of Warminster.)

The church rises steeply and immediately from the main road, seemingly in a profusion of crests, carvings and gargoyles. The hand of T. H. Wyatt was heavy here, making a Victorian Gothic interior out of the thirteenth-century chancel, but keeping the Early English sedilia. The twelfth-century font is square with four different motifs arranged in double bands around its surface. But the gem in this church is a piece of ninth-century sculpture, on what is thought to be part of a Saxon cross-shaft which was built into the north side of the chancel arch until the alterations of 1864. It shows a dancing man, his head thrown back at an impossible angle. Is it drunkenness, hilarity, ecstasy? Has it a biblical significance, or is it folklore? He has a band about his head and is dressed in a short, belted smock with deeply cut folds, and a cape around his shoulders secured by a large pin. His feet have slippers on them, in his left hand is a mallet, and his right hand grasps a branch with cones and leaves. There are leaves, animals and fishes on the piece, key ornament and banded shafts with square capitals.

Colerne: St John the Baptist. (North of A4 between Bath and Chippenham.)

The tower, built in 1450, draws on Somerset and Gloucestershire influences. Aubrey remarked: 'Here is a most noble prospect, a stately, high, well built tower which, when the bells are new cast, ring, shakes much. A very faire church, but nothing of Antiquity left, unless the three seats in the chancel for the Bishop, and others...' Much else is Victorian, but there are three fragments of a Saxon cross-shaft with entwined serpent motif in the north wall of the nave, and the nave arcade is transitional Norman with pointed arches springing above circular pillars and bases. In the north wall of the chancel are three sedilia with fourteenth-century canopies, restored and replaced in 1903.

Collingbourne Kingston: St Mary. (On A338 north-west of Andover.)

On the outside of this church are little starlight clerestory windows, put there in 1861, and whimsical, to say the least. Pevsner describes them as 'pentagon and hexagon surrounds, cinquefoil and sexfoils', which gives at once a good idea of their oddity. Also Victorian is the mighty pointed chancel arch. But the nave arcades are late Norman, the chancel is Early English and the tower Perpendicular. The church has some fine monuments and a brass of 1495. Under a fine canopy with a double arch, Tudor roses and flowers are the recumbent effigies of Thomas Pile and his wife, together with the kneeling effigies of Sir Gabriel Pile, his wife Anne and their two sons.

Compton Bassett: St Swithin. (Off A4 northeast of Calne.)

Here is a beautifully kept village church, on a rise from the roadway and nestling amidst downland; it is Perpendicular and Victorian outside, thirteenth- to fifteenth-century within. But it has both a curio and a thing of great beauty. The former is an hourglass in its iron frame, attached to the east respond of the north arcade and still in working order. Close by is the early fifteenth-century double rood screen, made in Caen stone, small but richly carved.

Coombe Bissett: St Michael and All Angels. (On A354 south-west of Salisbury.)

Despite the early promise of a Norman south doorway, the church is mainly of the fifteenth century. It nestles in a little valley, overlooking a medieval bridge. The land climbs sharply to the south and the river Ebble breaks suddenly into tributaries to the north. The chancel is of the thirteenth century, of the same period as the font. The greatest interest in this cruciform church is the Norman south arcade, and particularly the centre pier capital, which is finely decorated. Large foliated volutes curl around the angles and the surfaces between have delicate fleurs-de-lis.

Corsham: St Bartholomew. (On A4 southwest of Chippenham.)

Here is an excellent textbook example to illustrate the development of parish churches generally, for Corsham has not missed out on any period and retains something of most. It retains its original Saxon proportions, its Norman nave arcade, its twelfth-century chancel enlarged in the thirteenth, its fourteenth-century aisles and its general fifteenth-century rebuilding and enlarging. A fine screen was put up at the end of the north aisle when Thomas Tropenell rebuilt the Lady Chapel for his own heavy ornate tomb and that of his family, including the south transept in his design. The Methuen Chapel, made out of the north transept in 1876-8, contains an effigy of a child and a seventeenth-century tomb with six kneeling figures in alabaster.

Cricklade: St Mary. (Off A419 north-west of Swindon.)

Neatly tucked in between the houses of the main street, near to the river Thames, this picturesque building, with little dormer windows beneath their red roofing tiles, is a gem. Originally a little Norman church, to which was added a low thirteenth-century tower, most of it is now fifteenth-century work. The four-centred arches of the Tudor arcade are particularly striking. There is a well-carved Jacobean pulpit, and elsewhere the light-coloured pews have doors and interesting hinges, which were a development of the seventeenth-century cockshead type and the 'H' hinge of the eighteenth century. The chancel arch, put up *c*.1120-50, is all that is left of the Norman church – but how impressive it is.

Cricklade: St Sampson. (Off A419 north-west of Swindon.)

Although the church is tucked away behind the main street, the great Tudor crossing tower dominates the little town and commands attention. John Dudley, Earl of Warwick and later Duke of Northumberland, financed it *c*.1519-34. Lit up at Christmas, it is a joy to behold from miles around. Externally the tower needed its massive flying buttress of 1569 to resist the outward thrust. Below, the ribs of the elaborate lierne vault end in seventy-two bosses and the walls display a unique collection of heraldry. On sunny days all of this is illuminated in a bowl of light at the crossing, painting the walls a bright gold and bouncing shafts of sunlight into the thirteenth-century nave. Above the south arcade is a complete Anglo-Saxon pilaster strip still *in situ*, where the arcade was cut out of the walls of an earlier church. Of this period too are fragments of Anglo-Saxon decoration in the sixteenth-century porch.

Devizes: St John.

Both within and without, this church is a happy union of heavy Norman and lighter, if more ornate, fifteenth-century work. The churchyard is hard pressed by interesting little houses and is a wonder at blossom time. The original cruciform church was built by Bishop Roger of Sarum *c.*1130, at about the same time as he was completing his rebuilding of Old Sarum cathedral. The tower, crossing, chancel and transepts are almost as they were when the work was first done and comprise some of the most important Norman church architecture and decoration in England. The great tower had its embattled parapet and crocketed pinnacles added in the fifteenth century, and in the sixteenth century Richard Beauchamp, Lord St Amand, built the richly decorated chantry chapel to the south-east.

Downton: St Lawrence. (On A338 south of Salisbury.)

A very long building with a wide frontage, the church is built predominantly of flint with some brickwork and brown stone. The approach is through a fine lychgate dated 1892 and set off by a number of table tombs and a churchyard cross. The strange blind parapet above the south aisle is made of red bricks and gives the structure a top-heavy appearance. The tower is Perpendicular; it was raised some 30 feet (9 metres) in 1791 at the expense of the Earl of Radnor, restored to its original height with a new upper storey in the nineteenth century and once again topped by the Earl of Radnor's pinnacles. Here are a porch of 1648, some good Norman and Early English work in the five-bay nave arcade, Early English transepts with good lancets and some early fourteenth-century windows in the chancel.

East Knoyle: St Mary. (On A350 between Warminster and Shaftesbury.)

The Reverend Dr Christopher Wren, father of the famous architect, himself designed the decorative plasterwork in the chancel for which this church is well-known, paid for it and had it put up by Robert Brockway, a plasterer from Quinton in Dorset. Jacob's dream, the Ascension and the sacrifice of Isaac are all here, together with texts and verses. Some thirteenth-century work remains from when the north and south transepts were put up and the chancel lengthened. There are fourteenth-century windows and a fifteenth-century tower, but the chancel arch was called 'modern' in 1825, and so much was done throughout the nineteenth century that the bulk of the interior is Victorian. Yet there are Saxon dimensions to the nave.

Ebbesborne Wake: St John the Baptist. (South-west of Salisbury in the Ebble valley.)

This is a barn-like church overshadowed

Plasterwork designed by the father of Christopher Wren decorates East Knoyle church, where Wren was baptised.

Over the Lewis monument in Edington priory church a hovers an angel.

by the downs which hereabouts line the course of the Ebble valley. The tower was put up in the fifteenth century; the chancel and nave are separated by a wooden screen and in the former are canopied sedilia and piscinas of the fourteenth century, the general date of the church.

Edington: St Mary, St Katherine and All Saints. (On B3098 west of Westbury.)

In all Wiltshire there is no greater surprise than one's first sight of this church. Suddenly at a curve in the narrow road to the north-east of the village is this great building, totally unexpected and quite breathtaking. On one side it is protected by the sharp rise beyond which is Salisbury Plain; on the other it is open towards the distant Vale of Pewsey. William of Edington, Bishop of Winchester, built his great priory church here in 1352-61 at a time when the Decorated style was developing vertically into the Perpendicular. Built like a miniature cathedral with a nave some 75 feet (23 metres) long, but embattled like a fortress, it is a fusion of both styles, as seen to no better advantage than in the windows. The Lady Chapel has fine medieval stained glass, and there is good fourteenth-century decora-

tion in the chancel, separated from the nave by the magnificent double screen of *c*.1500. The building has many consecration crosses and masons' marks, a seventeenth-century pulpit and a number of noteworthy monuments and tombs.

Enford: All Saints. (Off A345 north of Amesbury.)

The exterior is mostly of flint and stone blocks in very narrow horizontal bands, a quite unusual discipline in this area, where the tendency is towards random flint. The spire of the fifteenth-century tower came down in 1817. The gem of the church is in the chancel under the kingpost roof: an arrangement of sedilia-like recessed blind arcading of nine bays with integral piscina. The nave arcades are early twelfth-century and the chancel arch a little later. The treatment of these features and the variety of decoration on them make the church well worth a visit.

Farley: All Saints. (East of Salisbury.)

An unusual church for Wiltshire, built of pink bricks and roofing tiles with neat rusticated stone quoins at all the angles, it was completed at a time of little church building in the countryside, *c*.1689-90, inspired by the Italian Renaissance. The church and the almshouses on the opposite side of the road form a homogeneous group set behind brick walls. There are restrained classical styles and decorative motifs, a modest collection of monuments and simplicity in design throughout. The fine oak chancel screen has turned balusters.

Fifield Bavant: St Martin. (South-west of Salisbury, in the Ebble valley.)

This is a lonely building in a small plot with few tombstones, surrounded by ranch-type fencing. It stands on a rise with its south face to the downs and is approached through a farmyard. This single-celled building with its tiled bell turret at the west end is the smallest parish church in Wiltshire and one of the smallest in England. The fabric generally, one lancet window and also the gable cross at the east end appear to be almost entirely the original thirteenth-century work. Of its other three windows, two are fifteenth-century and one was put in during the seventeenth.

Great Bedwyn: St Mary. (South of A4 between Marlborough and Hungerford.)

This spacious cruciform church, built of flint in the thirteenth and fourteenth centuries, is of interest to students both of heraldry and of church history. Here are the effigies of Sir John Seymour, whose daughter married Henry VIII in 1536, and of Sir Adam de Stokke who died *c*.1312. The church has rich and flamboyant Decorated windows. But its chief glory is the nave arcades, fine if a little over-restored Transitional Norman work with a riot of decoration.

Great Chalfield: All Saints. (North-east of Bradford-on-Avon.)

Here is one of the loveliest settings of any church in the county. Hard by the forecourt of the manor house (page 106) and within its moat, this little building is made all the more picturesque by its attractive bellcote, which is precariously balanced on the west gable. Inside, one is confronted by a floor so uneven that it seems to ripple like cross-currents on a beach. Plain panelling abounds and there is a

three-decker pulpit of unusual style, with tester. The most lavish item in the church is the six-light stone screen with heraldic devices which separates the chancel from the nave.

Great Durnford: St Andrew. (South of Amesbury, in the Avon valley.)

This small twelfth-century church is built of flint and stone and has a rare example of a thirteenth-century western tower. The original Norman north and south doorways are still there and one enters the church beneath a tympanum of alternating green and white stone blocks. The nave is exactly twice the length of the chancel and there are traces of red medieval wall painting. There is a pulpit dated 1619 and the font almost beneath the Georgian gallery is a fine example of twelfth-century work.

Ham: All Saints. (Off A338 south of Hungerford.)

The pebbledash exterior and little dormer windows with their clear glass colour up a warm gold in the evening sunlight. There is an interesting arrangement of seventeenth-century cambered tiebeams, collars and queen posts in this aisleless country church. The box pews, gallery and altar rails are of a quality, colour and design somewhere between the plush joinery of Mildenhall and the rusticity of Old Dilton. The fabric of the church is thirteenth-century, the low tower fourteenth-century.

Hankerton: Holy Cross. (Off B4040 north-east of Malmesbury.)

The little thirteenth-century church stands isolated in a field of its own, its Perpendicular tower tall in relation to the rest of the building. What could have been in the mind of the creator of the beasts of Hankerton – two frightening crocodile-like endings which carry the hood moulding over the south door? The chancel was put up in 1906.

Hardenhuish: St Nicholas. (Just north-west of Chippenham.)

Standing on a grassy rise beside a fast main road just north of Chippenham is this Georgian building of 1779 in Bath stone. It is of more interest outside than within. The exception to the low gravestones and memorials in the grounds is the railed monument to David Ricardo, the member of Parliament and political and social economist who died in 1823. The diarist Francis Kilvert was born at the nearby rectory in 1840. He delighted in the views to the south from the church, across the valley of the Avon towards Salisbury Plain. The church is a fine, if restrained, classical building with an apsidal sanctuary and Venetian windows.

Heytesbury: St Paul and St Peter. (Off A36 south-east of Warminster.)

This is a large cruciform church, mainly Early English, once collegiate, with a number of interesting windows. The late Perpendicular west window dominates – a tall piece of five lights in two horizontal rows separated by a transom. The east window is a huge lancet. Each aisle has a quatrefoiled roundel to the west and there are fine clerestories.

Highworth: St Michael. (On A361 north-east of Swindon.)

Built at the highest point for miles around, the fifteenth-century tower soars in five stages, taking full advantage of the eminent position. At the top is an unusual feature outside East Anglia: the buttresses which rise the full height of the tower are crowned by figures, in this case crouching animals. The porch, with the priest's room above, was built in the fifteenth century. Above the south door is a fine Norman tympanum which, in its time, has been put up above the fireplace in the room over the porch and above the vestry door. The church was besieged by Thomas, Lord Fairfax, who, fresh from his victory at Naseby for Parliament in the Civil War, was mopping up pockets of Royalist resistance. Cannonballs were used against the church, and one reputed to have struck the outside is preserved in the south chapel.

Hinton Parva: St Swithin. (East of Swindon.)

This pretty little downland village is on the edge of the Vale of White Horse and its church is a picturesque gem. The little two-stage tower, of Saxon foundation, used to be completely covered in ivy – only its pyramidal cap distinguishing it from a rectangular bush! From the outside, the building seems to be bursting out of true from every perspective. The interior is cool and chalky white. The solid Jacobean pulpit is an early twentieth-century remake of the original of 1637, and the arms of George III dated 1789 were put up to celebrate his recovery in that year. And here is one of the county's best Norman fonts, a curiously and extensively decorated tub which is well worth going out of one's way to see.

Hullavington: St Mary. (West of A429, south of Malmesbury.)

In 1917 the vicar decided to remove and replace an ancient wooden screen which was across the north of the Bradfield Chapel. Its lower part was thirteenth-century and above was a fourteenth-century traceried balcony front. Despite professional advice to the contrary, local controversy and muted rage from historians, the vicar convinced himself and the consistory court at Bristol that it was dangerous and down it came. Fragments were used in the modern screen and some are on display. Of other woodwork, there are some fifteenth-century bench ends and a plainly panelled pulpit of the seventeenth century. On the wall near the south door is a fine piece of medieval embroidery done predominantly in silver and gold. Thought to have been a priest's cope in the sixteenth century, it depicts Christ on the cross with angels, saints and a variety of decoration.

Inglesham: St John the Baptist. (On A361 south of Lechlade.)

In the north-east corner of the county, by the narrow Thames, is a wonderful little church much loved by William Morris, who lived at nearby Kelmscott and helped to restore it in 1888-9. Thames-side walks make it convenient to the boating and recreation areas at Lechlade. Tucked away almost in a farmyard, here is a towerless building beside its thirteenth-century churchyard cross, with a

St Nicholas at Little Langford has a notable Norman tympanum above the door.

mainly Transitional and Early English fabric, including the interesting little arcades. It is a church of important fragments of rustic woodwork, including fourteenth-century parclose screens, Carolean pews of varying heights, Jacobean pulpit and reading desk. There are wall paintings of the thirteenth, fourteenth, seventeenth and eighteenth centuries. Built into the inside of the south wall is one of the most interesting and important pieces of Anglo-Saxon work in England, a sculpture of the Virgin and Child. The figurework is well developed for its time, and the detail most intricate. The inclusion of a sundial in the piece indicates that it was once outside.

Knook: St Margaret. (Off A36 south-east of Warminster.)

This church, in an out-of-the-way place, is worth a visit for its Anglo-Saxon and Norman survivals. The east wall has an arrangement of three Norman round-headed windows in deep splays. Beneath them is part of the decorated side panel of a Saxon cross-shaft. The wooden chancel arch rests on Norman capitals, and the tympanum above the blocked-up south door is a carving which has

been ascribed to the early eleventh century, on account of its similarity to parts of illuminated manuscripts of the time.

Lacock: St Cyriac. (Off A350 south of Chippenham.)

This is an unusual dedication to an obscure child-saint. Even at first sight this church is no ordinary building. There is an embattled porch attached to the west wall of the two-stage tower, richly groined with a shield in the centre and put up in the fifteenth century. The low octagonal spire was added in the seventeenth century, but elsewhere the compact exterior is mainly Perpendicular – a profusion of battlements, crocketed pinnacles and a fine collection of grotesques. Inside, a wagon roof with tiebeams covers the high nave. But it is to the elaborate chantry chapel, evidence of a merchant's wealth, that one instinctively turns. Its grey fan vaulting is conspicuous from the moment one enters the building, and there remain in it fragments of the fifteenth-century colouring. Its arrangement of carved arches, little sculptures, rich mouldings and pendants was all done principally to set off the canopied tomb of Sir

William Sharrington, made in 1566 and acknowledged as one of the best of its kind in England.

Little Langford: St Nicholas. (Off A36 north-west of Wilton.)

This is a small out-of-the-way church built of flint and stone chequerwork with ashlar quoins and topped by a strange little wooden bellcote. Rebuilding in the nineteenth century brought into full view the tympanum, which with the doorway and carved lintel is an exciting tour of twelfth-century work. Monsters, a boar hunt, a bishop with representations of the Holy Trinity, knotwork and a wide selection of period decoration are all here.

Little Somerford: St John the Baptist. (Off B4042 south-east of Malmesbury.)

The narrow fifteenth-century tower is unusual in an area where they are generally much more substantial. Inside there is no structural division between the nave and chancel, just a stout Perpendicular screen of rather plain design. There are the arms of Elizabeth I, dated 1602, an interesting pulpit which has lost its tester, and a reader's desk which is unusually rectangular and dated 1626.

Ludgershall: St James. (On A342 north-west of Andover.)

This long cruciform church of random flint and rubble, basically Early English, was restored in 1675. The nave and chancel are one, nor are there arcades or aisles. In a south window are the arms of Henry Chichele, who founded All Souls College, Oxford, and was Archbishop of Canterbury from 1414 to 1443. The church is dominated by the magnificent tomb and monument of Sir Richard Brydges and his wife Jane. It was made of Caen stone in 1558 and is big in both size and decorative scope. It embodies a number of motifs ranging from strict and obligatory heraldry to the freedom of mythical beasts and capitals with wildly free foliage.

Lydiard Millicent: All Saints. (North-east of Wootton Bassett.)

There is Somerset tracery in the bell openings of the Perpendicular west tower, but the church is generally of the fourteenth century. There is a Norman font with interlaced arches and an old churchyard cross.

Lydiard Tregoze: St Mary. (West of Swindon.)

Closely adjoining the house of Lydiard Park, which now belongs to the Borough of Thamesdown and is open to the public (see page 114), and at the main entrance to the park, this is the old manor church packed full of delightful furnishings and monuments. Perpendicular on the outside, thirteenth- to fifteenth-century within, it has a wagon roof to the nave and a ceiling of c.1700, painted blue with stars, above the chancel. There are wall paintings and interesting furnishings, especially the seating in the nave and aisles. There are memorials to the St John family, several of which are the work of Sir John who died in 1648 and was buried at Lydiard. They include the 'Golden Cavalier' – the lifesize gilt figure in armour of Edward, who died in 1645, and the elaborately painted family triptych of 1615. There is a large canopied monument with lifesize effigies of Sir John and his two wives, and another has the kneeling likenesses of Nicholas and Elizabeth. Everything here is very ornate, and the whole feel east of the nave is of a private chapel. Yet this is a church of great character and interest throughout and is one not to be missed.

Maiden Bradley: All Saints. (On B3092 between Mere and Frome.)

Here the development of the pointed arch throughout the fourteenth century can be seen at its best. But it is to the white marble monument to Sir Edward Seymour that visitors will turn. Sir Edward (1633-1707) was Speaker of the House of Commons in 1678, and his memorial was put up in 1730 by his grandson Francis under the will of William Seymour, second son of the commemorated baronet. Note the catalogue of his attributes and accomplishments, which go as far as any in their praise, even for that age of affectation and pomposity. In contrast the pews are fairly plain Jacobean work, perhaps by Walter the Joiner of Maiden Bradley.

At Malmesbury Abbey a monk named Oliver achieved fame by trying to fly from the abbey tower.

Malmesbury Abbey: St Peter and St Paul.

The little town of Malmesbury clusters about the dominating remains of its abbey church. Its ruinous state is due largely to the collapse of the great crossing tower and spire in 1479, and of the western tower some time later. Its present bell tower, the steeple of nearby St Paul's, had lost the body of its church by the end of the seventeenth century, and what little remained was taken away in 1852. After the collapses the abbey church was sealed off to facilitate services, and the fallen masonry was left to be broken up and carted off by local people for secular use. But what remains has warmth and atmosphere belied by its apparently ruinous exterior.The massive, intricately carved, late Norman south porch of eight orders is a catalogue of twelfth-century decorative motifs and visual religious teaching. Inside the porch the sculptures of the twelve apostles are examples of fine figurework. Other Transitional decoration appears on what is left of the west front to the south and on the six bays of the nave. Short thick pillars support the original triforium of large arches, each enclosing four smaller ones

which are divided by small shafts with scalloped and cushioned caps. Elsewhere, the flying buttresses, nave vaulting, remade windows and associated decoration were all done in the fourteenth century. Visitors should notice the medieval table-tomb monument to Athelstan. The tenth-century king directed that he should be buried here near the body of the abbey's founder, St Aldhelm, the site of whose tomb at the abbey is unknown.

Manningford Bruce: St Peter. (Off A345 south-west of Pewsey.)

The church is built of widely spaced horizontal bands of small flint pieces placed in herringbone fashion. It has a nave of Saxon proportions and an apsidal ending, suggesting a very early church here; but what we see today is a complete twelfth-century church with Herefordshire tracery in the west window, and a seventeenth-century south door.

Marden: All Saints. (Off A342 south-east of Devizes.)

The pretty little village in the Vale of Pewsey was moved – perhaps on account of serious losses during the Black Death – and established again away from its medieval foundations. The Perpendicular tower was lowered in 1617 but raised to its former height at the Victorian restoration. It has the distinction of having been taken down stone by stone and rebuilt (with each stone having been marked) in exactly the same position. The twelfth-century south doorway, tall and narrow inside its shallow porch, is uniquely decorated. Just to the east of the porch is an interesting epitaph of 1770 to a man who was kicked to death by a horse, and a nearby table tomb has a skull and crossbones on one end.

Marlborough: St Mary.

With the exception of a large Norman doorway which has been rebuilt into the west side of the tower, and a pillar of the same period which is built into the west wall of the nave, there is nothing left of the earlier church on this site. The town suffered badly at the hands of Royalist troops in the Civil War. It was devastated by fire in 1653, which destroyed much of St Mary's and caused so much more to become unsafe that it had to be pulled down, leaving little more than a shell. Public subscription paid for the rebuilding on a large scale, giving Puritan views free rein. Everything was laid out simply, the altar came out into the nave and up went lofty round arches, supported by Tuscan columns.

Mere: St Michael. (Off A303, south-west of Warminster.)

This large town church is dominated by its huge fifteenth-century tower, and internally by a magnificent rood screen of the same period. The chancel is of the thirteenth century, built with material from an earlier church which seems to have been destroyed by fire. Of particular note, too, are the misericords in the chancel.

Mildenhall: St John the Baptist. (Just east of Marlborough.)

The church lies in a backwater of low country, its Anglo-Saxon windows and the rubble in the lower stage of the tower evidence of its age. The plaster-white interior is so sumptuously furnished in late Georgian dark oak that the eye is immediately drawn away from the stonework. But here is basically a Norman interior, with plain round Norman arches springing at little more than head height, above trumpet-scalloped capitals in the south arcade and round moulded capitals in the north. The furnishings, done in 1815-16 with local labour and money, crowd tastefully and generously into every available corner of floor space. The reredos, oddly headed altar piece, identical pulpits and reader's desks, with tall curving back panels and testers either side of the chancel arch, the delightful curving fiddler's gallery, the stalls and panelling are all a rare delight.

Netheravon: All Saints. (Off A345 north of Amesbury.)

The Anglo-Saxon tower here may well have been a tower-nave with round-headed doorways to the north and south which may have opened into porticus. The arch which opens into the nave is Norman and the church generally is from the thirteenth century.

Nettleton: St Mary. (Off B4039 north-west of Chippenham.)

Here is an oddity: a fourteenth-century attempt to make a Norman-style nave arcade. Parts of it may be original and some of it may be Norman-style carvings done later on older masonry. Between the arches, the nave is filled with dark Georgian box pews with 'H' hinges, all plainly panelled and seemingly leaning in sympathy with the pillars. The fifteenth-century stone pulpit with its little buttresses seems to come right out of the south wall of the nave at right angles to the congregation, and the priest reaches it via a spiral staircase through the wall. The circular Norman font is covered in fish-scale ornament and is scalloped on the underside.

North Wraxall: St James. (Off A420 west of Chippenham.)

Perhaps the most interesting part of this church is centred around the white marble tomb which Paul Methuen's family built for him on the north side of the nave *c*.1793. Above the tomb some forty painted coats of arms decorate the ceiling.

Ogbourne St George: St George. (Off A345 between Swindon and Marlborough.)

This low building of flint and stone in random coursing was built very much in the fashion of the area. It is mostly of the fifteenth century without and internally of the thirteenth. Of the latter, the capitals of the south arcade have some late and rather well-developed examples of stiff-leaf decoration.

Old Dilton: St Mary. (Just south-west of Westbury.)

Another of the county's little gems, the church stands hard by the road in lush pastureland. It is basically a fourteenth- and fifteenth-century building of rough coursed stones above larger blocks, supported by two-stage buttresses. The octagonal turret to the west has a spirelet and quaint bell openings. From the moment one enters through the little priest's door, what atmosphere there is! The flagstones are worn to a curve; light streams in from everywhere on to rustic Georgian woodwork, done in a jobbing fashion, patched up here and there and bleached with the years. The three-decker pulpit with its tester and hinged footstool stands centrally against the south wall of the nave; there are plainly panelled box pews with their original hinges and locks, and family pews. Everything is uneven. But there is nowhere else in the county which so evokes visions of a fiery preacher, high above his congregation, preaching eternal damnation to his small rural flock.

Pewsey: St John the Baptist. (On A345 south of Marlborough.)

Mighty sarsens support the buttresses of the north wall. The church's battlemented façade rises steeply from the busy roadway and encloses work from every period of church architecture since the eleventh century. The mahogany altar rails were made from timbers on the *San Josef*, a ship which Nelson took at St Vincent in 1797. Much of the woodwork in the church was done by Canon Pleydell Bouverie in the nineteenth century.

Potterne: St Mary. (On A360 south of Devizes.)

On a rising knoll which is almost an island stands one of the most beautiful cruciform churches in the county. It was built at one time in the thirteenth century, as a collegiate church on land then belonging to Salisbury Cathedral. With the exception of minor fifteenth-century work in the porch, with its interesting wind vane dated 1757, and the embattled parapet of the wide crossing tower, it is still a complete Early English building. Inside, the pre-Conquest font is one of the most famous in all England; it is a straight-sided tapering tub with a Latin inscription around the rim which translates as Psalm 42, verse 1: 'As a hart panteth after the water brooks, so panteth my soul after thee, O God.'

Preshute: St George. (Just west of Marlborough.)

The church was heavily restored by T. H. Wyatt in 1854. It has a monstrous, if unique, font some 11 feet (3.3 metres) in circumference. It was made of black Tournai marble from Calonne in Belgium in the thirteenth century and is reputed to have come from a chapel in Marlborough Castle.

Purton: St Mary. (Off B4453 north-west of Swindon.)

Together with Wanborough in the same county and Ormskirk, Lancashire, this is one of only three churches in England to have a central spire and a later western tower. Yet here the arrangement is unique as neither can be regarded as a secondary feature. The early fourteenth-century steeple was probably put up on the site of a low thirteenth-century crossing tower, and the west tower was put up late in the fifteenth century, when the porch, with its upper priest's room, and aisles were added and the nave heightened. Purton is an important church both in architectural terms and for the impressive collection of medieval wall paintings, which have been gradually coming to light over a number of years.

Ramsbury: Holy Cross. (Off B4192 between Swindon and Hungerford.)

This large wide building at the end of the village is mainly Early English, but with a massive Perpendicular tower and a clerestory of the same period. The font is an impressive goblet, carved in diamond diaper pattern with a small flower in the centre of each piece. Thomas Meyrick carved the four biblical scenes on the stem in the middle of the eighteenth century. Although nothing structural remains of any Anglo-Saxon church here, the restoration disclosed some early stonework, which is displayed in the church. The most important pieces of this are from the shafts of two different crosses which were made in the ninth century.

Salisbury Cathedral: the Virgin Mary.

Wherever one is in Salisbury or the surrounding countryside, the magnificent spire of the cathedral is visible. Close to, it is remarkable. The cathedral sits in perfect symmetry on a wide smooth lawn – the result of levelling late in the eighteenth century, when all the outside tombs were removed. Something similar occurred inside when James Wyatt cleared out the internal furnishings, fixtures and fittings that had accumulated over six centuries or so and rearranged the tombs.

Richard Poore began the cathedral in 1220 to his brother's design, laying the foundation stone on Easter Monday. It took thirty-eight years to build and by the end of the thirteenth century the spire, 404 feet (123 metres) high, had been added. Having been built entirely at the same time in a comparatively short period, it is a textbook example of Early English architecture. The cathedral was built in Chilmark stone in the form of a double cross with two pairs of transepts. Wren discovered that the spire was off centre, and the iron tierods he used to straighten it were replaced only in 1951. It is the finest spire in England and the cathedral is possibly the best-proportioned ecclesiastical building.

The imposing façade of five tiers is packed with inhabited niches, although the figurework is a nineteenth-century replacement for the medieval sculpture. Internally the nave arcade has ten bays of pointed arches on clusters of columns in Purbeck marble. The choir is similar and the whole is vaulted and illuminated by lancet windows. The vaulted cloisters are the largest in England.

There are many interesting tombs and memorials, perhaps the most noteworthy being the oldest, that of William Longespée, Earl of Salisbury, who was laid here in 1226. It was he who witnessed the signing of the Magna Carta and is reputed to have brought to Salisbury the copy in the cathedral library, one of only four in Britain. In the north transept is the oldest clock in Britain. It is dated 1386, made of wrought iron and still strikes the hour.

Salisbury: St Thomas.

This is a spacious and almost entirely fifteenth-century town church. There is a dramatic view from the alley at the back where, all buttresses and panelled battlements, it rises in waves towards the south tower. Buildings crowd against its brown walls, yet light streams through the wide aisle and clerestory windows, highlighting each cluster of four slender shafts with foliated caps which make up the piers of the nave arcades, and illuminates the Doom painting. One of the largest and most crowded scenes of its type in England, the Doom was painted around the raised chancel arch late in the fifteenth century by a thankful traveller come home. It was brought to light in 1819, having been under whitewash for a century and a half from the Reformation.

Sherston: Holy Trinity. (On B4040 west of Malmesbury.)

Here is a whole central tower built in 1730 in Georgian Gothic; its huge clasping buttresses, like neatly piled stone slabs, preclude any pretensions to true medievalism. Yet what a lively pattern the openwork pinnacles and battlements make on the skyline. The north arcade is late Norman; there is also much thirteenth-century architecture and decoration within, as well as a Jacobean pulpit and some interesting monuments. Of interest, too, is the Norman figure known as 'Rattlebone', who legend says fought the Danes and, when wounded in the stomach, staunched the flow of blood with a tile and carried on fighting.

South Wraxall: St James. (Off B3109 north of Bradford-on-Avon.)

Although there is not a lot of interest in this church, it has an eyecatching exterior. Set on an island, the short fifteenth-century tower rises

Salisbury Cathedral was built completely in the Early English style of architecture.

in three stages to a stone saddleback roof. The builders went on to accentuate the point by building a big square stair turret against the south-west side of the tower and topped that with a saddleback roof at right angles to the other. Monuments inside the church commemorate members of the Long family.

Stanton Fitzwarren: St Leonard. (Off A361 north-east of Swindon.)

A beautiful setting enhances this church, especially in the spring, when daffodils cascade down the bank opposite amidst the little orchard, and the lake beyond the church shimmers gently between the trees. It is an enlarged Norman building; the chancel arch was put up in the first half of the twelfth century, about a hundred years after the nave, which has typical Anglo-Saxon proportions. In the chancel is a detached piscina, its bowl formed of a hollowed-out Norman cushion capital set on what resembles a Saxon shaft. The late twelfth-century bucket-shaped font is one of the most famous in England, its rich figurework depicting the triumph of named virtues over vices. The interior of the church has much magnificent panelling and carved woodwork. It is a testimony to the love and skill of a former vicar here, the Reverend W. C. Masters, whose dominating Art Nouveau is packed with symbolism and teaching.

Stanton St Quintin: St Giles. (Off A429 north of Chippenham, close to M4.)

Norman work and Victorian Gothic applied with a heavy and serious hand live out of harmony here. But there is a rare Norman sculpture at the west end, well worth a visit. It depicts the seated Christ with his feet firmly placed on the back of the Serpent, which is writhing in an attitude of obvious restraint. Inside the building there is a Norman door and a thirteenth-century south arcade. The font is a small Norman tub.

Stapleford: St Mary. (On B3083 north-west of Wilton.)

A picturesque building peeps from between the neatly kept trees which line the approach. The south doorway, sharply cut south arcade of about 1160 and font are fine Norman work.

The arcade, with its low round arches springing from thick round pillars of alternating green sandstone and grey and white Chilmark stone, is a joy, and the decorative motifs employed throughout make this church one not to be missed. The rest of the church is mostly fourteenth- and fifteenth-century, except for the Perpendicular two-storey porch and clerestory.

Steeple Ashton: St Mary. (Off A350 east of Trowbridge.)

Large houses in groups around the approach road curve past the market cross to where the tower rises high above the village. This was the centre of the fifteenth-century wool trade hereabouts, when people like Robert Long and Walter Lucas had the money to pay for the north and south aisles respectively, c.1480-1500. It once had a spire, but that came crashing down in 1670. What we see today is an entirely Perpendicular church, for it was then that affluent rebuilding swept away all that was there before. It has flying buttresses, Somerset tracery in the tower, and within all is light, spacious and lofty, with tall pointed arches beneath magnificent vaulting.

Steeple Langford: All Saints. (Off A36 north-west of Wilton.)

This pleasant church of flints and stone in the Wylye valley has a little Anglo-Saxon sculpture from a cross-shaft, some Norman remains and rather more from the thirteenth century. The corbel tables outside and the square font within are Norman. The stiff-leaf and water-leaf decoration on the responds beneath the chancel arch are particularly fine examples of about 1200. There is also a Jacobean pulpit and reader's desk dated 1613.

Stratton St Margaret: St Margaret. (North-east of Swindon.)

In a backwater on the edge of the village is a small village church, looking very much as one might have done at the beginning of the fourteenth century. It is curious inasmuch as the 'Early English' tower, which has deceived some authorities, was actually put up early in the nineteenth century together with a low spire. The south porch was a fourteenth-century addition and has stone seats, its origi-

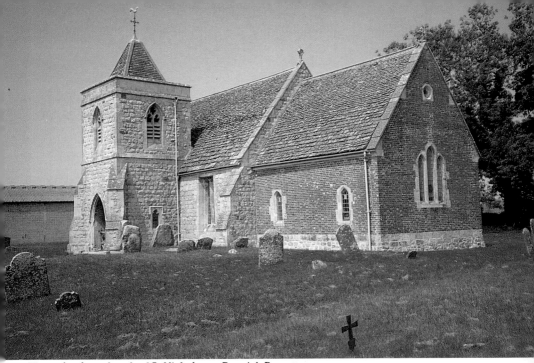

The redundant church of St Nicholas at Berwick Bassett.

The royal coat of arms displayed at the church of St Mary in Potterne.

nal roof and a newel stair which once led to an upper room of which there is no longer any trace. Inside, the church is mostly late thirteenth-century and there are some good bell caps in the four-bay nave arcade of *c.*1280.

Swindon: Christ Church.

In the grounds of The Lawn, the old Swindon estate of the lords of the manor, now a public parkland, are the refurbished chancel and ruined sections of the nave arcades from Holy Rood, the town's medieval church. Most of it was taken down in 1852, just after Sir Gilbert Scott's new parish church was built by public subscription a little further down the hill. Christ Church was built in the late thirteenth-century style. It is a big church with tower and spire in such a prominent position that it is still a landmark from most approach roads into the town.

Swindon: St Mark.

The Great Western Railway Company paid for this church, and railway employees built it in 1845. New Swindon was in its infancy and the old town's medieval church, annexed to the house on the lord of the manor's estate, was too far away from the new centre of things to have been of much use to the railwaymen. So here we have a wholly Victorian church, on a site west of Brunel's station and hard by the railway workshops. It was built in the Decorated style of the fourteenth century, which the designers Scott and Moffatt would have called the Middle Pointed, in some respects modestly but in others showing creative flamboyance.

Tidcombe: St Michael. (Off A338 south-west of Hungerford.)

This quaint little church, built of flint and rubble on its own rise at the foot of the downs, is in a very rural setting, seemingly at the bottom of the manor-house garden. The fabric dates from the thirteenth century, although the greater part of the interior is a good example of fourteenth-century rebuilding on a small scale.

Tilshead: St Thomas of Canterbury. (On A360 between Salisbury and Devizes.)

This is a small building of random flint and stone with chequerwork. There is a low thirteenth-century central tower topped by a short tiled cap. The chancel is Early English; the nave arcades are Norman with a fourteenth-century clerestory above. There are a number of small lancet windows set in deeply splayed openings, some with rere-arches in shaped timber above them – a rustic touch. A small window on the south side has a pointed wooden shutter, studded and clasped. Seven stained glass windows in the church are the work of the Reverend Joseph Holden Johnson, who made them at home in the vicarage during his incumbency in the nineteenth century.

Upton Lovell: St Peter. (Off A36 south-east of Warminster.)

This tiny church of Norman origin comprises just a chancel of *c.*1200, a nave and a low square west tower, both of 1250-1300, although the upper part of the latter is seventeenth-century work. The tower arch is from the fourteenth century and the north porch, west door, vestry and roof are dated 1633.

Urchfont: St Michael. (On B3098 south-east of Devizes.)

Lying exceptionally low and long behind fine table tombs, the church is built well back from the road, just out of sight of the village pond. The chancel should be visited both within and without; there is fine work from the fourteenth century, vaulted and ribbed, the other side of the thirteenth-century chancel arch. Of note, too, are the excessive buttresses with their saddleback tops. The tower is early Perpendicular, the transepts early fourteenth-century. The chancel was repaired in 1840, 'beautified' in 1864, and restoration took place in 1900.

Wanborough: St Andrew. (South-east of Swindon.)

Wiltshire's other church with both a tower (early fourteenth-century) and a spire (1435) is more of curiosity value than architectural interest (see also Purton). The hexagonal tower and little spire were put up above the east end of the nave when the church was first rebuilt. Both the tower and the spire are open from beneath, and the view of the crossing is quite exciting. The restoration of 1887 uncovered some frescoes, of which the painting on the north wall of the nave is the only one to survive.

Wilcot: Holy Cross. (North-west of Pewsey.)

Beneath the downs, near wooded country and the Kennet & Avon Canal, this hamlet with its red-brick gabled manor house is dominated by the church's interesting fifteenth-century tower, embattled and pinnacled. The church was built in the thirteenth century and retains its chancel arch of *c.*1200. It was restored in 1858 but had to be rebuilt following a devastating fire in 1876. There is a stone altar tomb with low canopy, dated 1574, in the north wall.

Winterbourne Bassett: St Katherine. (Off A4361 south of Swindon.)

The church stands at the end of a drive behind well-kept lawns and looks today as much of a private church as it was to the Despensers, who acquired the manor in 1271 and were probably responsible for building it. For a small village church it is surprisingly rich in fine Decorated work: ogee arches, four-leaved ballflower, reticulated tracery, wave mouldings – there is much to delight the visitor. The north transept was probably used as a private chapel, which accounts for the concentration of detail in that area.

Wishford Magna: St Giles. (At Great Wishford, off A36 north-west of Wilton.)

Visitors wishing to see how the price of bread has fared since 1800 are directed to the east churchyard wall, where this little bit of history is published. The Perpendicular tower with its older, lower stage is a surprisingly slim example and the open, stepped battlements are also unusual hereabouts. Otherwise the church is architecturally of little interest, although it has some notable fixtures, fittings and monuments. There is a fine Jacobean chest and a red and black hand fire-engine of 1728. The flamboyant overpowering Renaissance-style monument of 1629 to Sir Richard Grobham is colourfully made of several marbles.

Wootton Rivers: St Andrew. (South of Marlborough.)

Close by the north bank of the Kennet & Avon Canal and on the edge of Savernake Forest, this little church has perhaps the most beautiful approach lane in the county. Built of flint with stone dressings, it has a shingled broach spirelet above a wooden bell turret. This houses a clock which was made by the village craftsman Jack Spratt in 1911 out of odd bits and pieces, put up to commemorate the coronation of King George V. As if this was not unique enough, he gave it a different chime every quarter of an hour over a six-hour period. The dial on the south side has the words GLORY BE TO GOD instead of figures. The church itself is basically fourteenth-century with some good window tracery, sedilia, piscina and tub font.

Wroughton: St John the Baptist and St Helen. (On A4361 south of Swindon.)

The church stands on a ridge above the village, with fine views to the north. In 1977 it had a thorough internal renovation; the tower, north aisle and west end of the south aisle were refloored, revealing interesting fragments of masonry, medieval coffin nails and opaque glass. The tower was gutted whilst the bells were taken away for retuning, and a new baptistery was created. This included recreating, in what is thought to have been its original shape, a Norman font bowl which had been lying around the church for some time. Also Norman is the south doorway. Otherwise the building is very much Decorated with fine sedilia of the period in the chancel.

Wylye: St Mary. (Near intersection of A36 and A303, between Warminster and Wilton.)

Near Grovely Wood and in the Wylye valley, the church is almost entirely the product of restoration and building in 1841, a little earlier than the main wave of restoration in Wiltshire. It kept its low fifteenth-century west tower and east window of *c.*1230. The pulpit is dated 1628 and, together with the lectern and clerk's desk, came from the old church at Wilton. The altar table is Jacobean and there is a baluster font of 1765.

7

Historic buildings and gardens

Avebury Manor, Avebury, Marlborough SN8 1RF. Telephone: 01672 3388. National Trust.

Open subject to the progress of renovation; telephone for information about opening hours.

Reputed to be built on, or close by, the site of a Benedictine cell, the present house dates from the late 1550s and was added to early in the seventeenth century. The gabled front of grey stone and plaster with its stone-tiled roof has a most pleasing appearance. The manor is one of the most unpretentious, homely and atmospheric of the county's historic houses. Queen Anne stayed here, as did Charles II. Many of the rooms are oak-panelled and some have coved plasterwork ceilings, all forming perfect settings for the fine period furniture. The collection includes portraits of the Wiltshire gentry, the Queen Anne bed and Mary Tudor's travelling chest. The manor forms a picturesque group with its circular dovecote and former stables, now a museum.

Avebury Manor Gardens, Avebury, Marlborough SN8 1RF. Telephone: 01672 3388. National Trust.

Open April to November, Tuesday, Wednesday, Friday, Saturday and Sunday.

Avebury Manor has long been known as a romantic English garden, planted in the traditional manner, where one may encounter peacocks and other domestic breeds of birds oblivious to the footfalls of visitors. The well-kept medieval walled gardens include the formal Monks' Garden, gentle topiary of box and yew, exquisite borders, a wishing well, a fountain and a sundial on its Corinthian capital.

Bowood, Calne SN11 0LZ. Telephone: 01249 812102.

Open April to October, daily.

Although the 'Big House' at Bowood was demolished in 1955, the Earl of Shelburne's home remains a fine eighteenth-century building by Henry Keene and Robert Adam. It includes the laboratory where Joseph Priestley discovered oxygen in 1774, Adam's library and a mid nineteenth-century chapel. There are collections of sculpture, paintings, ceramics, furniture and statuary, Victoriana and Indiana. However, Bowood is primarily a garden of extraordinary beauty, with a 100 acre (40.4 hectare) pleasure garden and parkland laid out by 'Capability' Brown in the 1760s, Italian-style terraces, and spring flowers, roses, azaleas and rhododendrons providing colour throughout the season. The rhododendron walk is open during the flowering season in May and June. There are over two hundred types of trees and shrubs in the arboretum, as well as a pinetum and fine specimen trees. There are walks around the 40 acre (16 hectare) lake, rockwork, caves, a cascade, a Doric temple and a mausoleum. A magnificent adventure playground completes a visit for the children, and there is a plant and gift centre.

Bradford-on-Avon Tithe Barn, Barton Farm, Bradford-on-Avon.

Open Easter to October, daily.

Across Barton Bridge at Bradford-on-Avon is one of the most important medieval buildings in the county – the fourteenth-century tithe barn at Barton Farm. The second largest of its kind in England, the great barn is 168 feet (51 metres) long and 33 feet (10 metres) wide. The side walls are 2½ feet (70 cm)

Opposite: *The rose garden at Avebury Manor.*

thick and the end walls are 4 feet (1.2 metres) thick and rise to 39 feet (11.8 metres) at the apices. The walls are made of oolitic limestone and there are some thirty thousand stone tiles on the roof. Arched entrances to the north and smaller porches to the south are gabled; the building is of fourteen bays and is heavily buttressed. The interior is of cruck design with big oak timbers and an interesting arrangement of roof braces. Originally built as a granary for the Abbess of Shaftesbury, it has been continuously used as a barn into modern times.

Broadleas Gardens, Devizes SN10 5JQ. Telephone: 01380 722035.
Open April to October, Sunday, Wednesday and Thursday afternoons.
   Lady Anne Cowdray's beautiful valley garden, which she bought in 1946 and has been creating and developing since the early 1960s, is an inspiration and a joy. The inspiration comes from the knowledge that many of the plants which flourish here might not have been expected to survive, and the joy is of discovery, for here are secret gardens, winter gardens, a woodland, sunken rose gardens, a silver border – packed with plants which are unusual or rarely seen. Many are normally thought to be too tender for central southern England and more at home in the far west. Broadleas has the National Collection of Euonymus, and amongst the plants for sale are many from the garden stock.

Chalcot House, Dilton Marsh, Westbury BA13 4DF.
Open July and August afternoons.
   This small seventeenth-century Palladian-style manor house is on rising ground where a medieval building once stood, close by a Romano-British settlement. It is built of brick with stone dressings and its compact classical façade of about 1680 is particularly pleasing. At first sight there appear to be three stages of windows of five bays, each flanked by a pair of pilasters with bases and caps which link vertically. The lower two stages are variously pedimented, but three of the upper bays are actually panels with classical decoration, whilst that immediately above the central

doorway is a recess with an urn bearing the crest of the Phipps family. The house was altered in the eighteenth century and again in the nineteenth, when a wing was added. It was beautifully restored in the 1970s and won a European Architectural Heritage Award for the owner and architect in 1975. The Victorian rooms have fine plasterwork and chimney pieces, as well as good collections of eighteenth- and nineteenth-century furniture and Boer War memorabilia. There are a number of family pictures and other works of art, including an amount of twentieth-century work.

Charlton Park House, Malmesbury SN16 9DG.
Open May to October, Monday to Thursday afternoons.
   This is a splendid Jacobean mansion with Georgian alterations. It was apparently built for the Countess of Suffolk in 1607, altered in the same century and again in 1772-6 by Matthew Bressingham the younger for the twelfth Earl. The house is built foursquare around a centre court, solid and imposing. It is a riot of big square-headed windows, corner turrets with pointed caps, chimneys, heavy string courses and most exuberant parapets everywhere, including the gable ends to the projecting wings. The most important Jacobean feature is the long gallery above the colonnade of Tuscan columns on the west front. Viewing is limited to the hall, staircase and saloon.

Corsham Court, Corsham SN13 0BZ. Telephone: 01249 712214.
Open January to November, daily except Monday and Friday, afternoons only.
   The present building, home of the Lord Methuen, was originated by Thomas Smythe in 1582 on the site of a former royal Saxon manor house. Paul Methuen bought the house and estates in 1745 with a family fortune accumulated in the wool trade. The north side was remodelled on Palladian lines in 1749, enlarged by John Nash in 1800 and reconstructed by Bellamy in 1845. In 1760 'Capability' Brown built the state rooms and laid out the park, but Humphry Repton made ex-

Corsham Court houses one of the finest private collections of art in Britain.

tensive alterations to the park in 1800. Although the building has been extended around Smythe's house, the later south face still retains its Elizabethan Cotswold appearance in Bath stone, with gables, mullioned windows, pediments and pinnacles breaking the skyline from every angle. Former owners specialised in collecting sixteenth- and seventeenth-century Italian and seventeenth-century Flemish paintings, including Van Dyck, now displayed in the Georgian state rooms. They comprise one of the best private collections of old masters in Britain, in a 72 foot (22 metre) picture gallery designed as a triple cube. There is a famous collection of English furniture, including Chippendale and Robert Adam. The extensive gardens and parkland include fine lawns, specimen trees and Brown's 'Decorated' style bath-house of 1760 with ogee arches, niches and crocketed pinnacles.

The Courts, Holt, Trowbridge BA14 6AR. Telephone: 01225 782340. National Trust.
Open 1st April to 1st November, every afternoon except Saturdays.

This National Trust property is set in the pretty village of Holt, centred on its green. Holt was once a spa, but little of this now remains. The Courts were the place weavers in the cloth industry brought their disputes for settlement. The early eighteenth-century house (not open to the public) is grossly over-pedimented and exuberantly stone-wrought. The 7 acre (2.8 hectare) gardens include a small lake and a lily pond with aquatic and water-tolerant plants, a lawn with herbaceous borders, a recently restored terrace, a conservatory, hedged vistas and topiary gardens, and a small arboretum of trees and shrubs, with wild flowers.

Fonthill Abbey Ruins, Fonthill Gifford, Tisbury, Salisbury. South of Fonthill Bishop along minor roads to the west of the lake; at Fonthill Gifford turn along an unfenced road leading into woods and passing close to the ruins.

Deep within the woods lie the remains of what was the ultimate in follies. In 1796 William Beckford, the writer and eccentric, began his Gothic abbey in grey Chilmark stone. It was to be partly habitable and partly ruin, the commission being given to James

The Doric Temple is one of many fine garden features at Bowood.

Stonehenge.

West Kennett Long Barrow.

Wyatt. He put up a cruciform building with a central tower 275 feet (84 metres) high. The work, although unfinished, had progressed far enough by Christmas 1800 for Beckford to welcome Nelson, with Sir William and Lady Hamilton, and to hold an extended celebration in recognition of Nelson's victory at the battle of the Nile. Although Beckford lived in the abbey for sixteen years it was never completed and in 1825, two years after he sold it and moved out, the tower collapsed. Part of the battlemented cloisters and a turret room survive, as well as walls at the north end of the abbey and some of the stone flower beds.

Great Chalfield Manor, Melksham SN12 8NJ.Telephone: 01747 840224. National Trust.
Open (for guided tours only) April to October, except public holidays, Tuesday to Thursday afternoons. Historical societies and kindred groups at other times by written appointment.

The moated medieval manor house, centred on its great hall, was built about 1465-80 by Thomas Tropnell and restored in 1905-11 by Robert Fuller. It forms a perfect group with the adjacent church (see page 87) and Elizabethan farm buildings, the brown mellowed stonework in complete harmony. The house was once larger in ground plan, fell into disrepair, was altered in the nineteenth century and restored in the twentieth. It is pleasantly gabled, with fine windows, including two oriels. Inside the medieval north front fine vaulting, the chimney piece of the hall and concealed spy-holes to allow people to see what was going on within are noteworthy. Note also the screen and the contemporary mural painting of the builder. A timber-framed wing runs south from the south-west side.

Hamptworth Lodge, Landford, Salisbury SP5 2EA Telephone: 01794 390215.
Open during April, daily except Sundays.

Nestling in a wooded area off a minor road between Redlynch and Landford is this timber-framed, Tudor-style brick building of 1910-12. The house and garden are open.

Hazelbury Manor, Wadswick, Box, Corsham SN14 9HX. Telephone: 01225 812952.
Open late May to September, Thursday, Saturday and Sunday.

The manor house, originally of about 1400 but much rebuilt and restored, has a very attractive façade. Even the two prominent features, the wonderful two-storey porch and the oriel window to the hall, were removed and are now rebuilt on their old foundations. Set amidst terraces, the house forms an interesting focal point for the gardens, 8 acres (3.2 hectares) which are open to the public. There are formal gardens with a topiary chess set, a series of garden rooms, a laburnum walk, colourful herbaceous borders, clipped beeches, a rose garden, a stone ring, ponds and a plantation of specimen trees.

Heale Gardens and Plant Centre, Middle Woodford, Salisbury SP4 6NT. Telephone: 01722 782504.
Open daily all year.

Situated in the beautiful valley of the Salisbury Avon, and now with 8 acres (3.2 hectares) of gardens, the seventeenth-century Heale House sheltered Charles II for five days before he escaped to France after the battle of Worcester in 1651. It is said that he came there via Stonehenge, where he failed to count the same number of stones twice, thus giving credence to the legend that they cannot be accurately counted. The manor house is pedimented, of brick with stone dressings, set off by mellow stonework and formal hedging in the gardens. Here the centrepiece is an authentic Japanese tea house and Nikko bridge, surrounded by a water garden planted with magnolia and acers. A fine rose collection grows amongst the clipped hedges and there are lovely borders of shrubs and herbaceous plants. Many unusual plants from the garden may be bought in the Plant Centre and there is also a gift shop.

House of John à Port, 8-9 Queen Street, Salisbury SP1 1EY. Telephone: 01722 320311.
Open during shop hours.

This gabled timber-framed three-storey

The bridge over the river Frome at Iford, with Iford Manor beyond the parapet.

house of about 1425 was built for the wool merchant John à Port, who was six times mayor of Salisbury. Both internally and externally, layers of plaster were built up over the years and much of the carved woodwork was painted. Remarkable restoration in 1930 revealed the original beamwork, well-preserved. The premises are now a shop but visitors are welcome to inspect the stone fireplaces and the carved oak overmantel of about 1620, attributed to Humphrey Beckham. The stairs were put up early in the eighteenth century and one of the upstairs rooms has fine Jacobean panelling.

Iford Manor Gardens, Iford Manor, Bradford-on-Avon BA15 2BA. Telephone: 01225 863146.
Open: April and October, Sunday afternoons; May to September, all afternoons except Monday and Friday.

This Grade I listed 2 acre (0.8 hectare) garden is situated in a lovely riverside setting by the river Frome, 3/4 mile (1200 metres) west of Westwood. The garden lies on a steep hillside which rises in terraces. There are 15 acres (6 hectares) of woodland. Harold Peto, the architect and landscape gardener, bought the medieval manor with its eighteenth-century façade in 1899 and designed the gardens between then and 1933. He introduced statuary and fragments of ancient architecture and sculpture mostly from Italy and France. In consequence this is an Italian-style garden with a cloister, colonnade and summerhouse. There are also fine mixed borders of herbaceous plants and shrubs. The Acanthus National Plant Collection is kept here.

King Alfred's Tower, Kingsettle Hill, near Mere. Telephone: 01985 844785; or the Stourhead estate manager: 01747 841152. National Trust. 2 miles (3 km) north of Stourhead; 3 miles (5 km) by road plus a 300 yard (275 metre) level walk over grass from the car park.
Open April to October, every afternoon except Monday and Friday (but open bank holiday Mondays and Good Friday).

This 160 feet (49 metres) high brick tower stands on Kingsettle Hill, 854 feet (260 metres) above sea level, on the edge of the

Devizes Wharf on the Kennet & Avon Canal has been skilfully developed as a visitor attraction.

Opposite: *Westbury White Horse.*

The restored Crofton Pumping Station still houses its original 1812 beam engine.

The west front of Lacock Abbey, a monastery that was converted into a private house.

escarpment overlooking the Somerset plain and offers fine views over Somerset, Dorset and Wiltshire. It is a triangular structure with round projections at the corners, one of which contains a staircase leading to a platform with a crenellated parapet. The interior is hollow and open to the sky. Its only ornaments are three stone bands, an inscription and a statue of King Alfred. It stands on the county's border with Somerset, at the spot where Alfred mustered his troops before his defeat of the Danes at Edington in 878. Built in 1772, and designed by Henry Flitcroft, it was commissioned by Henry Hoare of Stourton to commemorate the peace with France and the succession of George III.

Lackham Country Attractions, the Gardens, Lacock, Chippenham SN15 2NY. Telephone: 01249 443111.
Open 1st April to 29th October, daily; at other times by arrangement for groups and societies.

Lackham House, now the Agricultural College, lies well back from the road in its own grounds. Apart from the family attractions described on page 128, it has a number of distinctive gardens and important collections. The house is surrounded by Italian-style gardens with beds and borders, collections of old roses on the rose terraces to the south and the Victorian-style herbaceous border which sweeps down from the house towards the museum complex. There are good collections of rhododendrons, other shrubs and trees and in the walled garden there are more than thirty separate displays of ornamental plants and flowers, fruit and vegetables. There is also a patio garden as well as a glasshouse and hothouses.

Lacock Abbey, High Street, Lacock, Chippenham SN15 2LG. Telephone: 01249 730227. National Trust.
Open 1st April to 30th October; house, Wednesday to Monday; cloisters and grounds, daily; all closed Good Friday.

At Lacock the meadows running down to the Bristol Avon provided an ideal spot for Ela, Countess of Salisbury, to establish her nunnery and the abbey was founded in 1232. Of this there remain the medieval cloisters, sacristy, chapter-house and nuns' warming room. The fifteenth-century monastic buildings were converted into a private house after 1539, following the Dissolution, by Sir William Sharington. Of his time, many important features survive, including the octagonal corner tower and the courtyard with its half-timbered gables and clock-tower. The great hall was rebuilt by Sanderson Miller for John Ivory Talbot in the Gothick style of the mid eighteenth century. In the nineteenth century there were further changes and in 1835 William Henry Fox Talbot, the pioneer photographer, made the latticed oriel window in the south gallery the subject of his first known photograph. A curiosity of note within is the huge Mechlin pot of 1500, reputedly the nuns' cooking vessel.

Littlecote House, Hungerford RG17 0SU. Telephone: 01488 62170.
Open Easter to end of September, daily.

This Tudor manor house was built of red brick, stone and flint about 1490-1520 by the ill-fated Darrell family. Chief Justice Popham, whose family acquired the property, added the south front in 1590. It is situated in the picturesque Kennet valley. The river runs through the surrounding lush and rising parkland, with green water-meadows and walled gardens beyond, providing a fine setting for the building's long, gabled façade, its win-dows mullioned and transomed. Within, the oak-panelled great hall has a collection of armour from the Civil War period. Cromwellian, too, is the chapel with its interesting furnishings. The library, haunted bedroom, long gallery and Chinese drawing room are also open to the visitor. Jane Seymour, whose father lived at Wolf Hall near Burbage, is said to have been entertained at Littlecote by Henry VIII before their marriage. Elizabeth I slept here. Charles II was entertained here by the turncoat Colonel Alexander Popham. William of Orange dined at the house with King James II's commissioners in 1688. The interior has moulded plasterwork, nowhere better than in the long gallery, where there are collections of paintings, china and glass. Of note, too, are the painted Dutch parlour, carpets and tapestries, panelling and oak furniture, the haunted bedroom and landing. Minor artefacts of interest include Judge Popham's fingerstocks and the shovel-board table. As a tourist attraction, Littlecote is amongst the finest. Although it offers two thousand years of history in the house and around the 100 acre (40 hectare) estate, it is – in its diversity – difficult to categorise. A mosaic pavement was found on the estate in 1727, part of a Roman villa (see page 71). This was rediscovered in 1976 and there have

Littlecote House on the Berkshire border is now the centrepiece of a parkland of attractions and amusements.

The garden landscape at Stourhead is one of the finest in Britain.

Wardour Old Castle was twice besieged in the English Civil War.

been extensive excavations, and now a Roman museum, which alone would make any visit worthwhile. But Littlecote has long been famed for bringing history to life with spectacle, demonstrations, tableaux and special events which run throughout the season. There are train rides, an adventure playground and picnic areas, walled gardens, a rose garden, lavender bothy and garden centre. In outbuildings too, a craft village, craft shops, stable yard, blacksmith and classic motor-car collection are amongst a host of other attractions.

Long Hall Gardens, Stockton, near Warminster BA12 0SE. Telephone: 01985 850424.
Open May to August, first Saturday of the month, afternoon only. Nursery open from the end of March to the beginning of October, Wednesday to Sunday.
In the grounds of an attractive thirteenth-century timber-framed and eighteenth-century brick-fronted house (not open), near the village church, is this mainly formal 4 acre (1.6 hectare) garden. There are many yews and other old trees. The plants in the garden have been collected by the same family since the 1920s and include flowering shrubs, spring bulbs and a fine hellebore walk. Adjacent is Long Hall Nursery, specialising in organically grown plants and bulbs which are featured in the garden.

Longleat House, Warminster BA12 7NW. Telephone: 01985 844400.
Open daily except Christmas Day.
Longleat was the first stately home in Britain to open its doors to the public as a commercial proposition, first doing so in the spring of 1949. The family seat of the Marquess of Bath is set in vast parkland with superb approaches, which includes some 5000 acres (2000 hectares) of estate woodlands. Sir John Thynne's house of 1550, built on the site of a thirteenth-century Augustinian priory, was largely destroyed by fire. The four-square rebuilding of about 1567-79 features rectangular windows, mullioned and transomed, and each of the façades is similarly designed. There are more than a hundred rooms, not all open to the public, and many were altered during the nineteenth century. Some internal rearrangement was done by Sir Jeffrey Wyatville. Of particular interest are the Elizabethan Great Hall full of sporting paintings, the saloon or long gallery and the state drawing room. These, and other rooms, show the influence of the Italian Renaissance in their ornate plasterwork, magnificently moulded ceilings and choice of paintings. Also on view are the grand staircase by Wyatville, the minstrels' gallery, the dining rooms with their interesting fireplaces and other state rooms. The library is one of the greatest private collections in Britain, and the well-equipped Victorian kitchen should not be missed. In 1757 'Capability' Brown cleared away the former gardens, created a formal garden and landscaped the area much as we see it today. He was also responsible for the stable block and the orangery.

The famous lions were introduced at Longleat in 1966, to be followed by rare white tigers and a whole range of animals. Apart from the Safari Park (see page 140) and boats, Longleat offers one of the most exciting packages of entertainment for all the family to be found anywhere in Britain. Since Alexander Thynne became the seventh Marquess of Bath in 1992, he has opened the murals in his private apartments to adults only. Other attractions include the largest maze in the world and a tropical butterfly garden. The estate is famous for its permanent exhibitions of vehicles and bygones, the narrow-gauge railway and a whole host of semi-permanent attractions, as well as a Postman Pat village, Dr Who exhibition, pets' corner, adventure castle and various other activities for children.

Luckington Court, Luckington, Chippenham. Telephone: 01666 84205.
Viewing on Wednesday afternoons only, strictly by prior appointment.
To the east of the village, off the B4040 road between Malmesbury and Bristol, Luckington Court with its farm outbuildings and stables forms an attractive group with the church and rectory. It is said that Earl Harold had a hunting box here before he became king in the eleventh century, and at the time of the

Lydiard Park, near Swindon, is a fine Georgian house in an attractive public park.

Domesday survey it was known as the Peach House. Of the present house the interior is early Tudor and the five-bay exterior is Queen Anne. In 1994 it was chosen as the site for 'Lambourn' in the television version of *Pride and Prejudice*. There are formal gardens with ornamental trees and flowering shrubs including ornamental cherries and cedars.

Lydiard Park, Lydiard Tregoze, Swindon SN5 9PA. Telephone: 01793 770401.
Open variously all year, daily except Christmas, Boxing Day and Good Friday.

Lydiard Tregoze Park was the site of a Domesday manor which subsequently passed to the St John family, who held it for five hundred years until 1943. The Tory statesman Henry St John, a friend of the writer Swift, and Secretary of State to Queen Anne, was created Viscount Bolingbroke in 1712. During his lifetime the house was remodelled in the classical style evident today. Swindon Corporation purchased Lydiard Park in a near-derelict state in 1943, restoring the house and returning many of the original furnishings and family portraits. The ground-floor state rooms are open to the public and contain fine mid-Georgian plasterwork throughout and an

unusual seventeenth-century painted window. The adjacent church of St Mary (see page 90) houses exceptional St John monuments. The large park has an icehouse, ha-ha, lake and children's adventure playgrounds with an aerial runway within the woodlands. There are also walks and nature trails around the estate, and an information centre and refreshment complex. The stable block has been converted into a hostel for youth groups and there is a conference centre within the house. Open parts of the estate are used for a variety of public amusements throughout the year. Lydiard Park is owned by the Borough of Thamesdown, the successor to Swindon Corporation.

Malmesbury House, The Close, Salisbury SP1 2EB. Telephone: 01722 327027.
Open April to October, Tuesday to Saturday; in winter by appointment.

An exquisite interior lies behind the seven-bay limestone façade of Malmesbury House, but the house's origins are much older. Three canonry houses, built in 1228, were replaced in 1399 by a three-storey house. In 1698 the house was enlarged by the addition of four west-facing rooms and a magnificent entrance hall with rococo plasterwork. The architect was Mr Fort, Christopher Wren's master builder. This work was commissioned by a member of the Harris family, whose descendant became the first Earl of Malmesbury. Amongst the many notable visitors to the house were Charles II, who brought his court from London to escape the plague, the composer Handel, the Duke of York and writers and artists of the period. The house is privately owned by Mr John Cordle, who lives in it with his family.

Manningford Gardens and Nursery, Manningford Abbots, Pewsey. Telephone: 01672 62232.
Open daily all year.
A special feature here is the maze planted in 1990. In spring and summer the gardens are divided into coloured rooms – the pink and red garden, the blue and gold garden, and the yellow and white garden, showing a wide variety of perennial plants and unusual shrubs. There is an astrological garden in the making and a French potager garden. The nursery has stocks of the interesting plants and shrubs displayed in the garden.

Manor House Garden, Milton Lilbourne, Pewsey SN9 5LQ. Telephone: 01672 63344.
Open May to October, Wednesday afternoons.
This is a typical English country garden belonging to an eighteenth-century house, pedimented and gabled. Only the garden is open to visitors, with its flower borders, azaleas, roses and lawns.

The Merchant's House, 132 High Street, Marlborough SN8 1HN. Telephone: 01672 511491.
Open by appointment. Shop open daily except Sunday.
Marlborough High Street is impressive, and its architecture a delight, especially the houses of the colonnade on the north side. One of the finest, the Merchant's House, was built in 1656 for a silk merchant; it later became the printing works where the town's first newspaper was produced in the 1770s and was latterly a bookshop and lending library. The gabled building retains a fine fireplace of the period, a staircase and some good panelling. In 1992 the Merchant's House (Marlborough) Trust was formed to restore the house and open it to the public as a museum of seventeenth-century urban life. Restoration has revealed painted plasterwork, hidden for over two hundred years. The Trust hopes ultimately to include a local museum on the premises as well as meeting and exhibition rooms.

Mompesson House, Choristers Green, The Close, Salisbury SP1 2EL. Telephone: 01722 335659. National Trust.
Open April to November, Saturday to Wednesday.
One of the finest eighteenth-century houses in the cathedral close, this is an exceptional small Queen Anne town house with a stone and brick frontage and hipped roof, facing the cathedral. It was built on the north side of Choristers Green in 1701 for Charles Mompesson, lawyer and MP for Old Sarum. Later it became a residence of the Bishop. The conservative but well-proportioned exterior gives no hint of the riot of classical decoration within. There is superb moulded baroque plasterwork in the ceilings, overmantels and panelling, particularly in the area of the elegant oak staircase hall, where there are classical motifs dating from about 1740. The house contains much period furniture, put together for the house, and the National Trust has the Turnbull Collection of eighteenth-century English drinking glasses on display. Although the house presses hard on The Close at the front, the garden at the rear is a paved oasis of herbaceous plants and shrubs, climbers, a covered pergola and specimen flowering trees.

National Plant Collections
Nine of the National Plant Collections are held in Wiltshire.
Acanthus: Leon Butler, Iford Manor Gardens, Iford Manor, Bradford-on-Avon BA15 2BA. Telephone: 01225 862840.
Open: April and October, Sunday afternoons; May to September, all afternoons except Monday and Friday.
Leon Butler, who started his collection of acanthus plants in the mid 1960s, keeps them

now in the gardens at Iford Manor, where he is the head gardener. Acanthus is a small family and the collection comprises only about half a dozen varieties, growing in a pleasure garden within the walled garden of the house. This is a good place for the collection, for Leon's favourite *Acanthus spinosus* – native to Italy and Greece – is the form mirrored in the classical stone capitals hereabouts.

Digitalis: Terence Baker, The Botanic Nursery, Atworth, Melksham SN12 8HY. Telephone: 01225 706597.
Open daily except Tuesdays.

Terence Baker has always loved foxgloves and this love led him to form the collection, which now numbers about twenty-five species and *purpurea* forms. They are growing in pots at the nursery (not the nursery plant centre just behind the Jubilee clock-tower of 1897 in the village). Because of the need for purity it is not possible to keep a display garden fully stocked, but the nursery has a good descriptive list; both plants and seeds are for sale. Different *Digitalis* plants flower at different times, so anyone visiting between May and August will find some in flower.

Euonymus: Lady Anne Cowdray, Broadleas Gardens, Devizes SN10 5JQ. Telephone: 01380 722035.
Open April to October, Sunday, Wednesday and Thursday afternoons.

In the woodland area of the gardens there are twenty-four species and cultivars of *Euonymus*. Their owner believes that not many people know what a beautiful plant *Euonymus* can be or much about it. She began her collection simply because she liked the shrub. When she offered to have the National Collection she did not realise that there were so many species, let alone varieties and hybrids, nor how difficult plants and seeds are to obtain. *Euonymus* are rather slow growing and, although the collection includes several now flowering, berrying and colouring, some are still fairly small.

Helleborus: Jeremy Wood, Lower House, Whiteparish, Salisbury. Telephone: 01794 884306.
Open by appointment February and March.

Jeremy Wood and his wife began growing hellebores in the 1960s. Their interest was stimulated when they saw and collected seeds of a number of hellebore species growing in the wild, in such countries as Yugoslavia, Turkey and Spain. The National Plant Collection was started in 1984, and it now contains twenty species and subspecies, ten primary hybrids, sixty-seven named cultivars and a quantity of unnamed cultivars identified by serial numbers. Each year seed is sown of the better cultivars and species, and there is a limited amount of breeding. The plants, when they come into flower two or three years later, are either added to the collection (if of sufficient merit) or are sold (to personal callers only) to bring in funds necessary for maintaining and increasing the collection.

Oenothera: John d'Arcy, The Old Vicarage, Edington, Westbury BA13 4QF. Telephone: 01380 830512.
Open by appointment, and on National Garden Scheme opening days.

The collection of approximately twenty species and cultivars is part of a 1.5 acre (0.6 hectare) garden on greensand, situated on the northern escarpment of Salisbury Plain with fine views. The garden is intensively planted with herbaceous borders, shrubs, a small arboretum, woodland plants, bulbs and some recently introduced species from abroad. John d'Arcy's interest in *Oenothera* stems from finding an interesting family of plants which grows well in the dry soil and which in 1982 was not already the subject of a National Collection.

Populus: Lackham College, Lacock, Chippenham SN15 2NY. Telephone: 01249 443111.

The collection of poplar trees is sited in several areas of the college grounds, where it was built up in three stages between 1986 and 1990. There are four species at River Field, twelve at Plucking Grove, and seven on the Engine Ground/Oxenleaze site. Quantities of each species vary from a single specimen to groups of two or three. The Dews Field site is

The village street in Potterne is dominated by the timber-framed Porch House.

scheduled for further planting to increase the collection.

Primula, Pyrus: Charles Quest-Ritson, Highfield House, Shrewton, Salisbury SP3 4BU. Telephone: 01980 621396.
Open by appointment only.

Charles Quest-Ritson is a well-known plantsman and horticultural journalist, who with his wife Brigid began both the *Primula* (European species) and *Pyrus* collections in about 1984. Their interest was in primulas: cowslips, oxlips and their natural hybrids and alpine species. They have moved both collections from the southern edge of the county to the 1.5 acre (0.6 hectare) garden of a Georgian and early Victorian village house in the middle of Salisbury Plain. It will take some years for the *Pyrus* to become established, and the primulas are best seen in March or April.

Scabiosa: Sylvia Parrett, Pear Tree Cottage, Upper Woodford, Salisbury.
Open by prior appointment only.

When she lived in Yorkshire, Sylvia Parrett began to grow scabious plants as reminders of her home county of Wiltshire. The collection moved with her to Lancashire, and in 1992 she brought them all back to Wiltshire. Although the climate and growing conditions to be found in the south of the county favour the perennial scabious, the collection will need time to establish well. There are currently about twelve varieties (no annuals) in Sylvia's collection, and she is still experimenting with a genus which is botanically difficult to classify because of different leaf shapes on the same plant.

Newhouse, Redlynch, Salisbury SP5 2NX. Telephone: 01725 20055.
Open August, daily except Sundays; also May to August by appointment only, for groups of fifteen or more.

An austere brick building of unusual ground plan, made all the more imposing by its elevation, Newhouse has three wings arranged in a Y shape with a hexagonal central core. The main front is of three bays and three stages, gabled and flanked by two-storey wings. These were added in 1742 and 1760. All the windows are rectangular and the entire façade is devoid of ornamentation. It is reputed to have been built early in the seventeenth century as a hunting lodge for Sir Thomas Gorges of Longford Castle, and it was sold to Giles Eyre in 1633. The Lord Chief Justice, Sir Robert Eyre, further enlarged the property in 1689 and is commemorated in a series of likenesses in the house. There are other family portraits and sculpture, a collection of Nelson miscellanea and some costume. Note the Georgian staircase and the rococo ceiling in the dining room.

Philipps House, Dinton, Salisbury SP3 5HJ. National Trust.
Open by written arrangement only.

Within Dinton Park, this simple country house is of neo-classical design, done with dignity in Chilmark stone. It was designed and built in 1814-17 by Sir Jeffrey Wyatville for William Wyndham. The house was acquired by Bertram Philipps in 1917 and has been a National Trust property since 1943. The most pleasing features are the huge portico with its Ionic columns and pediment and, inside, the simple but impressive central staircase of Portland stone with a lantern window above. The state rooms are light and open with attractive moulded ceilings and fine Regency furniture.

Porch House, Potterne, Devizes.
Open by written appointment only.

This small, late fifteenth-century timbered house is supposed to have been a church house and, at some time, the Pack Horse inn. It is also reputed to have been a brewery, a bakehouse and barracks before being divided into dwellings. Well-loved by the romantic artist Samuel Palmer, it was bought at his recommendation in 1872 by Sir George Richmond, who restored it four years later. This is a hall-house, timbered, gabled and tiled, with carved bargeboards above little projecting oriel windows. Internally, it has been considerably reconstructed, mostly by means of partitioning, with the addition of staircases and fireplaces, needed when the house became tenements. There are good beam arrangements within, although the original pendants

in the hall were cut off to allow sufficient headroom when an upper floor was put in. It is well worth a visit.

Pyt House, Tisbury, Salisbury SP3 6PB. Telephone: 01747 870210.
Open May to September, Wednesday and Thursday afternoons.

This early nineteenth-century, late Georgian stone-built mansion stands on the site of an earlier house of some importance. Steps lead up to a Palladian-style façade with Ionic columns. There are a number of fine paintings. It was on the Pyt House estate in 1830 that four hundred rioting agricultural labourers, incensed at the poor quality of their existence, engaged a troop of yeomanry. Many were arrested, tried at Salisbury and transported.

Sheldon Manor, Chippenham SN14 0RG. Telephone: 01249 653120.
Open April to October, Sundays, Thursdays and bank holidays.

Wiltshire's oldest inhabited manor house is all that remains of a medieval village which is now lost beneath the undulations of a nearby field. The Plantagenet manor house dates from 1282 and is therefore one of the oldest in Britain. It retains the large, buttressed entrance porch, vaulted and ribbed, which was put up by Sir Geoffrey Gascelyn in the thirteenth century. The detached chapel was built in the fifteenth century and wings were added to the house in 1431 and 1659. Continuously lived in since it was built, Sheldon Manor retains the atmosphere of a home, where the past is met at every turn. Nothing squares up; passages undulate, sloping floors give under foot, great oak beams, out of true and roughly hewn, support converging rafters. The interior has fine woodwork, oak furniture and panelled rooms. There are collections of Nailsea glass, porcelain and Persian saddlebags, English and foreign glass and china. A speciality is the home-made cooking to be had in the Georgian stables. The surrounding gardens are a series of outdoor rooms: the water garden, Judas-tree garden, elm-tree garden, terraced gardens, shrub gardens and old-fashioned rose collection – each with its own character and features.

There is a maze of edible plants in the old kitchen garden.

Stourhead Gardens, Stourton, Warminster BA12 6QD. Telephone: 01747 841152. National Trust.
Open all year daily.

There are no landscaped gardens in Britain to compare with the National Trust's property adjacent to Stourhead House. Laid out by Henry Hoare II between 1741 and 1785, with the addition of exotic trees and shrubs in the nineteenth century, the gardens are centred on a magnificent lake. Around its edges is a series of classical buildings, eccentric buildings and various shrines to eighteenth-century romanticism and ideas of classical beauty. The Observatory, like the Temple of the Sun with its Corinthian capitals, stands high on the wooded hill. From it can be viewed the whole amazing panorama, virtually unchanged since it was laid out. Most of the work was done by 1770, during which time Flitcroft designed the Temple of the Sun and the Pantheon. The 1¼ mile (2 km) walk around the lake crosses the Palladian-style stone bridge, near the fourteenth-century Bristol Cross, which was brought to Stourhead in 1765. Statuary in the Grotto, en route, includes Neptune and nymphs. The whole area was laid out as pleasure gardens, not to look at but to walk in or drive around (in coach and horses). To this end the various elements provide a series of breathtaking vistas. There are beeches, conifers and other trees and shrubs in abundance, including magnificent rhododendrons. The village of Stourton is included in the overall design, and the view of its little church from high above on the estate is as breathtaking as any.

Stourhead House, Stourton, Warminster BA12 6QD. Telephone: 01747 841152.
Open April to October, afternoons daily, except Thursdays and Fridays.

Colen Campbell's model Palladian-style

Sheldon Manor is Wiltshire's oldest inhabited manor house. This is the thirteenth-century entrance porch.

Stourhead House was the home of Henry Hoare II, who laid out the remarkable Stourhead Gardens.

villa was built in 1721-4 for the banker Henry Hoare I. The two wings, which give it a well-balanced and impressive east front, were added about 1800 for Sir Richard Colt Hoare, the Wiltshire historian. The central portico was built in 1840, after Campbell's original design. The core of the house was gutted by fire in 1902 and rebuilt by Sir Henry Hoare, the sixth baronet, from photographic evidence. The library in the south wing and the picture gallery in the north wing both survived, but elsewhere the eighteenth-century interiors perished in the blaze. The present ornamentation and plasterwork were crafted to match the original. The picture gallery, which contains many of Henry Hoare II's collection of paintings, copies and commissions, also has furniture by Thomas Chippendale the younger. The paintings include works by Gainsborough, Reynolds, Canaletto and Raphael. The music room has furniture of the William Kemp period, and in the cabinet room is Pope Sixtus V's marble cabinet, dated 1587.

Stourton House Garden, Stourton, Warminster. Telephone: 01747 840417.
Open April to November, Wednesday, Thurs-day, Sunday and bank holiday Mondays.

This is a 4 acre (1.6 hectare) 'all seasons' garden with much to see and smell in a number of areas. It is noted for the unique cupressus hedge surrounding the herbaceous garden and the collection of over 230 varieties of hydrangea. There is a woodland garden and good collections of bulbs, herbaceous plants and shrubs, many of which may be bought on site. Stourton House is also the home of the famous Dried Flower Garden. There is a programme of garden events each year, including special Plantsmen's Days.

Wardour Old Castle, Tisbury, Salisbury.
Open April to October, daily; November to March, Wednesday to Sunday.

Originally built late in the fourteenth century for John, fifth Lord Lovel of Titchmarsh, and remodelled in the sixteenth century, the castle is now in ruins around its hexagonal courtyard. It is a design unique in Britain and it is thought that the owner was inspired by similarly arranged structures in France, where he had been a veteran campaigner during the Hundred Years War. It is situated on rising wooded ground to the east of a small lake. The west side of the castle was blown up in the English Civil War, when it was twice besieged. In May 1643 Lady Blanche Arundell, in the absence of her Royalist husband and with only about fifty fighting men and servants, held out for six days against Sir Edward Hungerford, Colonel Strode and thirteen hundred Parliamentary troops. They installed Edmund Ludlow, who was in his turn besieged by Royalists for ten months from March 1644. The campaign secured the castle, and although the ruins were made habitable they were not rebuilt. What is left today is austere and impressive, yet romantically situated between woodland and water, where a lakeside Gothic pavilion provides a stark contrast.

Westwood Manor, Lower Westwood, Bradford-on-Avon BA15 2AF. Telephone: 01225 863374. National Trust.
Open April to September, Tuesday, Wednesday and Sunday afternoons.
    A small early fifteenth-century stone manor house, Westwood Manor is gabled with a stone-tiled roof and retains some late Gothic tracery. Although the small house which probably existed here in about 1400 was suc-

cessively enlarged by its owners during the next century or so, it was the coming of the rich clothier Thomas Horton in 1518 that made it into a real manor. He began a reshaping of the ground plan, which was further altered and extended by John Farewell, who bought the property in 1616. At that time the buildings were ranged on two sides of the forecourt; Farewell built a stair turret at the angle between them and made alterations to the rooms. Two centuries later it became a farmhouse and was not restored until 1911. The most noteworthy features include the Great Hall of about 1490 and the Great Parlour and King's Room from the extensive work done in the seventeenth century. These have fine decorative plasterwork in the ceilings, wood panelling and a plaster overmantel of about 1609. There are Jacobean windows, furniture and decorative features. Outside are modern topiary gardens.

Wilton House, Wilton, Salisbury SP2 0BJ. Telephone: 01722 743115.
Open Easter to October, daily.
    The original building of about 1550, on the site of a ninth-century nunnery founded by

Westwood Manor, near Bradford-on-Avon, has a topiary garden which includes a cottage cut out of yew.

Wilton House contains the famous Single Cube Room and Double Cube Room.

King Alfred, was devastated by fire in 1647. Inigo Jones and John Webb were called in to undertake the reconstruction and the present house was completed about 1653. The central east front, which remains from the Tudor building, was incorporated into this new design. The principal subsequent changes were made by James Wyatt in the early nineteenth century, including alterations to the north and west fronts and the addition of the cloisters about 1810-14. Here, as well as in the state rooms, is a remarkable collection of treasures, including what is reputedly one of the finest private art collections in Britain. The house is built around a hollow square and has been called the most beautiful stately home in Britain. Best of all are the Single Cube Room, 30 feet (9 metres) long, wide and high, and the Double Cube Room of twice the length, which was built to display the collection of Van Dyck paintings. As the operations room for Southern Command, it was visited by Churchill, Eisenhower and Montgomery as preparations were made for the Normandy landings in the Second World War. The six state rooms contain a priceless collection of paintings and furniture, including work by Chippendale, Rubens, Lely, Brueghel and Reynolds.

The Triumphal Arch, surmounted by an equestrian statue of Marcus Aurelius, at the entrance to the Memorial Gardens and the grounds, was designed by Sir William Chambers in 1755 and placed in its present position by Wyatt in 1801. The river Wylye crosses the estate and the Nadder flows beneath Roger Morris's covered Palladian bridge of 1737. The grounds are noted for their spacious lawns, landscaped parkland and rose and water gardens, with several cedar trees dating from the seventeenth century.

Other attractions include a display of model soldiers from the nineteenth century. Modern interpretative displays have been added to complement the architectural and artistic splendours of the house. In the film theatre, visitors are transported back to the times of earlier Earls of Pembroke, who have been at Wilton House since the sixteenth century. The reconstructed Tudor kitchen and the estate's old Victorian laundry also offer a glimpse of life in times gone by. With a massive adventure playground, children's quizzes and a collection of miniature dressed teddy bears, Wilton House provides interest for all ages.

8
Museums

The majority of the county's museums are either in private hands or belong to local history societies. The Wiltshire Library and Museum Service (Bythesea Road, Trowbridge; telephone: 01221 43641) offers pastoral care to some which do not have professional staff. This is part of the stated intention to 'foster better care and availability of Wiltshire's heri-tage, in particular the recording of environmental information and the professional care of museums in the county'. It also encourages the work of the Wiltshire Buildings Record (c/o Devizes Library, Sheep Street, Devizes; telephone: 01380 3610) and the Wiltshire Biological Record (Devizes Museum, 41 Long Street, Devizes; telephone: 01380 2765). Other museums in the county belong to central government, private companies, school societies and local authorities. The Wiltshire Library and Museum Service has a Conservation Centre (Wyndham House, 65 The Close, Salisbury; telephone: 01772 331321) which is open to the public by appointment.

The visitor should not be discouraged by those collections which are listed as being available 'by appointment only'. All are freely available, even where access is through government property, and often outside official public viewing times where these are normally restricted. In addition, the Wiltshire Museum and Library Service maintains a Sites and Monuments Record and a photographic record of the county at museum headquarters, whilst there are also good collections of archives and contemporary photographs in the libraries at Sheep Street, Devizes (telephone: 01380 3610); Market Place, Salisbury (telephone: 01722 24145); Regent Circus, Swindon (telephone: 01793 616277); and Mortimer Street, Trowbridge (telephone: 01221 461171).

Atworth

Atworth Museum, The Barn, Poplar Farm-house, Bradford Road, Atworth, Melksham SN12 8HZ. Telephone: 01225 702043.
Open last Sunday of the month, or by appoint-ment.

This small village collection is run by the Atworth History Group. There are some permanent exhibits, but as this enterprising group works on specific topics the themes and exhibits are constantly changing. Permanent material includes farming hand tools, old bottles, a 'then and now' collection of photographs, and objects relating to various institutions such as the church, school and shop. There is a specially commissioned colour-coded historical map of the village linked to aerial photographs, and a collection of objects, photographs and records concerning the immediate locality. There are also annotated displays on walks in the area.

Avebury

Alexander Keiller Museum, Avebury, Marlborough SN8 1RF. Telephone: 01672 539250. National Trust.
Open daily.

The museum was founded in 1938 in the early eighteenth-century coach-house and stables which belonged to the manor. These had been especially converted for the Morven Institute of Archaeological Research in order to display pottery, bones and other artefacts recovered during the excavations at Avebury, nearby Windmill Hill and the adjacent West Kennett Avenue. Alexander Keiller and his team excavated between 1924 and 1929, and again between 1934 and 1939. He then owned many of the prehistoric sites thereabouts, as well as part of the village, and undertook the work at his own expense. The museum is a record of the archaeological team's achievements and of the people who used beaker pottery. Keiller raised fifty of the Avebury stones. The remains of a barber surgeon, trapped beneath one when it fell late in the thirteenth century, yielded his instruments and some coins of the day. The result is one of the most important collections of its kind in Britain today.

The Great Barn Museum of Wiltshire Life,
Avebury, Marlborough SN8 1RF. Telephone: 01672 539555.
Open late March to early November, daily; winter, weekends only.

Avebury Great Barn is the museum of the Wiltshire Life Society and is devoted to the rural and domestic life of this county. It is housed in a seventeenth-century aisled threshing barn and is situated on a farm site including dovecote, green and dewpond. It was opened in 1979 when the Society raised funds to renovate and rethatch the building. Displays include a recreated country kitchen, dairying equipment, agricultural machinery and hand tools, shepherding, rural crafts (the thatcher, blacksmith, wheelwright and saddler) and a range of old local photographs. A temporary exhibition space includes a display on Avebury past and present, new in 1995. Throughout the season there are a variety of rural craft demonstrations. The barn also houses a tourist information centre and a craft shop and bookshop, with a 'Wiltshire Larder' selling local produce. A study centre is available for school use and for commercial bookings. Adjacent to the barn is Stones restaurant, providing an excellent range of food which should not be missed.

Bradford-on-Avon

Bradford-on-Avon Museum, The Library, Bridge Street, Bradford-on-Avon BA15 1BY. Telephone: 01225 863280.
Open: Easter to October, Wednesdays to Saturdays, also Sunday and bank holiday afternoons; November to Easter, Wednesday to Sunday afternoons, also Saturday mornings.

This general collection relating to the area includes a reconstructed chemist's shop, which was in use for 120 years and preserved when it closed down in the town. Otherwise the museum is an interesting mix of natural and local history from around the area.

Calne

Atwell-Wilson Motor Museum, Downside, Stockley Lane, Calne SN11 ONF. Telephone: 01249 813119.
Open all year daily except Fridays and Saturdays; times vary.

This is a fine collection of about sixty vintage, post-vintage and classic cars, motorcycles, some old lawnmowers and motoring miscellanea which Richard and Hasell Atwell have been putting together since the early 1960s. It is housed in custom-built premises of over 8000 square feet (743 square metres),

The Great Barn at Avebury now houses the Museum of Wiltshire Life.

which were completed in 1989 on part of the old Blackland Park estate. Many of the exhibits were extensively restored on site and are working vehicles, for their owners also operate a hire company. The oldest car in the collection is a Model T Ford Tourer of 1924, and the most recent is a 1983 white Ford Granada. These vehicles are beautifully restored, and many are young enough to revive happy memories in visitors. The collection includes a number of American classics, such as the 1961 Chrysler Plymouth convertible and 1980 Cadillac Fleetwood Broughton diesel. Earlier cars include the only known 1937 Albemarle Buick from McLaughlin, Canada, with an English body. Some have interesting stories. Fully restored antique play equipment for children has been set up at the museum.

Castle Combe
Castle Combe Museum, The Hill, Castle Combe SN14 7HU. Telephone: 01249 782295.
Open Easter to October, Sunday afternoons.
   The Castle Combe and District Historical Society's collection is housed in the Congregational Chapel schoolroom of about 1806, which also used to serve as the village telephone exchange. Opened in 1985, the collection includes artefacts from neolithic times to the present day arranged in showcases, and it presents the history of this most beautiful village on good wall displays. It is easy to miss on the way down from the public car park.

Chippenham
Sevington School Museum, Sevington, Chippenham SN14 7LD. Telephone: 0249 783070. About 2 miles (3 km) north of Yatton Keynell, turning east off the road to Grittleton, towards Leigh Delamere.
Open June and July, Sundays.
   At the west end of the village, on the green, is the old village school with the teacher's cottage attached. The schoolroom dates from 1849. It was closed in 1913 but has now been reopened as it was. There are desks, books, school uniforms and photographs, including one of the last three boys to be educated there. Visitors can use slates at the original desks

and see the reconstructed kitchen and living rooms of the old schoolhouse. The garden is being restored to how it was a hundred years ago. The big bell turret is from Leigh Delamere old church, as are the fourteenth-century chancel arch used as the porch doorway and other features inside. Joseph Neeld rebuilt Leigh Delamere church in 1846 and the following year had James Thompson build Sevington School.

Yelde Hall Museum, Market Place, Chippenham SN15 3HL. Telephone: 01249 651488.
Open mid March to end of October, Monday to Saturday.
   A small collection of local photographs, scrapbooks and geological and archaeological items is housed in one room of the sixteenth-century timber-framed Guildhall, where the original council chamber and lock-up may also be seen. The restored timber-framed building has fine braces and roof arrangement; it is twin-gabled with a little wooden turret. It was used as a meeting place by the bailiff and burgesses of the town, then by the mayor and council, until the present town hall was built in 1841.

Chittoe
Spye Park Stables Museum, Spye Park, Lacock, Chippenham SN15 2PS. Telephone: 01249 730247.
Open Sunday afternoons; at other times by appointment to parties of ten or more.
   The collection is housed in a stable block of about 1654. It contains the family coach of about 1800, a wagonette and two smaller coaches. Also included are a horse-drawn model fire-engine, harnesses and stable tackle, hunting and military relics, amongst them helmets of the 9th Lancers and the 3rd Dragoon Guards. There are also local history items in the collection.

Corsley
Longhedge Collection, Longhedge Farm, Corsley, Warminster BA12 7QZ. Telephone: 0137 388205.
   This is a large private collection of farming bygones from about 1858. It includes a work-

ing portable flour mill, machinery and hand tools, much of which is on loan to other country life museums. The owner began the collection in 1972. Although it is not displayed at the farm, visitors are welcome by appointment.

Cricklade

Cricklade Museum, Calcutt Street, Cricklade SN8 6BB. Telephone: 01793 750756.
Open Wednesday afternoons and Saturday mornings.

Formed in 1950, this collection was moved in 1986 to a disused chapel. The town lies within Alfred's fortifications against the Danes, and the museum holds the records of the excavation of the town wall. There are items from the Roman period, including pottery and coins. Its greatest prize, although not kept at the museum, is a quantity of Saxon silver pennies which were made at the Cricklade mint. A hoard of two hundred coins from another excavation is on display, and there is a Roman roofing tile that bears the stamp of its maker. Of the same period are an axe, wine flagon and mixing bowl which were buried in a stone coffin. Other exhibits include a large archive of documents, poll books, church records, maps, over two thousand photographs and prints of the town and its environs.

Devizes

Devizes Museum, 41 Long Street, Devizes SN10 1NS. Telephone: 01380 727369.
Open all year, Monday to Saturday, except bank holidays.

This is the museum of the Wiltshire Archaeological and Natural History Society. It was founded in 1854 and archaeologists have been adding to it ever since. The museum includes many of the discoveries made during the major archaeological excavations around the county. The collection is particularly rich in material from palaeolithic to Anglo-Saxon times, and there are dedicated neolithic, bronze age, iron age, Roman, Anglo-Saxon and medieval galleries. There are collections of local and natural history and geology and the Buckler Collection of watercolours depicting churches and country houses as they

were early in the nineteenth century. A local history gallery, telling the story of Devizes from about 1600, was opened in 1988. A new bronze age gallery opened in 1993 and a Roman gallery in 1994. The natural history gallery is particularly good, illustrating and explaining the range of geology and natural habitats within the county, and the influences of each upon the other.

Kennet & Avon Canal Museum, The Wharf, Devizes SN10 1EB. Telephone: 01380 729489.
Open daily from Easter to Christmas.

Devizes Wharf was one of the most important places on the working canal. Now it is an equally important resource centre, dealing with the creation of the Kennet & Avon Canal through the groups of people who conceived, designed, built, operated and latterly restored it. The exhibition features photographic displays and other audio-visual presentations and is a useful interpretative centre for canals in general.

Fovant

Fovant Badges Society Collection, Pembroke Arms, Fovant, Salisbury SP3 5JH. Telephone: 01722 714201.

At the end of 1944 the Fovant Home Guard Old Comrades Association first met at the Pembroke Arms and the tradition has continued with its successor, the Fovant Badges Society. Over the years a collection of medals, cap badges, buttons, letters, postcards, etcetera, relating to the First World War, and in particular to the regiments camped around Fovant at the time, has built up. These are displayed on the walls of the lounge/dining room at the pub.

Great Bedwyn

Great Bedwyn Stone Museum, 91 Church Street, Great Bedwyn, Marlborough SN8 3PF. Telephone: 01672 870234.
Open on weekdays during normal business hours. Visitors are welcome, although, because this is a working monumental masonry business, groups should telephone in advance.

The Lloyd family came to Wiltshire from the Midlands to help construct the Kennet &

The work of a family of monumental stone masons is on display at Great Bedwyn Stone Museum.

Avon Canal. In the 1880s they built East Grafton church. The house at Great Bedwyn which is the centre of their business as monumental stone masons was once the village post office. The museum in the yard includes items collected by seven generations of this family firm. There is plasterwork reputed to have been on show at the Great Exhibition, restored and painted headstones and texts, fonts, statuary and fossils. The collection includes stonework created by the family throughout the twentieth century, and items are constantly being added. There is also a collection of old tools of the trade.

Highworth

Highworth Musem, Highworth, Swindon. Telephone: 01793 763121.
Open by appointment only.

The Highworth Historical Society's collection has nowhere to be displayed but may be viewed by appointment with the keeper. It comprises documents (including land enclosures of 1779), postcards and about seven hundred photographs relating to the town, as well as to Inglesham, Hannington and Stanton Fitzwarren. There is some archaeological material including a complete and rare Roman dish, made in Gaul and signed by the maker.

Lacock

Fox Talbot Museum of Photography, Lacock, Chippenham SN15 2LG. Telephone: 01249 730459. National Trust.
Open March to October, daily, but closed Good Friday.

Located at the entrance to Lacock Abbey estate and housed in a sixteenth-century barn, the museum celebrates the achievements and life of William Henry Fox Talbot (1800-77), who founded in principle and practice the positive/negative process, the basis of modern photography as we know it today. The main display shows all aspects of the life and work of this nineteenth-century polymath, whilst the upper gallery area exhibits a range of contemporary and historical work. Within the museum is a shop selling specialist photographic publications and prints. The shop is one of the best in the region for specialist books on photography.

Granaries raised on staddle stones are among the preserved farm buildings at Lackham Agricultural Museum.

Lackham Country Attractions, the Agricultural Museum, Lackham College, Lacock, Chippenham SN15 2NY. Telephone: 01249 443111.

Open April to October, daily.

Set in the grounds of Lackham College, the agricultural museum is housed in a reconstructed threshing barn and granaries, with exhibition areas concentrating on rural crafts, engines and machinery. The museum was founded in 1946 by J. O. Thomas, a former principal of the college, and the collection has grown to encompass a range of farming and rural life items. There are magnificent gardens on the site (see page 110) and fun for the children in the adventure playground and the rare breeds centre. The threshing barn, refurbished for the 1995 season, houses exhibitions on the Victorian farmer, ploughing and threshing, milking, butter and cheese making. Other subjects covered include traps and trapping, livestock, the blacksmith, wheelwright and carpenter, tractors and engines and a display on the changing seasons.

Ludgershall

Ludgershall Museum, Andover Road, Ludgershall, Andover.

Open by appointment only.

The Ludgershall History Society's museum, founded in 1958, comprises a collection of local photographs and documents. There are a number of farm implements, material to do with shepherding and old bottles from the Ludgershall Mineral Water Company and the Crown Mineral Water Company.

Malmesbury

Athelstan Museum, Town Hall, Cross Hayes, Malmesbury SN16 9BZ. Telephone: 01666 822143.

Open Easter to September, daily, except Mondays; Wednesday, Friday and Saturday afternoons in winter in winter.

The museum is situated within the town hall, in a former fire (and later ambulance) station, and appropriately it has an eighteenth-century manual fire-engine. The collection mostly relates to the industry and topography of the town: items recalling the Radcliffe Engineering Works, a collection of lace and lacemaking, early bicycles, and stone jars used by the town's brewers. There are costumes, coins and archaeological and geological material. Local drawings and photographs include some of the Malmesbury branch railway, now defunct, and there are a number of floor tiles which were once in the abbey.

Malmesbury Abbey Parvise Museum, The Abbey, Malmesbury. Telephone: 01666 2075.
Open when the abbey is open.
The abbey has a wealth of treasures from exquisite items in precious metals to fragments of medieval masonry. It has twelfth-century manuscripts written in Anglo-Norman and a huge, beautifully illuminated manuscript Bible of 1407 as well as numerous lesser works. Roman and medieval tiles, very early photographs, prints, drawings and paintings are exhibited in the large room over the great porch at the abbey. Here gunpowder was stored during the Civil War, and children did their schooling for a hundred years. There are also some musical instruments including the organ of 1714.

Market Lavington
Market Lavington Village Museum, Church Street, Market Lavington SN10 4DT. Telephone: 01380 818736.
Open May to September, Wednesday, Saturday and Sunday afternoons, or by appointment.
A once derelict cottage houses a collection of objects gathered from no further away than the village. The kitchen and sitting room have been decorated in the late Victorian and early Edwardian style, and items on display include tools, local photographs and clothes, with a particularly good and very comprehensive local history filing system. Work files for primary schools fit in with the national curriculum.

Marlborough
Marlborough College Natural History Collection, Marlborough College, Marlborough SN8 1PA. Telephone: 01672 515511.
Open by appointment only.

Part of the former Marlborough College Natural History Society Collection, these fine exhibits may be viewed by serious students only, by appointment.

Melksham
Melksham Historical Collection, Rachel Fowler Centre, Melksham. Telephone: 01225 703422.
Open by appointment.
The material belonging to the Melksham and District Historical Association is housed in part of a former Congregational church which has been converted into an arts centre. It has documents, photographs and slides relating to the history of the area, including papers concerning Rachel Fowler, a benefactor of the town. Amongst its other exhibits are a set of village stocks and a quantity of old medical instruments.

Mere
Mere Museum, Public Library, Barton Lane, Mere, Warminster BA12 6JA. Telephone: 01747 860546.
Open Mondays and Fridays in the afternoon and evening; Tuesdays in the morning and afternoon.
This small museum contains material relating to the trade and local history of Mere and its neighbourhood, natural history, geology and fossils. It also includes a large part of the former Mere Church Museum. Miscellaneous artefacts include Roman and later coins and tokens, keys, brass-rubbings, eighteenth-century prints and nineteenth- and twentieth-century photographs.

Monkton Farleigh
Monkton Farleigh Mine, Monkton Farleigh, Bradford-on-Avon. Telephone: 01225 852400.
Open Easter to October, daily; winter weekends.
Here are 80 acres (32 hectares) of bomb-proof tunnels built by the Royal Engineers from an abandoned stone mine. They were once used to store 12 million tons of ammunition in what was the biggest underground arsenal in Europe. The tunnels are up to a mile long with a concrete supporting struc-

ture. Visitors are told how it all came about and can see the 1940s generator and switchgear, the underground power house, the haulage systems and the air-conditioning plant.

Pewsey

Pewsey Heritage Centre, Whatley's Old Foundry, High Street, Pewsey SN9 5AF. Telephone: 01672 62051 or 62404.
Open May to October, weekends.

Started by Michael Duckenfield in 1992 as a registered charity, this collection is housed (by courtesy of the directors of Whatley's) in a stone building (unusual for this area of brick and flint), which was a foundry from the 1870s. Inside it still has something of the feel of a Victorian workshop. The Heritage Centre encompasses both the social and the engineering interests of Pewsey's past. Here you will find machine tools with belt drives, a large range of domestic items, farm machinery, photographs and documents as well as large-scale models. Amongst the exhibits are some unusual ones: a hook device for retrieving buckets from wells when they come off the rope, and an early American kitchen import – a hand bread or meat slicer.

Potterne

Bert Watts Museum, George and Dragon Inn, High Street, Potterne, Devizes SN10 5PY. Telephone: 01380 722139.
Open during pub opening hours.

A resident of the village and long-time farmworker, Bert Watts began making his collection of old agricultural hand tools in the early 1980s. He exhibited them at vintage shows and the collection grew to around two hundred items, which are now displayed in an outhouse at the pub. Donations by visitors go to charity.

Wiltshire Fire Defence and Brigade Museum, Fire Brigade Headquarters, Manor House, Potterne, Devizes SN10 5PP. Telephone: 01380 723601.
Open April to September, first Wednesday of month. Intending visitors should telephone in advance.

This collection is displayed in the foyer and stables at the brigade headquarters, and some items are in other fire stations in the county with access on open days. The nucleus is a miscellany of small firefighting equipment: hand lamps, hoses, branches, buckets, extinguishers, breathing apparatus. There are uniforms, tunics, belts, axes and buttons, extinguishers on cast-iron wheels, hydrant installations and hydrant plates (each town had its own design), manual fire-engines and later appliances.

Purton

Purton Museum, Purton Library, 1 High Street, Purton, Swindon SN5 9AA. Telephone: 01793 770567.
Open Tuesday and Wednesday; also Friday afternoons.

The Purton Historical Society's collection of documents relates to the Earl of Shaftesbury's estates. A curio is a prayer book reputed to have been held by the last man to be hanged in Purton. There is also the disbursement book of the overseer of the poor. Otherwise it is a collection of archaeological and agricultural interest.

Salisbury

Bishop Wordsworth School Museum, Bishop Wordsworth School, 11 The Close, Salisbury SP1 2EB. Telephone: 01722 333851.
Open by appointment only.

The museum has two sections. The first is a collection of mostly prehistoric flint implements from local archaeological sites which is owned by the Bishop Wordsworth School Archaeological Society and housed in a large wooden shed. There is some Roman and medieval material, and later items include an eighteenth-century turret clock from the stables of the Bishop's palace. The second section comprises the school archives including memorabilia relating to the school's founder, John Wordsworth, Bishop of Salisbury at the end of the nineteenth century and the beginning of the twentieth. There are photographs, letters, magazines and a wide range of other items relating to the history of the school and the achievements of Old Wordsworthians. It is housed in number 11, The Close.

The Wardrobe in The Close at Salisbury houses the museum of the Royal Gloucestershire, Berkshire and Wiltshire Regiment.

John Creasey Museum, Salisbury Library, Market Place, Salisbury SP1 1BL. Telephone: 01722 324145.
Open daily except Thursday and Sunday.

The museum comprises Creasey memorabilia including non-book material such as pottery relating to the writer and framed book jackets. There are also copies of all the writer's works in all editions and the languages into which they have been translated. The Creasey Collection of Contemporary Art, important work by modern artists, funded by the Creasey Trustees, is being constantly added to as funds and grants become available.

The Royal Gloucestershire, Berkshire and Wiltshire Regiment's Salisbury Museum, The Wardrobe, 58 The Close, Salisbury SP1 2EX. Telephone: 01722 414536.
Open April to October, daily; February, March and November, Monday to Friday; December and January, closed.

The 'Bishop's Wardrobe' is a fine house of medieval origins in The Close with an extensive riverside garden and views of the watermeadows beyond. The museum tells the story of the infantry regiments of Berkshire and Wiltshire since 1743 – hence its more usual name of 'Redcoats in The Wardrobe'. The museum is housed in a large building of stone, flint and brick, which dates from 1254, still with many medieval features, and originally used as a storeroom for the Bishop and as a private house in more recent times. Of particular note are the eighteenth-century stucco and classical chimney piece. The exhibits include fine collections of medals and silver, uniforms and other militaria. There are also the stuffed remains of Bobbie, a dog decorated by Queen Victoria for campaign service in Afghanistan.

Salisbury and South Wiltshire Museum, The King's House, 65 The Close, Salisbury SP1 2EN. Telephone: 01722 332151.
Open all year, Monday to Saturday; also Sunday afternoons in July and August.

The museum was founded in 1860 by Richard Fowler, based on a large collection of medieval artefacts discovered in 1852 when the city's canals were filled in. This drainage collection includes material from the seventeenth century to the eighteenth. The museum is especially rich in archaeological collections including the Wessex material of Pitt-Rivers and the Blackmore Museum. The latter was originally a collection of international exhibits opened by William Blackmore in 1867. There are fine models of Stonehenge and Old Sarum, and items from excavations of the latter, English pottery and porcelain, costume, flint implements, local prints and drawings. There is much former local street furniture and many artefacts, a great medieval processional model of St Christopher once used by the Guild of Merchant Tailors in pageants, and the skeleton of one of the people who used beaker pottery. Of particular interest is a mounted group of great bustards, shot on Salisbury Plain and now extinct in Britain.

A splendid gallery, opened in 1983, displays the Pitt-Rivers Collection. There is much relating to early man hereabouts and Stonehenge in particular, as might be expected, the history of Salisbury and a mass of artefacts and pictures of note, including five Turners. It is all housed in a fine Grade I listed building, which was once the home of the Abbots of Sherborne and latterly part of a teachers' training college. It includes a gift shop and coffee shop, the famous giant Hob Nob, and the 'Stitches in Time' gallery with costume, lace and embroidery of Wiltshire.

Swindon

Great Western Railway Museum, Faringdon Road, Swindon SN1 5BJ. Telephone: 01793 493189.
Open daily.

The imposing building, with its twin stone turrets and modern frontage let into the Victorian Gothic, was built about 1850 as a lodging house for workers and known as 'The Barracks'. It later accommodated engine crews and subsequently became a Wesleyan chapel for ninety years. It was opened as a railway museum in 1962, after considerable alterations to house the large exhibits. Locomotives in the main hall include the famous *King George V*, a 'Dean Goods', a 94xx tank locomotive and a replica of the broad-gauge engine *North Star*, as well as diesel railcar number 4. There is a fire engine of 1912 and a collection of models, prints, paintings and miscellaneous items relating to the history of the Great Western, as well as much of general railway interest. The Brunel Room has material connected with the engineer Isambard Kingdom Brunel. Upstairs, the Gooch Gallery has an exhibition which celebrates Swindon's former importance as a railway town. Swindon was at the centre of 'God's Wonderful Railway' and the Great Western Railway was to dominate employment in the town for more than a century. The railway workshops began to decline in the 1960s and now they are no more, their site absorbed into urban development.

Railway Village Museum, 34 Faringdon Road, Swindon SN1 5BJ. Telephone: 01793 526161 extension 4527.
Open Monday to Saturday; also Sunday afternoons.

This is an end-of-terrace railway foreman's house built of Bath stone in about 1842, as part of Swindon's planned village for the Great Western Railway employees, and renovated externally and refurbished within to show how it might have been during the last quarter of the nineteenth century. The accommodation comprises three bedrooms upstairs, and a front room, parlour and washroom downstairs, with a privy in the yard at the rear. The rooms are gaslit and packed with the paraphernalia of Victorian living. The view of the lesser cottages across the alley at the rear is exactly as it would have been seen by the original occupants.

Richard Jefferies Museum, Marlborough Road, Coate, Swindon. Telephone: 01793 493188.
Restricted opening.

The museum is in part of the seventeenth-century stone-built farmhouse where the naturalist writer was born in 1848. The countryside hereabouts – Coate Water, Hodson Woods, Liddington Hill – provided the inspiration for much of his work and many of his characters. Coate farmhouse was added to in the nineteenth century and opened as a museum in 1960. The collection includes objects and furniture used by Jefferies, as well as manuscripts and first editions. Amongst the exhibits are items connected with Alfred Williams, the scholarly railway hammerman from South Marston, who was well-known as a social writer and poet.

Swindon Museum and Art Gallery, Bath Road, Swindon SN1 4BA. Telephone: 01793 493188.
Open Monday to Saturday, and Sunday afternoons.

Apsley House, which has been the museum since 1930, is a limestone building of about 1830 with three bays and a Doric south porch. The art gallery was built on to its east side in 1964. It has important collections covering geology, archaeology and local history with a temporary exhibition space and a manually propelled early eighteenth-century fire-engine. The Swindon Collection of work by twentieth-century painters and potters is one of the best collections outside London.

Trowbridge

Trowbridge Museum, The Shires, Court Street, Trowbridge BA14 8AT. Telephone: 01225 751339.
Open Tuesday to Friday afternoons, and Saturday; closed bank holidays.

This museum is housed in a former woollen mill. In telling the story of this wool town, the museum produces its own cloth and the process can be seen by visitors on Saturdays. Displays, which have grown considerably since this site was opened in 1990, include reconstructions of Samuel Salter's mill office, a weaver's cottage and a shearman's workshop. The museum also contains material relating to the social and industrial history of the town and the locality, fossils, archaeology, natural science and geology. The Crabbe Collection of fossils, rocks and pressed flowers is also here. So too are the domestic artefacts, library and records of a family business in Bratton from the early eighteenth century to the mid twentieth. Herbert Garlick's collection of local photographs, prints and paintings and a section on

The farmhouse at Coate where Richard Jefferies was born is now a museum (left), as is the Victorian lodging house (right) built in Swindon for railway workers and now devoted to the Great Western Railway.

Isaac Pitman, who invented the much used method of shorthand, can also be seen.

Warminster

Dents Glove Museum, Fairfield Road, Warminster BA12 9DL. Telephone: 01985 212291.
Open by appointment.

The permanent exhibition was set up in 1986 by Robert Yentob and includes antique (mainly leather) gloves from the sixteenth, seventeenth and eighteenth centuries with a particularly good Victorian section and fine representative collections up to the present day. There are also antique sewing machines, glovemaking tools and various documents. Dents factory shop is adjacent to the museum.

Dewey Museum, Warminster Library, Three Horseshoes Mall, Warminster BA12 9BT. Telephone: 01985 215640.
Open daily, but at various times.

The museum is within Warminster library and takes its name from H. N. Dewey, whose personal archive is deposited there. It mounts monthly displays from its own collection of local and natural history and the geology of the area including Westbury and Battlesbury Camp. Much of this relates to the eighteenth and nineteenth centuries, including Halliday's notes on Warminster. There are also the Manley Collection of local fossils, mainly of the Jurassic and Cretaceous periods, a collection of marine and land shells, and a number of archaeological exhibits including a bronze age palstave.

Infantry and Small Arms School Corps Weapons Museum, Warminster BA12 0DJ. Telephone: 01985 842487.
Open to the public but because the museum is located on Ministry of Defence property an appointment is necessary and all visitors are escorted.

This comprehensive collection of military firearms was started when the School of Musketry was established in Hythe, Kent, in 1853. Approximately 2500 exhibits are displayed, illustrating the development of small arms from the sixteenth century to modern times. Of particular interest are a pair of pistols once the property of Napoleon, a rare Tinker's mortar dated 1681, sporting firearms dating from the sixteenth century, an exceptional collection of experimental breech-loaders, the rifle fired by HM the Queen at Bisley in 1993 and a selection of modern assault rifles. Additionally anti-armour weapons and mortars are displayed. A fine reference library contains manuscript trial records dating back to 1853. The museum has an active role within the Army Training Organisation and expert advice on firearms is available.

Westbury

Donne Collection, Leighton House, Westbury. Telephone: 01373 822832.
Visitors received by prior arrangement only.

This is an international collection of nineteenth-century watercolour paintings made by Colonel D. A. Donne (1856-1907), grandfather of the present owner. The collection is on Ministry of Defence property so it is essential that intending visitors make arrangements in advance. The present owner has added a collection of tropical butterflies and shells, as well as some archaeological material discovered when his home was being built on a former Roman settlement. He also has a quantity of old newspapers, which include reports on the battle of Trafalgar and the death of Nelson.

Woodland Heritage Museum, The Woodland Park, Brokerswood, Westbury BA13 4EH. Telephone: 01373 823880.
Open all year daily; times vary with season.

The museum building was put up at the southern end of the Woodland Park in Conservation Year. In it, 'the wood is brought to the museum but also the museum is brought to the wood'. Here are permanent exhibits, diorama displays of the fauna of Europe and reference collections of woodland fauna and flora including birds' eggs and lichen. There are displays of animals, birds, trees and insects, a feature bird wall, and an exhibition on conservation, forestry and natural history, which aim to promote public interest and concern in natural history conservation. Lectures may be provided in a lecture room. An educational programme is available for

The town hall at Wootton Bassett houses a museum of local history.

schools and there are on-site laboratory and audio-visual theatre facilities. At the interpretation centre, visitors of all ages are encouraged to participate and learn about conservation. The museum is a registered charity, administered by trustees as a centre for education studies in natural history and forestry. It has outdoor displays, including work at a sawpit. Together with the Woodland Park (see page 141), the museum provides a perfect day's visit.

Wootton Bassett

Wootton Bassett Museum, Town Hall, High Street, Wootton Bassett SN4 7AF.
Open Saturdays only.

The little building which houses the museum is an oddity. It comprises a dark timber-framed upper storey supported on fifteen Tuscan columns. These, in three equal rows, have an exaggerated entasis and little caps. The upper storey is reached by an open oak staircase with heavy balusters. It was put up in 1700 by Laurence Hyde, first Earl of Rochester, considerably restored in 1889 by Sir Henry Meux and given to the town by his widow in 1907. The restoration was responsible for the west Midland 'magpie' effect of white panels separated by dark woodwork including decoratively curved pieces. The museum houses items of local history and in the open space between the pillars are the stocks and an old fire-engine.

Wroughton

Science Museum, Wroughton Airfield, Swindon SN4 9NS. Telephone: 01793 814466.
Open selected days throughout the summer.

Public access to the museum, which forms part of the National Museum of Science and industry, is limited. Rarely seen exhibits include road transport, particularly commercial and specialist vehicles, civil aviation, space science and technology, and agricultural machinery. The museum is also the venue for a number of major public events each summer, usually to do with aeronautics and transport.

9
Industrial archaeology

Box Tunnel, Box (OS 173: ST 850694).

The Great Western Railway, built originally to the broad gauge (abandoned in 1892), had cost £5 million by the time it reached Bristol in 1851. Part of that cost had been spent on building Brunel's tunnel under a hill at Box in 1831-41, using up to four thousand men and one thousand horses. It was constructed simultaneously from both ends, and about one hundred men died and many were injured in the final push to link up. Measuring 3212 yards (2937 metres) in length, it was, when opened, the longest tunnel in the world and in some places it is 100 yards (91 metres) beneath the surface. The entrances are classical and ornate. Despite its reputation as a feat of Victorian engineering, many travellers at the time were cautious of the experience. They forsook the railway at that point in favour of a coach and horses!

Bradford-on-Avon Wharf, Bradford-on-Avon (OS 173: ST 826603). Kennet & Avon Canal Trust, telephone: 01380 721279.
Open Easter to October.

Bradford-on-Avon lock to the south of the town, the deepest in the Wiltshire section of the Kennet & Avon Canal, was built in order to raise the level of the canal to that of the Wilts & Berks Canal at Semington. Beside the lock is the wharf, with a slipway, dry dock, workshop with machine tools, canal shop and café in a most attractive cluster of stone buildings, which include an original warehouse. A boat show takes place here every September, and it is the starting point for pleasure cruises on the canal.

Caen Hill Locks, Devizes (OS 173: SU 979614).

About 1½ miles (2.4 km) west of the town is Rennie's engineering masterpiece on the Kennet & Avon Canal. It is the flight of twenty-nine locks, sixteen of them close together in one straight staircase at Caen Hill, which overcomes the rise of 237 feet (72 metres) from the Avon valley to the town of Devizes. Large deposits of clay found on Caen Hill whilst the locks were being built provided the raw material for an important brickmaking industry in the locality. The locks were opened to traffic in 1810 and nineteen years later the canal company, which had its own gasworks nearby, put up gas lighting so that the canal would be navigable at all hours. Left to rot in 1951, they became the very heart of the restoration and the focal point of the reopening by Queen Elizabeth II in 1990.

Canal Forge, Lower Wharf, Northgate Street, Devizes SN10 1JN (OS 173: SU 002616). Telephone: 01380 721759.
Open weekdays.

Visitors are welcome at any time during normal business hours to John Girvan's forge, where he carries on the traditional craft of the blacksmith, using old traditional tools. He is also a fairground historian, and there are a number of fairground panels as well as a small exhibition on the premises. He has two hearths, one a military hearth with foot-operated leather bellows. Private demonstrations of blacksmithing can be arranged in the evenings.

Crofton Beam Engines, Crofton, Marlborough SN8 3DW (OS 174: SU 262622). Telephone: 0672 870300.
Open Easter to end of September, Saturdays, Sundays and bank holiday Mondays.

Crofton Pumping Station is situated on the Kennet & Avon Canal near to Great Bedwyn and Wilton Windmill. This brick-built pumping station is a four-storey Georgian engine house with a separate round chimney. It was restored and reopened in 1970. There are two early Cornish beam pumping engines: an 1812

Boulton & Watt and an 1845 Harvey of Hayle. These have also been restored, and the former is said to be the oldest working beam engine in steam in the world still in the original building. They are still used to raise water to the summit level of the canal, their original purpose, when in steam on six weekends between Easter and the end of September. The pumping station also houses a small display of other stationary steam engines. The station is run by volunteers of the Crofton branch of the Kennet & Avon Canal Trust (telephone: 01672 851639).

Devizes Wharf, Devizes (OS 173: SU 005617). Telephone: 01380 721279.
Open February to Christmas, daily.

The Kennet & Avon Canal passes Devizes on the north-west side of the town. There the long, timbered granary building of 1810 houses the Canal Trust headquarters, a canal exhibition, information centre and shop. This is the best place to study the history of the

The Barge Inn on the Kennet & Avon Canal at Honey Street.

canal from planning up to the present day. Under a series of linked topics, the exhibition describes how the canal came about, the people who were involved in all aspects of its construction, how it was built and the trades that operated along its length. It tells, too, of the reasons for the canal's decline, the work which faced the restorers, and how the renaissance was achieved. A second extant wharf building, the old warehouse, is now the Wharf Theatre. It was here that goods, particularly coal which came via the Somerset Coal Canal, were unloaded by crane from the canal barges. The complex also has crafts, shops and the Wharfside restaurant. There are guided walks from Devizes Wharf on Sunday afternoons in summer.

Honey Street, Alton Barnes (OS 173: SU 105615).

Honey Street is a small hamlet in the Vale of Pewsey on the Kennet & Avon Canal about half a mile (800 metres) south-west of Alton Barnes. Here a picturesque collection of industrial buildings was put up in association with the canal, on a stretch of particular beauty. It came about specifically to build barges and narrowboats which worked on the waterway, and the nearby Barge inn provided sustenance to boatbuilders, boat crews and the local community. There was also a timber yard. Part of the wharf, built in 1811 and rebuilt after a fire in 1854, is still there.

Kennet & Avon Canal: Kennet & Avon Canal Trust, Canal Centre, Couch Lane, Devizes SN10 1EB. Telephone: 01380 721279.

Running 87 miles (140 km) between Bristol and Reading, the Kennet & Avon was the longest and most important of the canals within Wiltshire. Authorised in 1794 and completed under the supervision of John Rennie in 1810, it was the last to decline and well into the twentieth century was still navigable, although little used, and to some degree maintained. There was no regular traffic along it after the 1930s; it was eventually closed to traffic in 1951 but was gradually brought back to life by a combination of public pressure, an organisation formed in 1955 which was to become the Kennet & Avon

Canal Trust, local authorities and British Waterways. In 1990 Queen Elizabeth II reopened the canal at Devizes.

Once crucial to the economy of the county and its limited industrial development, the canal is now a linear parkway, the longest in southern England. It is one of the county's most important green corridors – both for the wildlife which has re-established itself on and around the water and the leisure activities it offers. Amongst these are public boat cruises operated by the trust from Hungerford (telephone: 01488 683389), Pewsey (01672 62147) and Bradford-on-Avon (01225 864378). In addition there are extensive private charter cruises (including horse-drawn boats), day and holiday hire facilities on day boats, rowing boats, narrowboats and electric boats. The canal towpath is a public right of way.

Pewsey Wharf, Pewsey (OS 173: SU 158612).
The Kennet & Avon Canal passes to the north of Pewsey, where the wharf has attractive brick-built warehouses. Here the Canal Trust operates waterside tea rooms.

Swindon & Cricklade Railway, Blunsdon Station, Tadpole Lane, Blunsdon, near Swindon SN2 4DZ (OS 173: SU 110897). Telephone: 01793 771615.
Open every weekend during the year, but 'in steam' to a timetable.
Started in 1979 off a minor road west of Blunsdon St Andrew near Swindon, on the course of the disused railway to Cricklade, the Society now has a quarter of a mile (400 metres) of track and offers steam trips along it throughout the year. Every weekend visitors can see the restoration work being carried out on a number of locomotives and can walk the track, which is in the middle of the countryside and well-placed for spotting interesting fauna and flora.

The Underground Quarry, Park Lane, Corsham SN13 0QR (OS 173: SU 856704). Telephone: 01249 716288.
Open April, May, June and October, Sundays, bank holiday Mondays and summer half-term week; July to September, daily except Fridays.
At this outstanding underground quarry generations of quarrymen have dug the fashionable cream-coloured Bath stone to create fine buildings in Bath, elsewhere in Britain and around the world. The resulting labyrinth of caverns deep below the countryside is the only shaft stone mine open to the public in the world. All tours are guided tours; helmets and miner's lamps are provided and visitors are reminded that there are 159 steps up out of the quarry.

Westbury Cement Works, Trowbridge Road, Westbury (OS 183: ST 887526). Telephone: 01373 822481.
Two-hour guided tours are offered by appointment to groups of not more than twenty people, who must be at least of secondary school age.
On the plain outside Westbury, overlooked by the famous white horse, are the Blue Circle cement works, which have been in operation since 1962, and the nearby chalk quarry. The white complex sits low and long amidst its agricultural surroundings, identified by the 400 foot (122 metre) chimney. The works have the capacity to produce 700,000 tons of cement each year from the good-quality raw materials hereabouts.

Westbury Swimming Pool, Church Street, Westbury BA13 3BY. Telephone: 01373 822891.
Open daily except Christmas Day.
Visitors come here to look at the building as well as to swim. Built in 1887 by W. H. Laverton in the grounds of his mill for the use and relaxation of the millworkers, the swimming pool was subsequently presented to the town. It is said to be the only Victorian indoor swimming pool still in use and retains its ornate cast-iron roof supports, crests and hall with stained glass windows. In 1984 the interior of the building was completely refurbished and modernised when improving the water plant. The exterior of the building is unaltered. A programme is now under way to reconstruct the swimming pool in keeping with the original work. The premises have a

The only Victorian indoor swimming pool still in use is at Westbury.

resident ghost known as George whom people working at the pool claim to have seen.

Wilton Windmill, Wilton, Marlborough (OS 174: SU 276616). Telephone: 01672 870472. *Open Easter to September, Sunday afternoons, and bank holidays in summer.*

The county's only complete surviving working windmill stands on a chalk hilltop 550 feet (168 metres) above sea level overlooking Crofton, to the south of the minor road running north-east out of Wilton (near Marlborough) to Shalbourne. (This Wilton should not be confused with the town near Salisbury.) It is a five-storey brick tower mill, built in 1821 and worked until the 1890s. It fell into disuse and was closed down in the 1920s, when it became derelict. The machinery was taken down and the windmill stood in a dilapidated condition until 1971, when restoration began. When it was completed in 1976 the mill was in full working order, able to grind corn and produce the flour which is on sale throughout the summer. It has a domed cap, two common and two patent sails.

Wootton Rivers Lock, Wootton Rivers (OS 173: SU 199630).

A particularly interesting and well-kept lock-keeper's cottage stands in a picturesque setting on the Kennet & Avon Canal, to the south of the little village with its timber-framed thatched cottages. This lock once featured in a television series.

10
Other places to visit

Cholderton Rare Breeds Farm, Amesbury Road, Cholderton, Salisbury SP4 0EW. Telephone: 01980 629438.
Open April to October, daily.

The village lies on either side of the narrow river Bourne, just east of Amesbury. The farm, established in 1987, has 50 acres (20 hectares) and fine views across the southern part of the Plain towards Salisbury. The farm specialises in old breeds of British farm animals which are close to extinction and has featured several times on television. The abundance and diversity of the animals – from traditional farm animals to rare breeds of pets (the rabbit unit is one of the country's largest collections) – are the main attraction, but the farm also features conservation areas and a nature trail packed with wildlife. There are picnic areas in beautiful settings, gardens, orchards, ponds and water gardens.

Cotswold Water Park, Ashton Keynes and Lechlade (OS 163: SU 055965 and 190990). Telephone: 01285 861459.

The Water Park is in two sections along the valley of the upper Thames north of Swindon, where about a hundred lakes were formed by gravel workings, and some are still being worked for sand and gravel. The main group of those no longer being worked curves around the pretty village of Ashton Keynes, off the A419 Swindon to Cirencester road, where about 1000 acres (404 hectares) have been reclaimed. The other group barely touches the county at its most northerly point north and west of Lechlade and can be reached via the A361 Lechlade to Burford road or the A417 between Lechlade and Cirencester. Virtually any activity that can be done in or around water can be found here in season: game and coarse fishing, canoeing, sailing, windsurfing, water-skiing, powerboat racing and jet-skiing. The Water Park is the centre for a good many private watersport clubs and organisations.

Elms Cross Vineyard, Bradford-on-Avon BA15 2AL. Telephone: 01225 866917.
Open April to September, Monday, Friday and Saturday. Shop open all year.

According to the Domesday Book there was a vineyard at Bradford-on-Avon over nine hundred years ago. This one was established in 1976 and by the late 1980s had two thousand vines. Now there are 6 acres (2.4 hectares) with seven thousand five hundred vines able to produce fifteen thousand bottles of dry, medium dry and sparkling wines each year. The four varieties on sale in the shop are made in the fully equipped winery at the vineyard. There is parking, even for coaches.

Farmer Giles Farmstead, Teffont Magna, Salisbury SP3 5QY. Telephone: 01722 716388.
Open March to November, daily, and every weekend throughout the winter.

The pretty little villages of Teffont Evias and Teffont Magna lie adjacent to one other along a tributary of the river Nadder in a wooded area of south-west Wiltshire. Here a working dairy farm, with 30,000 square feet (2800 square metres) under cover, has not only opened its whole complex to visitors but has turned it into an exciting and educational experience. In the milking parlour visitors can see how cows are milked today and in the 'Dairying Through the Ages' and 'Farming Back in Time' exhibitions they can see how it used to be done. Visitors can bottle-feed sheep and hand-milk cows and enjoy all the sights, sounds and smells of a modern farm. There are a nature walk, restaurant and gift shop, a fishing lake and conservation pond, and an adventure area for children.

Longleat Safari Park, Warminster (OS 183: ST 821440).
Open late March to October, daily.

Longleat's safari park, a 100 acre (40.4

hectare) nature reserve with lions and 'white hunters', was established in 1966. Tigers were introduced in its tenth year. There is a pets' corner for children and a reserve where visitors can see giraffes, camels, zebras and cattle. There are monkeys and gorillas on their island. Visitors ride in safari buses or their own cars to get close to the wild animals, and boats take them to the hippopotamuses and sealions. There are also elephants, wolves, ostriches, antelopes and cheetahs. There are walks and places to picnic.

Roves Farm, Sevenhampton, Swindon SN6 7QG (OS 174: SU 211888). Telephone: 01793 763939.
Open: March to September, Wednesday to Sunday afternoons.

For about eight years Rupert and Joanna Burr welcomed visitors to their farm at lambing time. Then in 1993 they opened for the first time as a full-season visitor centre, offering sheep-shearing, spinning and weaving demonstrations, tractor and trailer rides. There is a guided farm trail to help visitors get the most out of this piece of countryside by the river Cole, as the seasons progress. Group visits of ten to fifteen people are available by appointment at any time, and during the season farmhouse cream teas or ploughman's lunches can be had in 'The Old Granary'.

Stert Vineyard, Barn Cottage, Stert, Devizes SN10 3JD. Telephone: 01380 723889.
Open by appointment.

In 1768 James Long of Wedhampton built a road which greatly improved the lot of the villagers of Stert, whose livelihood depended on access to nearby Devizes. The monument to commemorate this event, put up three years later, marks the thatched village which lies just off the A342, surrounded by narrow tracts of woodland. Since 1977 it has also been the home of a vineyard on an ancient site. In a good year Roy and Irene Sharman-Spiller might have just two thousand bottles of wine for sale. The owners fell in love with the cottage and acquired it in spite of the 1½ acre (0.6 hectare) vineyard! White wine is made from the Muller Thurgau grapes, and there is a small area planted with the red Wrotham Pinot vines.

Wadworth Shire Horses, Northgate Brewery, Devizes SN10 1JW. Telephone: 01380 723361.
Open (stables only) Tuesday and Thursday.

H. A. Wadworth, a farmer, took over the former cloth-factory site here in 1875, when it was already an established brewery. Wadworths bought up small local breweries, as well as inns and hotels, thus helping both to create and to supply an increasing demand for their product. The big brick building of 1885 (with 1990 additions) at one end of the market place is not open to the public, but the stables are. For more than a century Wadworth's beers have been delivered locally by a succession of Shire horses, and they are still to be seen working about the town and at shows and fairs.

The Woodland Park, Brokerswood, Westbury BA13 4EH (OS 183: ST 836523). Telephone: 01373 822238.
Open daily, all year.

Here is an 80 acre (32.3 hectare) forest which has been run by the Phillips family as a commercial undertaking since 1957. It is a working woodland which is managed to provide an ecological balance for fauna and flora and comprises a balanced mixture of self-seeded and planted specimens. The approach is by minor roads from the A350 or A36, the Warminster to Westbury or Bath roads. There are caravan and camping sites with services, ten nature trails, a 5 acre (2 hectare) lake with wildfowl and an adventure playground. Visitors may picnic in the woodland area or use the designated picnic or barbecue sites, and they may wander at will along the paths, with due regard for the wildlife. The woodland paths are named and this, together with the map, ensures that everyone derives maximum benefit and no one gets lost. Organised walks can be arranged, as may special facilities for schools. The trails range from less than 300 yards (275 metres) to more than a mile (1.6 km). There is also the enjoyable Smokey Oak Railway, which is over one-third of a mile (500 metres) long.

11
Famous people

It is not surprising that such an ancient county should produce many antiquarians, historians and archaeologists, notable in their chosen spheres but largely unrecognised in the larger context of fame. An example is **Sir Richard Colt Hoare** (1758–1838) of Stourhead, a traveller, scholar and book collector whose field studies with the archaeologist William Cunnington of ancient sites on Salisbury Plain resulted in a monumental work, *The Ancient History of Wiltshire*, followed by *The History of Modern Wiltshire*. **William Cunnington** (1754–1810), who lived at Heytesbury, came from Northamptonshire but adopted Wiltshire as an antiquarian and geologist. He is remembered by a tablet in the south transept of the church.

The arts are also well represented in the county, although most sojourns were fleeting. For example **John Gay** (1685–1732) is said to have written the book of his most famous work *The Beggar's Opera* in an artificial cave or stone room overlooking the river Avon from the abbey grounds at Amesbury. At the time he would have been visiting the Duke of Queensberry. **Joseph Addison** (1672–1719), the poet, essayist and writer of hymns (in which he was influenced by the countryside about), was born in the rectory at Milston, near Amesbury, where his father, Launcelot Addison, was rector. Joseph represented Malmesbury in Parliament in 1708 but never spoke in the House. The man who in 'Orchestra' wrote one of the great poems of the Elizabethan age, **Sir John Davies** (1569–1626) – poet, lawyer and political writer – was born at Tisbury. The Reverend **William Jay** (1769–1853), 'boy preacher', 'Jay of Bath', and arguably the most famous nonconformist preacher of his day, began life in a thatched cottage 'about an equal distance from Wardour Castle, Pithouse and Fonthill' and ended it at Bradford-on-Avon. In between he was for sixty-two years preacher at the Argyle Chapel, Bath.

The opium-addicted poet **Samuel Taylor Coleridge** (1772–1834) lived at Calne between 1814 and 1816, in a house owned by his friend John Morgan. He would have been completing *Biographia Literaria*, which was published the following year. The novelist **Henry Fielding** (1707–54) lived for a while at Salisbury, where his grandfather was canon of the cathedral. He occupied at least two houses in the city and eventually bought one there. It was at Salisbury, too, that he met Charlotte Cradock, with whom he was to contract a ten-year marriage. Critics believe that she may have been the original of Sophia Western in *Tom Jones* and the heroine *Amelia*. The poet **Sir Henry John Newbolt** (1862–1939), best remembered as the writer of 'Drake's Drum' and 'The Fighting Temeraire', lived at Netherhampton House, a seventeenth- and early eighteenth-century building in the Nadder valley. Newbolt was Comptroller of Telecommunications during the First World War and an official war historian.

The author and dramatist **Reginald Arkell** (1882–1959) was born just over the border at Lechlade and went to Burford Grammar School but lived as an adult in Marston Meysey in the far north of the county. A journalist before the First World War, Arkell wrote a biography of Richard Jefferies and enjoyed wide acclaim for a succession of theatrical reviews and musical comedies. The thriller writer **John Creasey** (1908–73) lived at New Hall, Bodenham, from 1958. Four times married, Creasey was a well-known figure in nearby Salisbury, and a writing phenomenon. A master of crime fiction, he produced more than 560 novels under his own name and a number of pseudonyms – Michael Halliday, Gordon Ashe, Jeremy York, Norman Deane and Anthony Morton. He gave us the Toff, the Baron, Gideon of the Yard, Inspector West, Dr Palfrey and Department Z, wrote on travel and philosophy and was Liberal parliamentary candidate for Bournemouth.

Aldhelm (c.640–709)

Great miracles were claimed for the founder of Malmesbury Abbey, said variously to have been the son of a weaver or a person of royal lineage. He was educated at Malmesbury and eventually entered the monastery there. Aldhelm was a scholar monk working in the so-called Dark Ages under the Irish influences of his teacher (said to be the hermit Maildulf, founder of the town), the thrust of Christianity from Ireland and the Saxon traditions of his ancestry. A poet and accomplished musician who mostly wrote in Latin, he was for a while at Canterbury under the strong influences of Rome. And so it was that when Maildulf died and Aldhelm succeeded him at Malmesbury it was the Christianity of Rome which came to Wessex.

Aldhelm established religious centres at Bradford-on-Avon and Frome; the plan and part of the wonderful little church of St Lawrence at Bradford-on-Avon is what is left of Aldhelm's centre there. His literary works included a translation of the Psalms of David and two treatises, *De Virginitate* and *Aenigmata*. He also set about building an abbey at Malmesbury, by all accounts with much royal and ecclesiastical sponsorship and patronage, and the cathedral church at Sherborne, having been consecrated that town's first bishop. Aldhelm died at Doulting, Somerset, and was brought back to Malmesbury in preference to the place of his bishopric for burial in a tomb held as a shrine and revered as a centre for miracles. At one time his festival day, 31st March, occasioned a four-day feast every year.

John Aubrey (1626–97)

Born at Easton Piercy in the parish of Kington St Michael near Calne, educated at Malmesbury Grammar School and Trinity College, Oxford, Aubrey the antiquarian's great claim to fame lay in his being a remarkable collector of gossip. (He was portrayed wonderfully in this guise in recent years by the actor Roy Dotrice, in a one-man stage production which gave Aubrey a new lease of fame!) A weakly child by his own account and once stricken by a 'grevous ague', he was fascinated by conversations from an early age and admitted to preferring the company of tradesmen and old men to the usual pursuits of childhood.

The young Aubrey inherited a large estate, which was subsequently whittled away by lawsuits which dogged him for decades, and was unlucky in numerous love affairs. He became an antiquary at college, was much taken by the ancient sites of Wiltshire and was responsible for reviving interest in Avebury, of which he made a plan in 1660. Between 1656 and 1670 he put together the *Topographical Collection of Wiltshire*. Famed for his 'cathedral' and 'parish church' comparison between Avebury and Stonehenge, it was at the latter that he noted the so-called 'Aubrey Holes' in 1666, which were rediscovered during excavations in the 1920s.

Aubrey published a book of fables, dreams and omens called *Miscellanies* in 1696 and wrote a history of Surrey (where he lived for many years), which was eventually published in 1719. But he is best-known for what became *Brief Lives* – a collection of tittle-tattle and anecdote about well-known people which he gave to Anthony à Wood together with other material which included a biographical work about his friend Thomas Hobbes, the philosopher. Anthony à Wood described Aubrey as 'a shiftless person, roving and maggoty-headed, and something little better than crazed' and in that may lie the key both to his failure to publish much of substance during his life and the enduring nature of *Brief Lives*.

William Beckford (1750–1844)

When his father, then the richest merchant in England, died in 1770 young William inherited the magnificent Palladian mansion where he was born at Fonthill, set in 4900 acres (1983 hectares) of land. Beckford senior had bought the manor in 1740, only to see it destroyed by fire. He spent £250,000 putting up the building which passed to his son, an eccentric semi-recluse who loved animals. With the estate came a £1m fortune plus £100,000 a year from business interests, which allowed William to travel extensively and accumulate a circle of influential friends. William was also well-educated and at the age of twenty-two wrote the eastern romance *Vathek* in French, saying it took him 'three days and two nights of hard labour. I never took off my clothes the whole time'. *Vathek* was published in English in 1786.

Beckford came home from his travels abroad to Fonthill in 1781 and two years later married Lady Margaret Gordon; but five years on she was dead and William went abroad again. It was to be another decade before he settled at Fonthill, to some extent a changed man. He had a 12 foot (3.6 metre) high wall put up around the estate and Beckford shut himself up with a handful of friends. And it was here that he conceived the idea of a Gothic building – 'a convent partly in ruins and partly perfect', which James Wyatt was commissioned to build (see page 103). The eccentric personality of the man is emphasised in the contrast between the solitude of his daily life and the way in which he launched himself into building projects and clearly revelled in the interest they promoted both locally and nationally. In 1822-3 he disposed of the estate and went to live at Lansdowne, Bath, with his collection of books and paintings.

William Lisle Bowles (1762–1850)

That William Bowles should be singled out as a worthy amidst any number of eighteenth- and nineteenth-century Wiltshire clerics who pursued similar interests is largely due to his associations. Bowles successfully entered the lists of poetry criticism with Byron and Campbell, was a friend of the poet Tom Moore and is said to have been admired by Coleridge, Wordsworth and Southey. Poet and critic himself, benefactor, antiquary and biographer, Bowles was vicar of Cricklade, of Bremhill from 1805 to 1845, and canon of Salisbury, where he died.

Notably retiring and very absent-minded, Bowles was a lover of nature, who wrote passionately of country matters in his poetry, and something of a gardener. His vicarage at Bremhill is now Bremhill Court, which owes its outward appearance largely to Bowles. Of his garden not much remains, but Moore wrote

of it: 'He has frittered away its beauty with grottoes, hermitages, and Shenstonian descriptions; when company is coming he cries "Here John, run with the crucifix and missal to the hermitage and set the fountain going." His sheep bells are tuned in thirds and fifths, but he is an excellent fellow notwithstanding.' Bowles's chief prose work was his two-volume *Life of Bishop Ken*.

John Britton (1771–1857)

The son of a baker and small farmer, the antiquarian John Britton was born at Kington St Michael, in whose church he and Aubrey are commemorated in a stained glass window of 1857. Britton had a hard childhood, first at home and then in servitude in London, where, spurned in love and disowned by his relatives, he lived in poverty and ill health whilst struggling to better himself. In 1801 he published the *Beauties of Wiltshire*, a monumental work in two volumes; between 1814 and 1835 he brought out *Cathedral Antiquities of England* in fourteen volumes. He also published a collection of Aubrey's material on Wiltshire. Britton is commemorated by a brass monument in the north transept of Salisbury Cathedral.

George Crabbe (1754–1832)

Most of Crabbe's writing was published between 1775 and 1812, so it was as a famous narrative poet that he came to the living of St James, Trowbridge, in 1814. During the latter part of his life his proximity to Bowood, a centre for literary debate at the time, attracted him back into the kind of society he had enjoyed as a young man. A friend of Tom Moore and William Lisle Bowles, Crabbe was also well acquainted with Wordsworth, Southey, Samuel Rogers and Sir Walter Scott, whom he visited in Edinburgh, where much of his earlier work was published. His only published work to come during the eighteen years he spent at Trowbridge – and it is considered one of his best books – was *Tales of the Hall* (1819). He spent a lot of his time pursuing his hobbies of geology and botany and was a familiar sight hammering out fossils from the local quarries.

Crabbe made friends with the rich cloth

Fox Talbot, who lived at Lacock Abbey, was a pioneer of photography and developed the paper negative.

merchants of the town, clearly liked his comforts and took opium. He was also very popular with the ladies, whose company he enjoyed. Sometimes naive and unworldly, he was also a man of strong principles and, once having made up his mind, adhered to them with some conviction. At Trowbridge he was moderate in his preaching, and although this was against the trend of the time he was preferred for it. At his death he left a substantial amount of unpublished work, which was collected in print by his son in 1834. George Crabbe was buried in the chancel of St James, where there is a memorial to him by E. H. Baily.

John Dryden (1631–1700)

It was to Charlton Park near Malmesbury, then a Jacobean mansion dating from the early seventeenth century, that the great dramatist, poet and critic came during the plague and the Great Fire of London. Charlton was the home of his friend Sir Charles Howard, also a composer of songs, sonnets and plays, and it was in the writing of the last that the two became friends. At Charlton in 1663 Dryden briefly but successfully courted Elizabeth Jane Howard, his host's daughter, a play, *The Indian Queen,* was completed, and the men indulged themselves in long literary discussions. It was at Charlton too, in 1666, that Dryden wrote *Annus Mirabilis,* one of his longer poems. He also perpetuated a connection with the county through his representation of Thomas Thynne, owner of Longleat from 1670, as the 'Wise' Issachar in *Absalom and Achitophel* (1681), his political satire in verse.

Stephen Duck (1705–56)

Born of lowly parents at Charlton in the Vale of Pewsey, Duck was encouraged to study literature whilst working as a farm labourer. He took to writing indifferent poetry, which was nevertheless approved of in Marlborough society, and the poet enjoyed the patronage of Frances, Countess of Hertford. He was introduced to Queen Caroline, who became his benefactor, gave him a house and a pension and in 1733 made him a Yeoman of the Guard. He published 'The Thresher's Labour' in a collection of 1736 and was thereafter known as the 'Thresher Poet'. His poetry continued to be criticised, as was his favour in royal circles. Swift wrote of his work: 'Tho' 'tis confessed that those who ever saw his poems think them all not worth a straw.' In 1746 Stephen Duck took holy orders but, just four years after becoming rector of Byfleet in 1752, drowned himself at Reading whilst very depressed.

Geoffrey Grigson (1905–85) and Jane Grigson (1928–90)

Poet, essayist, critic and country writer, Geoffrey Grigson was born in Cornwall but came to a cottage at Littletown, Broad Town, near Swindon, before the Second World War. He was in his thirties and the editor of a periodical anthology, *New Verse*. There he took on a picture researcher whom he later married, and from around 1965 Jane Grigson wrote a succession of cookery books which made her one of the most widely read cookery writers of her time. The couple later moved to the seventeenth-century Broad Town Farm, and the cottage was sold to Nikolaus Pevsner, the architectural historian. At both places the Grigsons created fine gardens. Geoffrey was the writer of several volumes of verse and prose works, compiler of a number of anthologies of poetry and the author of biographical and autobiographical works.

William Hazlitt (1778–1830)

In 1808 the essayist and literary critic married Sarah Stoddart, a friend of Charles and Mary Lamb, and came to live at her cottage in Winterslow near Salisbury. The marriage failed (although they were not divorced until 1822) and after about three years Hazlitt spent little time there. He is, however, also associated with the Pheasant inn, writing 'I can take mine ease at mine inn beside the blazing hearth... and seated around discourse the silent hours away'. It was at Winterslow that he wrote the *Winterslow Essays* and, whatever the state of his marriage, he clearly enjoyed living on Salisbury Plain. Charles and Mary Lamb visited him, and he used to take his various friends for long walks.

George Herbert (1593–1633)

The village of Bemerton near Wilton is renowned for its seventeenth-century rector, the poet and divine who was revered almost as a saint in his own lifetime and who came there in 1630. The rectory in which he lived and died still stands, although much changed. George was related to the Herberts, the Earls of Pembroke of Wilton House, and it was through family connections that he was offered the living of Bemerton. From there he frequently walked to Salisbury Cathedral, which he believed to have no equal on earth. Always a frail and consumptive person, he met his wife, Jane Danvers, as a result of a stay in Dauntsey where he was taking the air for his health's sake, and it must have been around this time that he began writing poetry. He wrote a single volume of poetry – *The Temple*,

a short account of the life and duties of a country parson called *A Priest to the Temple* and some collections of proverbs. The poems were published the year he died and were an instant success. Amongst his particular friends were Izaak Walton, who is best remembered for *The Compleat Angler* and his friendship of clergymen, and the theologian Nicholas Ferrar. As an English poet of the metaphysical school and one of the finest religious poets, George Herbert's work has gone in and out of fashion and it was not until the twentieth century that it was fully appreciated.

Thomas Hobbes (1588–1679)

The philosopher – sometimes called the father of materialism – and ardent royalist was born at Westport, Malmesbury, where his father was parish priest; his education was paid for by his uncle, a wealthy glover of the town. After Magdalen Hall, Oxford, he travelled through France and Italy on several occasions – sometimes in the role of tutor – meeting thinkers, mathematicians and scientists of the day including Galileo, Descartes and Mersenne.

At home he was befriended by Francis Bacon and Ben Jonson and collaborated artistically with both. In 1641 he went to France to avoid the English Civil War, which he had anticipated, and there began his best-known work, *Leviathan; or the Matter, Form, and Power of a Commonwealth, Ecclesiastical and Civil*. It was published in 1651 and did him few favours, either politically at the Restoration or in religious circles, wherein he was condemned as an atheist.

Otherwise Hobbes was a prolific writer on politics, mathematics and religion, a poet and a pioneer of modern political science. Amongst his better-known publications are *Elements of Law* (1651), *Philosophical Rudiments* (1651) and, in his old age, translations of Homer. He spent much of his life as tutor or companion to the Cavendish family (the Earls of Devonshire) at Chatsworth, Derbyshire, where he seems to have lived by a strict but comfortable regime of his own choosing.

Richard Jefferies (1848–87)

Born at Coate farmhouse (now a small museum to his memory) near Swindon, John Richard Jefferies was essentially a naturalist and prose poet. Much of his work derived from observing the wildlife around the nearby reservoir for the Wilts & Berks Canal which had been built in 1822, and from the sheer exhilaration he felt wandering around the Wiltshire Downs. His ability to recall and record the minutest of details and set them down accurately and in a beautiful writing style guaranteed success in his lifetime and continued interest to this day. (There is a flourishing Richard Jefferies Society.)

He became a journalist on the *North Wilts Herald* in 1866, and the lodgings he had close by the newspaper offices in Victoria Road, Swindon, are marked by a plaque. From here he learned shorthand and wrote for several newspapers, notably the *Swindon Advertiser* and *North Wilts Herald.*

Jefferies's early attempts as a novelist failed but were revived with *The Dewy Morn* and late in his short life became accomplished with *Greene Ferne Farm* (1880) and *Amaryllis at the Fair* (1887), his best-known work of fiction. His success was assured with publication of *The Gamekeeper At Home* (1877), the reprint of a series of pieces he had contributed to *The Pall Mall Gazette*. But it is the personification *Wood Magic* (1881) and the acutely observed *Bevis* (1882), the story of his own childhood, which have given their author a deserved place in English literature.

Richard Jefferies lived part of his life in London and Sussex, where he died at Goring, so ill that for two years he had to dictate all his work to his wife.

Hugh Latimer (c.1485–1555)

The Perpendicular pulpit from which Latimer preached as rector of West Kington, in the north-west of the county, can still be seen in the otherwise mid nineteenth-century church. Here Latimer lived in his 'little Bishoprick of West Kington' between 1530 and 1535, when he was appointed Bishop of Worcester. Aubrey tells us that on the way to the rectory there was a little scrubbed oak in which Latimer used to sit. And Latimer himself wrote how, living just half a mile from the Fosse Way, he watched 'flocks of pil-

grims' coming up from the West Country on their way to several venerated places, but chiefly Hailes Abbey near Winchcombe, Gloucestershire. It was during his time at West Kington that Latimer was accused of heresy but absolved. However, under Mary I he was convicted of heresy and burnt at the stake in Oxford.

Thomas Moore (1779–1852)

Sloperton Cottage near Bromham is where the little Dublin-born poet spent most of the second half of his life, coming to live there in 1817. A patriot who achieved status as the national poet of Ireland, Tom Moore enjoyed the friendship and patronage of the Marquis of Lansdowne. He achieved wide fame as a romantic poet, lyricist and collector of folk songs; he was also a notable biographer and novelist. In his lifetime he was second in popularity only to his friend Byron as a poet of the romantic period. Said to be 'genial hearted', he is also remembered as the person who destroyed Byron's own memoirs rather than have them published, whether as an act of kindness to his late friend's reputation or to the sensibilities of the reading public of the day we shall never know. Moore is buried on the north side of the churchyard at Bromham where the inscription recorded the details of himself, his wife and their three children, who all died tragically young. The west window is a memorial to him, put up in 1879, and in 1906 a tall Celtic cross was erected to his memory in the churchyard.

Joseph Priestley (1733–1804)

Clergyman, philosopher and chemist, Dr Priestley lived between 1772 and 1779 with his family in Calne, where he held the office of librarian and literary companion to Lord Shelburne, first Marquis of Lansdowne, at Bowood House. The arrangement gave him the time and the freedom to pursue his interests, including his experiments into the nature of chemical discharges, and it was at Calne that Priestley wrote some of his educational and religious theses. The laboratory at Bowood House, now open to the public, is the actual room where Priestley discovered oxygen on 1st August 1774.

Siegfried Sassoon (1886–1967)

The poet and prose writer Siegfried Loraine Sassoon was a countryman by inclination who adopted Wiltshire in middle age. Although born in London, he had been educated at Marlborough College before going to Cambridge and was the author of several published books of poems, even before the antiwar poetry for which he is more readily remembered. Sassoon had embarked on his semi-autobiographical fictional trilogy *The Memoirs of George Thurston* (1928-36) before he settled in Wiltshire. In 1933 he married and went to live at Heytesbury House near Warminster, a fine eighteenth-century mansion in its own grounds which was to be his home for the rest of his life. It was here that he wrote *Siegfried's Journey* (1945) in three volumes and continued to compose fine poetry as well as nostalgic prose works. These include *The Old Century* (1938) and *Weald of Youth* (1942). In 1948 he published a biography of George Meredith. Sassoon died at Heytesbury.

Arthur George Street (1882–1966)

Farmer's Glory (1932) was the hugely successful book for which A. G. Street is best remembered. *Strawberry Roan*, published in the same year and later filmed, and *To Be a Farmer's Boy* (1935) quickly confirmed his position as a pre-eminent chronicler of the countryside. Born at Wilton, where his father rented a farm from the Earl of Pembroke, Street was educated at the then newly rebuilt Dauntsey's School (founded 1543) at West Lavington, then lived abroad for some years before taking over the farm in 1918. Author, journalist, lecturer and broadcaster, he began writing only as a hobby when he was nearly forty. During the next thirty years he produced as many books of fiction or cameos of rural life and is regarded as one of the best interpreters of his subject in the twentieth century. He was a much read columnist in *Farmer's Weekly* and a popular team member of BBC Radio's *Any Questions*. From 1951 he lived at Milton Farm, South Newton.

William Henry Fox Talbot (1800–77)

The history of Lacock is inextricably linked to the story of the Talbot family and the earlier blood line who were owners of the village from the mid sixteenth-century suppression of the Augustinian nunnery. The tenth owner, W. H. Fox Talbot, was a pioneer of photography, whose 'Latticed Window', taken at his home at Lacock Abbey in 1835, is the earliest paper negative in existence. Other calotypes of those who lived and worked on the estate during the next few years are amongst the earliest taken in the world.

Fox Talbot in theory inherited both the family estate and the village on the death of his father, William Davenport Talbot, in 1801 when he was just a few months old. However, the family travelled abroad and did not return to the house until 1827. By this time Fox Talbot had enjoyed a privileged life in scientific, artistic and political circles and had made much of educational opportunities at Harrow and Cambridge. Said to be a shy, private person who was not fond of public life, he nevertheless became an accomplished scholar and scientist; he was made a member of the Royal Society in 1831 and represented Chippenham as a Whig in the reformed parliament of 1832.

Throughout the 1830s he was developing his interests in photographic processes and experimenting widely at Lacock. His work into the negative-positive process led to the developing of the subsequent image. Fox Talbot was the first to understand the effects of stabilising a negative with a fixing solution. The results of his researches were published in 1839 as a reaction to the work of Daguerre, whom he very much admired.

Ralph Whitlock (born 1914)

Of all the Wiltshire writers on country matters, Ralph Whitlock is undeniably the most expansive and probably the most widely known by people alive today. He is a crusader for our heritage, as defined by his own words, recorded by the present writer in 1965: 'We have a countryside littered with things that are going to disappear before long, and it is worthwhile making ourselves familiar with what is left, and in recording and making some kind of permanent record of what is now to be seen but what our grandchildren will not see.' Born at

Pitton (and latterly living close by at Winterslow), he was educated at Bishop Wordsworth School, Salisbury, and took up writing for the *Western Gazette* in 1932. A prolific and well-respected journalist, he was farming editor of *The Field* from 1946 to 1973. In more than a hundred books spanning six decades, Whitlock has informed, educated and amused adults and children alike in matters of country life, mythology, natural history, folklore, social history and topography.

William of Malmesbury (c.1090 to c.1143)

Learned, well-travelled and a figure of national importance, William of Malmesbury was a descriptive writer of strength and vigour who shaped much of our perception of early history. Preferring the role of librarian and precentor at Malmesbury Abbey, where he was educated, and refusing the post of abbot, William gave us *Gesta Regum Anglorum*, his anecdotal history of the kings of England from AD 449 to 1127, written in Latin and dedicated to Robert, Duke of Gloucester. This was followed by a contemporary history, *Historia Novella*, which continued the story into the reign of Stephen. Both are lively accounts of the times, spiced with the stuff of legend as well as historical fact and opinion, such as his comments about King Arthur. Amongst his other writings are *Gesta Pontificum Anglorum* (1125) and *De Antiquitate Glastoniensis Ecclesiae* (1129-39). A contemporary of Geoffrey of Monmouth, William's writing was much less fanciful and romantic and altogether more reliable.

Alfred Williams (1877–1930)

Known as the 'hammerman poet', self-taught scholar, linguist and market gardener, Owen Alfred Williams was born at South Marston near Swindon, and the cottage where he lived may still be seen in the centre of the village. Living in poverty after his father left the family, Williams was in full-time employment locally at eleven years old, and at fifteen he was at the forge of the Great Western Railway works in Swindon. There, in what was known as the stamping shop or 'hot shop', Williams spent his meal breaks behind the great furnaces teaching himself

Latin and Greek.

In 1915, the year after he retired to his market garden at South Marston through ill health, he published his most poignant and enduring book; *Life in a Railway Factory* was an exposé of a tough regime and remains a wonderful piece of industrial history. A poet of nature, Williams went on to write a number of good books on folk life: *A Wiltshire Village* (1912), *Villages of the White Horse* (1913), *Round about the Upper Thames* (1922) and *Folk Songs of the Upper Thames* (1923). He died just after receiving a civil list pension and is remembered on memorials to him on Liddington Hill and Barbury Down.

Sir Christopher Wren (1632–1723)

Son of Dr Christopher Wren, the rector of East Knoyle, Wiltshire's most famous native was born there in the old rectory, which was demolished in 1888. He was privately educated before going to Wadham College, Oxford. Said to be a mathematical genius in his mid teens, at a time when his father was losing his living in the Civil War and being indicted by Parliament, his progress seems not to have been checked by family problems. At twenty-five he was professor of astronomy in Gresham College; Charles II appointed him Surveyor of the Board of Works and he was elected a Fellow of the Royal Society.

Wren was hardly tried when he was given the job of rebuilding many of the churches of London and a number of public buildings following the Great Fire of 1666. His work is characterised by graceful interiors that provided for the central preaching position required by the change in liturgy at the time and for the increasing size of the congregations, and by a wide variety of spires. There was little church building outside the capital at the time, so the Wren influence is rarely felt. In his native county, only Farley church may have been built to a design of his influence, for he was known to both the sponsor and the builder, and the Choristers School at Salisbury was rebuilt in the Wren manner in 1717. The spire of Salisbury Cathedral was strengthened at his recommendation to his friend, fellow mathematician and astronomer Bishop Seth Ward.

12
Customs and folklore

Moonraking and smuggling

People born and bred in Wiltshire are called 'Moonrakers'. It all came about because sixteenth-century Dutch and Flemish wool merchants resident in the county were unable to import their favourite whisky and gin without paying heavy import duty. Wiltshire smugglers quickly established up-country routes between the deserted Hampshire coast and Swindon, from where the contraband was distributed into Gloucestershire. On one such overnight journey a group from **Bishops Cannings** and **All Cannings** were surprised by excisemen. Quickly they hid their kegs in Southbroom Pond and pretended to be raking the water with hay rakes for the 'cheese' apparently sunken in its depths. The excisemen decided that these were just a group of rustic simpletons, trying to fish out the reflection of the moon, and passed on. In another version the moonrakers claimed to be fishing for that part of the moon which had fallen from the sky. Just to complicate matters further, it has also been suggested that the contraband may have been tobacco, hidden in a Wiltshire cheese. Certainly rum, brandy, whisky, tea and tobacco were all regularly smuggled into Wiltshire and often delivered to important people throughout the county either to order or as payment for their silence.

Both **Collingbourne Ducis** and **Devizes** have claimed their ponds for the possible site of the Moonraker legend, and **Swindon** itself is not without possibilities. The Bell inn was once the clearing house for contraband at the centre of the smuggling trade and the kegs might have been hidden in underground tunnels, arteries which linked the cellars of private houses, inns and even the manor in Old Swindon. No one knows the extent of these tunnels and they have been blocked up or built over as they were discovered in recent years. Some time ago an employee of a wine merchant in The Square fell through the floor of what was believed to be the lowest cellar and found a drain. To discover where the drain led, a coloured dye was put down it – only to reappear in the pond of the nearby Goddard estate. The wine merchant's shop and a very old inn which was then next to it had both been built above the tunnels. Could the way in have been through the pond?

Villagers' names

'Moonraker' is not the only name by which Wiltshire people are known; some villagers have suffixes of their own. At **Aldbourne** villagers are known as Aldbourne dabchicks. It came about when a strange bird appeared on the pond. An ancient was brought in a wheelbarrow to identify it and after three revolutions of the water pronounced it to be a dabchick. The people of **Stratton St Margaret** are known as Stratton crocodiles after a group of men who, armed with agricultural implements, set out to apprehend the creature which one of their company thought had crawled out of a ditch. It turned out that the alarm had been raised over a lady's stole.

Wiltshire customs

The only ancient custom still taking place in the county is that enacted by the people of **Great Wishford**, who annually assert their right to gather wood and rear cattle in the woodlands of Grovely. The ceremony involves cutting an oak bough from the forest, decking it in ribbons and hanging it from the church tower. Before the Restoration this custom took place at various times between the morning of May Day and Whit Monday and was accompanied by feasting and merrymaking. Afterwards it was celebrated on 29th May, beginning before dawn. With it were associated the mystic cry of 'Grovely, Grovely and all Grovely', which symbolised the people's all-embracing claim to the forest, and processional dancing which con-

The Crammer at Devizes is one of the places claimed to be the Moonrakers' pond.

tinued as far as Salisbury Cathedral.

Exemption from paying tithes was first granted to villagers at **Wootton Bassett** by Cistercian monks in the twelfth century. Until late in the nineteenth century this was celebrated and re-established by a custom known as word-ale, hosted each year around All Saints Day by one of the tenants on the manor lands for all of the others. It consisted of much hymn-singing, some prayers of thanks and considerable ale-drinking. Then a notch was cut on a yard-long hazel rod, to be kept by the following year's host tenant.

Wiltshire flyers

People sometimes leap off high places to make a point. Most famous of the Wiltshire flyers was Oliver, a monk who in the year 1010 strapped wings to his arms and launched himself from the tower of **Malmesbury Abbey**. Oliver broke his hips and was crippled for the rest of his days, although he achieved further fame as a prophet. Then there was Olive Sharrington who in 1574 hurled herself from the battlements of **Lacock Abbey** because

her father refused to let her marry. Her billowing skirts acted like a parachute and her fall was broken when she landed on her lover. It all so upset her father that when both the young people had recovered he gave his permission for the wedding. Imagine, too, the awe with which the travelling steeple flyer Thomas Kidman was received by the villagers of **Bromham** in 1735. Kidman stretched his rope from the church spire to the ground, sat on his board and began the descent. Part way down, the steeple gave way, Kidman lurched off course and landed in a tree.

Myths and legends

In the early 1960s the present writer put together the first source list of recorded hauntings in the county, at a time of great interest in Wiltshire's folklore, myths and legends. What follows serves only to whet the appetite of those with such interests, because there are now a great many books which are dedicated to these matters. The best contemporary ones are noted on page 157.

Wiltshire tales

In **Broad Hinton** church – where it is claimed a man once watched his own funeral taking place — there is an elaborate monument of 1597 to Sir Thomas and Lady Anne Wroughton and their children. They are for ever kneeling in prayer, but only she has hands. It is said that the sight of her reading a Bible instead of attending to his meal so incensed Sir Thomas one day when he arrived home from hunting that he tore the book from her hands and flung it into the fire. At once his own hands and those of their children withered away. A hand, too, was involved at **Draycot Cerne** in 1610 when Sir Walter Long's second wife succeeded in getting her husband to change his will so that the manor would not be left to her stepson. Sir Walter employed a clerk to add the codicil, but each time he tried to do so a ghostly white hand cast a shadow over the parchment.

Children figure in plenty at **Great Wishford**, where the tomb of Thomas Bonham in the church is said to have been built from the offerings of travellers, thankful to be safely home through the forest. Bonham himself was so upset when his wife gave birth to twins that he went away for seven years. It is said that some time after his return she gave birth to seven children at one confinement.

In the eighteenth century a cobbler of **Bulford** so angered villagers by badly treating his apprentices that they made his effigy and daily marched it through the streets, to the accompaniment of much noise and derision, before stringing it up on mock gallows. Friendless and driven to despair, the poor man eventually hanged himself in deference to the will of the people. This kind of mob law is a parallel of wooset hunting, which went on all over the county in pursuit of married persons suspected of adultery. The mob usually formed a 'band' composed of farm and household utensils, which struck up outside the suspect's house. It continued all night, three nights on and three nights off, through fifteen nights. Infidelity was not something to be kept quiet in Wiltshire.

Littlecote Manor and more than a score of other estates were inherited by nine-year-old William Darrell in the mid sixteenth century.

His life became one of lawsuits, quarrels and debts, during which he pawned possessions, was charged as an accomplice to murder, spent time in jail on libel charges, had many mistresses, including, it is said, his own sister, and came to be known as 'Wild' Darrell. One night a local midwife named Mother Barnes was roused by a coachman, who promised her high payment to go with him. She had to be blindfolded and should never divulge anything of the event. She was taken to a big house where she met a ferocious man and delivered a lady of a child. The man immediately took the baby and flung it into the fire. Mother Barnes could not keep this quiet; she identified Littlecote Manor, correctly numbered the steps on the staircase and produced a piece of bed curtain which she had cut out whilst she was there. Darrell was accused of murder but allegedly bribed the judge and was acquitted. In 1589 he was thrown from his horse and killed, for ever to be seen on his phantom steed at night. The ghost of a baby is said to haunt an oak-panelled room at the house, and a bedroom has the ghost of Darrell's mistress.

Some tales of the Plain

The ghost of a murdered boy figures in the Wiltshire tale of a murderer caught by his own guilt. A sailor named Gervase Matcham was crossing **Salisbury Plain** with his friend John Sheppard in a storm in 1786. Suddenly Matcham began to see fearful visions, and the ghost of a drummer boy attached itself to the travellers. Matcham at once recognised the spectre as that of a child he had murdered some years previously, and when the presence could not be shaken off he confessed his guilt and pleaded to be taken before the magistrates. He was arrested and hanged whilst the ghostly drummer boy looked on.

There are many tales associated with the Plain, for example that of the travelling drummer who was arrested during the seventeenth century for begging and banging his drum in **Tidworth**. The instrument was appropriated by the local JP, in whose house banging was heard from that time on. An exciting event took place in 1816 at the old **Winterslow** tavern called The Hut, later to become the

The Grovely procession at Great Wishford recalls the rights of the villagers in the local woodlands.

Pheasant inn. The leading horse of the incoming mail-coach from Exeter was suddenly set upon by an escaped lioness, a particularly terrifying matter since it is unlikely that many of the people involved would have seen such an animal before. Her attention was diverted by a dog and the arrival of her owner, a travelling showman who was at pains to vouch for her docility, and the animal slunk off, quietened down and was relatively easily secured.

Travellers crossing the Plain in the eighteenth century did so in fear of the highwayman Thomas Boulter (1748–78), whose ghost is still to be seen on dark and stormy nights. Boulter was the son of a convicted horse-stealer, the miller of **Poulshot**. Although known for his courteous manner and sentimentality, this endearing rogue eventually got his come-uppance at Winchester assizes.

The mystery of Stonehenge

In modern times people gather at **Stonehenge** to witness sunrise on 1st May, the festival of the god Bel to whom sacred fires were lighted by the Druids. The intentions of New Age travellers, eager to hold their contemporary festivals at the summer solstice, are annually thwarted by the authorities, who are alarmed at the damage which people have caused to Britain's most enigmatic monument. Indeed the ruinous condition of the monument has in the past been attributed not to the hands of time or man but to that of God, angered by the pagan worship which has taken place there!

A contemporary of Caesar, Diodorus Siculus, made reference to a circular temple dedicated to the sun and under the auspices of the Druids; so too did Ninnius in *c*.617. Dr John Smith championed the Druids' claim in *Choir Gaur; The Grand Orrery of the Ancient Druids Commonly Called Stonehenge on Salisbury Plain*, published in 1771. It was he who first concluded that, when viewed from the Altar Stone, the midsummer sun would have risen over the Friar's Heel or Bowing Stone and that the large flat stone between this and the entrance might have been a sacrificial altar. The antiquarian John Aubrey agreed with this in his work *Monumenta Britannica*. It was he who introduced Charles II to the monument and claimed the king had tested the theory that it is impossible to count the same number of stones twice.

Dr Smith divided the temple into equal parts, representing each sign of the zodiac. He pronounced that it was a mathematical observatory for calculating the time, days of the year, etcetera, from the position of the sun in relation to the Friar's Heel. Nearly two centuries later, in 1966, the astronomer Gerald Hawkins developed a similar theory, producing credible calculations in support of its being an early computer linked to the movements of the sun and moon.

Writing in 1170, Geoffrey of Monmouth had even more fanciful ideas. The stones, it appears, had been taken from Africa to County Kildare in Ireland by a race of giants. They came to Salisbury Plain in the sixth century, when Aurelius Ambrosians was resisting the Saxons. The Saxon Hengist arranged a meeting with Vortigern at Amesbury, where he killed the Briton and 460 of his men. Some accounts say that Aurelius Ambrosianus erected the stones as a memorial over Vortigern's grave, others that it marks the spot where he took his revenge on Hengist.

Hearne, the sixteenth-century antiquary, attributed to John Gibbon the idea that Stonehenge was built by the Iceni to mark a battle associated with Boudicca, perhaps associated with her death. In 1676 Speed proposed that it was the burial place of Aurelius Ambrosianus, of Uterpendragon, who was Aurelius' younger brother and Arthur's father (hence the connection with Merlin, who before he was assigned to Arthur was said to have been in Vortigern's employ), and of Constance, King of Brittany. It was, said Speed, built in the shape of a crown to denote a royal burial.

In 1660 Dr Charleton, physician to Charles II, said that the Danes built Stonehenge as a place to crown their kings.

The Devil in Wiltshire

The Devil seems fond of flying around with heavy loads, so it is little wonder he occasionally drops them. **Cley Hill** near Warminster is said to be the result of one such accident when the weary Devil, intending to drop a load of earth on Devizes, lost his way. **Silbury Hill** at Avebury was a load intended for Marlborough until some strong magic by the priests at Avebury forced it out of his hands. Others, of course, know differently about Silbury: the burial place of King Sil (whoever he was), or the last resting place of a knight in golden armour. The fact that no archaeological dig has ever established its purpose allows the mystery of Silbury Hill to endure whilst moon maidens camp about its base and dance on its summit at midsummer.

The Devil has appeared in the form of a crow at **Blunsdon**, when challenged to put in an appearance at **Hindon**, in the shape of a black dog one Palm Sunday at **Longbridge Deverill**, and as a hare when two men were hanged at **Warminster**.

Spectacular spectres

Surely the most atmospheric of all sights must have been that which presented itself to the folklorist Edith Olivier at **Avebury**. Passing through the great stone circle one evening early in the twentieth century, she was confronted with all the paraphernalia of a fair taking place amidst the stones – a fair which had not been held there for fifty years! And perhaps the most thought-provoking apparition was that of the phantom leper colony observed at **Bradford-on-Avon**, in whose Saxon church fifteenth- and sixteenth-century people have been seen taking communion.

Most communities have a phantom or two, and some are quite spectacular. One may meet a spectral funeral on the Roman road near **All Cannings** – large black horses pulling a wagon with a golden coffin surmounted by a crown. Chariots and horses rattle beside the churchyard wall at **Stratton St Margaret**; a phantom coach and four rush across the meadows near **Driffield**. A headless coachman careers up Granham Hill near **Marlborough** on the stroke of midnight. Headless, too, is Reginald de Cobham, who was stripped and burnt as a heretic in 1413 and walks naked at midnight on moonlight nights at **Langley Burrell**. A Royalist carries his head under his arm on the road between Moredon and Haydon Wick near Swindon, as does the man who tramps about **Roundway Hill** near Devizes.

There are several ghosts associated with

the house and church at **Lydiard Tregoze**: an elderly gentleman who helps visitors to seats in the grounds when they are feeling the effects of the summer heat; Sir John St John who walks around the house; a cowled figure who inhabits the church; and even a phantom coach and horses. At **Longleat House** children haunt the minstrel gallery and there have been strange and unexplained noises in the stable courtyard. Louise Carteret, whose husband is said to have fought a duel and killed the man he thought to have been her lover, walks in a passageway, on the staircase and through a servants' corridor. **Avebury Manor** has a good share of ghosts, from white ladies to Benedictine monks, from the noise of a phantom coach and horses to doors and windows which unlock themselves. And in the nineteenth century a serving girl described the cavalier she had seen from a window.

At Watkins Corner, between **Purton** and Purton Stoke, Robert Watkins was hanged in 1819 for a murder to which his father later confessed. The moment of his departure was accompanied by thunder and lightning which so frightened the hangman's horse that it bolted, throwing the hangman and breaking his neck. Robert himself haunts the spot where he was hanged. A few miles away at **Rodbourne Cheney**, legend has it that a bricked-up tunnel beneath the church still holds a golden altar, put there in the sixteenth century. And nearby a spectral lady has been hunting for the grave of her baby since the fifteenth century. She might meet the Victorian lady who wanders around the same place with a baby in her arms. At **Hannington** Squire Montgomery roams around the old manor grounds looking for money he once hid. And at **Lydiard Millicent** the sad ghost of Madam Blunt, still bemoaning her unfaithful husband, can be seen seated beneath her favourite tree in the manor grounds at nightfall on the last day of October.

Many churches have some association with a black or, more frequently, a white nun. Tradition usually has it that the poor soul was bricked up alive as a punishment for doubtful behaviour. Such may be encountered at **Stratton St Margaret** – where a phantom stage-coach may be heard rattling along the old road by the churchyard wall – and at **Highworth**. The phantom little red man who makes his way towards the manor house at All Cannings is presumed to be a priest going in search of the priest's hole which was discovered in the chimney. The grounds of **Bradenstoke** Priory are patrolled by a black monk, and elderly ones haunt the area of the priory at **Cricklade**. A nun walks daily towards the priory of **Kington St Michael** at 1.30 a.m. In the graveyard at **Biddestone** you may encounter the ghost of a person reputed to have been hanged there.

Ghostly noises

The sound of a spectral coach can be heard approaching and departing from the area of Chalk Pit Hill near **Amesbury**. At a house in **Berwick St James** a ghostly carpenter has been heard at work at midnight, as well as the sounds of shuffling up and down the stairs and along passages. The old rectory at **Boscombe** is renowned for the presences felt there, the ghost of a man who hanged himself in the attic and the sounds of fighting. Once a night at **Bowerchalke** three chops can be heard at the site of a now demolished house in which its owner was murdered. Visitors to the Bell at **Malmesbury** may be told of the wailing woman supposed to have been walled up in the cellar, and folk may tramp up Saltern Hill near **Netton** in time to catch the rumbling wagon and the gallop of phantom hooves.

Phantom animals

All Cannings, **Cricklade**, **Moredon** and **Wootton Rivers** all have ghostly dogs which appear at dusk, and that at **Crockerton** breathes fire from its nostrils. The folklorist Kathleen Wiltshire has recorded forty-five phantom black dogs in the county. The one which appears at **Stourton** on Christmas Eve is associated with a headless horseman. **Amesbury** also has a phantom horse, and such have been reported galloping headless through **Crockerton**, through a flock of sheep at **Great Durnford** and at breakneck speed through **Norton**. And if you believe the twilight ramblings of the great phantom black sow of **Bishops Cannings**, you will probably believe anything!

13
Tourist information centres

Amesbury: Redworth House, Flower Lane, Amesbury SP4 7HG. Telephone: 01980 622833.
Avebury: *The Great Barn, Avebury SN8 1RF. Telephone: 016723 425.
Bradford-on-Avon: The Library, Bridge Street, Bradford-on-Avon BA15 1BY. Telephone: 01225 865797.
Chippenham: The Neeld Hall, High Street, Chippenham SN15 3ER. Telephone: 01249 657733.
Corsham: *Arnold House, High Street, Corsham. Telephone: 01249 714660.
Devizes: The Crown Centre, 39 St John's Street, Devizes SN10 1BL. Telephone: 01380 729408.
Malmesbury: Town Hall, Market Lane, Malmesbury SN16 9BZ. Telephone: 01666 823748.
Marlborough: **Car Park, George Lane, Marlborough SN8 1EE. Telephone: 01672 513989.
Melksham: Roundhouse, Church Street, Melksham SN12 6LS. Telephone: 01225 707424.
Mere: The Square, Mere BA12 6JJ. Telephone: 01747 861211.
Salisbury: Fish Row, Salisbury SP1 1EJ. Telephone: 01722 334956.
Swindon: 37 Regent Street, Swindon SN1 1JL. Telephone: 01793 530328.
Trowbridge: St Stephen's Place, Trowbridge BA14 8AH. Telephone: 01225 777054.
Warminster: Central Car Park, Warminster BA12 9BT. Telephone: 01985 218548.
Westbury: The Library, Edward Street, Westbury BA13 3BD. Telephone: 01373 827158.

National Trust: Regional Information Office, National Trust, Eastleigh Court, Bishopstrow, Warminster. Telephone: 01985 847777.
North Wiltshire District Council: Monkton Park, Chippenham. Telephone: 01249 443322.

Information is available to the public on a personal visit at:
Downton: The Library, Barford Lane, Downton.
Tisbury: Tisbury and District Sports Centre, Weaveland Road, Tisbury.
Wilton: The Library, South Street, Wilton.

*   Open summer only
** Restricted winter opening

14
Further reading

Chandler, John. *The Vale of Pewsey*. Ex Libris Press, 1991.

Gillam, Beatrice (editor). *The Wiltshire Flora*. Pisces Publications, 1993.

Jordan, Katharine. *The Folklore of Ancient Wiltshire*. Wiltshire County Council Library and Museums Service, 1990.

Marshman, Michael. *The Wiltshire Book*. Countryside Books, 1987.

Olivier, Edith, and Edwards, Margaret K.S. *Moonrakings*. Coates & Parker, reprinted 1979.

Perham, Molly (compiler). *Wiltshire Country Recipes*. Ravette Books, 1989.

Rawson, Angela, and Kedge, Nikki. *Wiltshire Cookery*. The Dovecote Press, 1984.

Street, Pamela. *The Illustrated Portrait of Wiltshire*. Robert Hale, 1971.

Tomkins, Richard. *Wiltshire Place Names*. Red Brick Publishing, 1983.

Underwood, Peter. *Ghosts of Wiltshire*. Bossiney Books, 1989.

Vile, Nigel. *Family Walks in the Downs and the Vales of Wiltshire*. Scarthin Books, 1988.

Watkin, Bruce. *A History of Wiltshire*. Phillimore, 1989.

Westaway, Charles. *Pub Walks in Wiltshire and Avon*. Greensward, 1990.

Whitlock, Ralph. *The Folklore of Wiltshire*. B.T. Batsford, 1976.

Whitlock, Ralph. *Wiltshire*. B.T. Batsford, 1976.

Whitlock, Ralph. *Wiltshire Folklore and Legends.* Robert Hale, 1992.

Wilson, Margaret. *Touring Guide to Wiltshire Villages*. Ex Libris Press, 1987.

Wiltshire, Kathleen. *Wiltshire Folklore*. Compton Russell, 1975.

Wiltshire, Kathleen. *More Ghosts and Legends of the Wiltshire Countryside*. Colin Venton, 1984.

Haycocks still stacked in the Vale of Pewsey in the 1980s.

Index